OPPORTUNITY, MOBILITY AND INEQUALITY

RESEARCH ON ECONOMIC INEQUALITY

Series Editors: Juan Gabriel Rodríguez and
Sanghamitra Bandyopadhyay

Recent Volumes:

Volume 31: *Opportunity, Mobility and Inequality*
Edited by Sanghamitra Bandyopadhyay and Juan Gabriel Rodríguez

RESEARCH ON ECONOMIC INEQUALITY VOLUME 31

OPPORTUNITY, MOBILITY AND INEQUALITY

EDITED BY

SANGHAMITRA BANDYOPADHYAY
Queen Mary University of London, UK

AND

JUAN GABRIEL RODRÍGUEZ
Universidad Complutense de Madrid, Spain

emerald PUBLISHING

United Kingdom – North America – Japan
India – Malaysia – China

Emerald Publishing Limited
Emerald Publishing, Floor 5, Northspring, 21-23 Wellington Street, Leeds LS1 4DL.

First edition 2025

British Library Cataloguing in Publication Data
A catalogue record for this book is available from the British Library

ISBN: 978-1-83549-545-2 (Print)
ISBN: 978-1-83549-544-5 (Online)
ISBN: 978-1-83549-546-9 (Epub)

ISSN: 1049-2585 (Series)

Printed and bound by CPI Group (UK) Ltd, Croydon, CR0 4YY

CONTENTS

ABOUT THE EDITORS

Sanghamitra Bandyopadhyay is Professor of Development Economics and the Deputy Director of the Centre for Globalisation Research. She specializes in the economics of growth and development, measurement of inequality and poverty and applied econometrics. She has held previous academic appointments at the University of Oxford, University of Birmingham and the London School of Economics. She holds a PhD from the London School of Economics. She has been a Visiting Professor/Visiting Fellow at the Toulouse School of Economics and Cornell University (2015), and is currently Visiting Professor at the International Inequalities Institute at the London School of Economics. In addition to editing *Research on Economic Inequality*, she is also Co-Editor for the *Review of Development Economics,* and is Fellow of the Royal Society of Arts, UK. https://orcid.org/0000-0003-4299-9599

Juan Gabriel Rodríguez is Full Professor of Economics in the Department of Economic Analysis at the Complutense University of Madrid and Member of the research groups ICAE, EQUALITAS and CEDESOG. He has participated in projects funded by the La Caixa, BBVA, Ramón Areces, and COTEC Foundations, and different Spanish Public Administrations at the National and Regional levels. Between 2008 and 2010, he was Deputy Assistant Director General of the Institute of Fiscal Studies (Ministry of Finance). He has published scientific articles in journals such as *Journal of Economic Theory*, *Journal of Development Economics*, *European Economic Review*, *The Scandinavian Journal of Economics*, *Scientometrics*, *Regional Studies*, *Journal of Economic Inequality*, *Economic Letters*, *Social Choice and Welfare*, *Review of Income and Wealth*, and *Oxford Bulletin of Economics and Statistics*. He has been a Visiting Scholar at Yale University, the World Bank, Brown University, East Carolina University, Oxford University and Laval University. He is currently co-editor of the Research on Economic Inequality series. https://orcid.org/0000-0002-0256-8789

ABOUT THE CONTRIBUTORS

Gordon J. Anderson is an Applied Econometrician, a Fellow of the *Journal of Econometrics* and *Journal of Applied Econometrics* Distinguished Author. He works on wellbeing, inequality and poverty measurement in the fields of health, human resources and incomes and has published over 60 refereed articles and books on those topics.

Kenzo Asahi is an Associate Professor at the Pontificia Universidad Católica de Chile (PUC-Chile) School of Government. He is a Principal Investigator at the Millennium Nucleus in Intergenerational Mobility (MOVI) and an Investigator at the Centre for Sustainable Development (CEDEUS). His research lies at the intersection of urban and labour economics, examining how urban policies, such as regulations and transport investments, affect the human and economic development of city dwellers. He holds a PhD in Social Policy from the London School of Economics and Political Science (LSE), a Master's degree in Research in Economics from University College London, a Master's in Public Administration in International Development (MPA/ID) from Harvard University, and both a Master's and a Bachelor's in Engineering from PUC-Chile. https://orcid.org/0000-0001-7838-4647

Raquel Sebastian, Universidad Complutense de Madrid, ICAE and EQUALITAS, Spain. Raquel Sebastian is a Postdoctoral Researcher at Universidad Complutense de Madrid and member of ICAE and EQUALITAS. She holds a PhD in Economics from University of Salamanca where she has been a Marie Curie Fellow. She has been Visiting Researcher at the Institute for New Economic Thinking (Oxford University), the European Foundation for the Improvement of Living and Working Conditions (Eurofound) in Dublin, and the Central European Labour Studies Institute in Bratislava. She has worked on projects for several governments and international organizations, including the European Commission, and the International Organization for Migration. Her fields of research are employment, structural change and inequality. She has also published book chapters in *Handbook of Labor, Human Resources and Population Economics* (Editorial Springer). https://orcid.org/0000-0003-4420-7604

Ángel S. Marrero is an Assistant Professor in the Department of Economics at the University of La Laguna (ULL). He holds a Ph.D. in Economics from ULL. His work has focused on two research areas: discrete choice models applied to transport demand and the revision of convergence hypotheses under economic growth theory. Currently, his main focus is studying inequality of opportunities in education. This research has resulted in the publication of several papers included in the Journal Citation Report (JCR), including Review of Income and Wealth, Transportation Research Part A, Energy Economics, and Energy Policy. https://orcid.org/0000-0003-0093-9571

Cosmas Bernard Meka'a is Associate Professor and Dean of the Faculty of Economics and Management (FSEG) at the University of Bertoua. He is a senior researcher at the Research Centre on Innovation, Institutions and Inclusive Development. He is the author and co-author of numerous scientific articles published in international journals as such as *Travail & Emploi, Région et Développement, Revue d'économie du développement, Journal of the Knowledge Economy, Renewable Energy, Heliyon*. Its areas of research include labour economics, migration, gender, inequality, digitization, environmental economics and human capital. He is also Editor-in-Chief of the *Cameroon Management Review* of the Advanced School of Economics and Commerce at the University of Douala. He is also co-founder and Chairman of the Microeconomics of Development Laboratory. Finally, he is the PhD thesis director of Romus Noufelie and Astride Claudel Njiepue-Nouffeussie

Francisco Meneses is the Director of Corporate Finance at Banco Estado in Chile. He is an Investigator at the Millennium Nucleus in Intergenerational Mobility (MOVI) and an Investigator at the Centre for Sustainable Development (CEDEUS). He holds a PhD in Public Policy from the Duke University, a Master's in Public Administration in International Development (MPA/ID) from Harvard University, Master in Arts in Agriculture and Applied Economics from the University of Wisconsin-Madison and a B.A in Business and Economics from PUC-Chile.

Romus Noufelie is currently a PhD candidate at the University of Ngaoundéré-Cameroun, working on the economics of migration and inequality and that of energy and technology. He has published in journals such as *Renewable Energy, African Scientific Journal and Helivon Review*. He has also taught at Cameroon's Institute of Social Sciences. https://orcid.org/00000002-2269-0888

Astride Claudel Njiepue Nouffeussie is a PhD candidate in economics at the University of Douala-Cameroon, where he is due to defend a thesis on the *Effects of social capital on the labour market in Cameroon* before the end of 2024. He holds a Research Master's thesis in Economic Policy and Development from the same University. He is tutorial instructor at the FSEG of University of Bertoua. He has co-authored several scientific articles published in international journals such as *Journal of the Knowledge Economy, Heliyon review*. His areas of research include labour economic, digitization, industrial economy, inequality, energy and accommodation. He has familiarised himself with data analysis using STATA, SPSS and R software. He has also taken part in several international conferences, including the 1st Euro-African conference organised by the University of Tours (France), the Conference on the Digitisation Economy 2023 organised by

CESifo (Germany) and ICDE 2024 organised by AFEDEV (France). He is also a member of several learned societies including, Microeconomics of Development Laboratory, AFEDEV, ERMA, RCIIID, Econometric Society and Cameroonian Economic Society. https://orcid.org/0000-0002-0268-8078

David Pérez-Mesa is a Postdoctoral Researcher in the Research Center of Social Inequality and Governance (CEDESOG) at the University of La Laguna (ULL). He holds a Ph.D. in Economics from ULL. His research focuses on the areas of Health Economics and Development Economics, in particular on the analysis of health determinants and health inequality in both children and adults, as well as on the study of inequality of opportunity in health. https://orcid.org/0000-0003-2454-2990

Fernando Pinto, Universidad Rey Juan Carlos de Madrid, EQUALITAS, Spain. Fernando Pinto is a Professor and Researcher in the Department of Business Economics, Applied Economics II, and Fundamentals of Economic Analysis at the Rey Juan Carlos University in Madrid. He holds a PhD in Economics and a Master's in Economic Analysis of Law and Public Policies from the University of Salamanca. His main research areas are labour economics and public economics. He has conducted research visits, among others, at the Oxford Department of International Development at the University of Oxford (Oxford, United Kingdom) and the Department of Economics at San Diego State University (San Diego, California, United States). Additionally, he has participated as a speaker in numerous national and international conferences and seminars within his field of study. Additionally, he has participated as a speaker in numerous national and international conferences and seminars within his field of study. He has also published book chapters in prestigious editorials such as Thomson Reuters and Edward Elgar. https://orcid.org/0000-0003-1525-3206

Juan Prieto-Rodriguez is Full Professor of Economics at the Oviedo School of Economics and Business (at the University of Oviedo), one of the seven Spanish Business schools accredited by the AACSB. He has coordinated and been member of projects of the Spanish National Research Plans or EU programs. He has published articles in Spanish and international peer-reviewed journals such as *Cambridge Journal of Regions, Economy and Society*, *Economics Letters*, *European Economic Review*, *European Journal of Operational Research, Industrial & Labor Relations Review*, *International Journal of Forecasting*, *Journal of Economic Psychology*, *Journal of Cultural Economics*, *Journal of Sport Economics*, *Kyklos, Marketing Science, Transportation Research Parts A and D* and *Transport Policy*. He has been a Visiting Scholar at the University of Strathclyde in Glasgow, Trinity College Dublin, the University of Portsmouth and the Johns Hopkins Carey Business School. He has been the Executive Secretary-Treasurer of the Association for Cultural Economics International (ACEI) for more than 10 years and the Coordinator of PUCK, a multinational project fund by the European Union. https://orcid.org/0000-0001-9163-3011

Inna Skriabina did her Bachelor's degree in Commerce in the MGIMO University in Moscow, Russia, and her Master's degree in Sustainable Development in St Andrews University in Scotland, UK. Later she moved to Spain to continue her academic pursuit and to focus on the research in income inequality and economic development. She earned her PhD degree in Economics in the Complutense University in Madrid in 2020. Her thesis 'Opportunity, Inequality and Growth: The Case of Russia' was directed by Professor Juan Gabriel Rodríguez. Currently she works in management and finance in fine dining and hospitality business in Spain.

Pablo De la Vega Suárez holds a Degree in Economics from the University of Oviedo and a Master's degree in Economics from the Complutense University of Madrid. He has worked as teaching and research staff at the latter university for several years. He currently works for Next Educación, as coordinator of master's programs. He has published in international journals in the fields of inequality and cultural economics. He has developed part of his work in the field of network economies, applying techniques and new approaches to the existing literature.

INTRODUCTION

Sanghamitra Bandyopadhyay[a] and
Juan Gabriel Rodríguez[b]

[a]*Queen Mary University of London, UK*
[b]*Universidad Complutense de Madrid, Spain*

Research on Economic Inequality: Opportunity, Mobility and Inequality comprises seven papers each of which present original research using novel data and empirical methods to uncover new findings about intergenerational mobility, inequality and welfare. The chapters in this volume reflect the contribution of newly published rich datasets that deepen our understanding of these issues, as much as novel innovations about how we conceive and measure these economic entities.

We open the volume with empirical evidence from Chile, which uses for the first time novel administrative panel data to measure intergenerational mobility in a developing country. The authors generate a panel data set using a national educational test with surveys of students in the eighth grade and analyses their intergenerational income mobility in their late twenties. The significant addition to the literature stems from the article's use of administrative data from Chile's Ministry of Labour of wage data tracked by the Department of Unemployment Insurance to obtain their cohort members' salaries between 2007 and 2018. The administrative surveys are the national mandatory SIMCE test, and the national voluntary college selection test provided by the Ministry of Education and DEMRE (Department for the Educational Testing, Measurement, and Records of the University of Chile). Using social class and role model proxies, they show that college educational outcomes are related to early years' social and educational environments. The authors use panel regression methods to reveal that remarkably 8th grade students placed in the lowest income quartile have a probability of 9% of rising to the top income decile in their late twenties. These students are, however, not immune from difficulties in future economic mobility due to having low college enrollment and graduation rates.

Opportunity, Mobility and Inequality
Research on Economic Inequality, Volume 31, 1–4

Published under exclusive licence by Emerald Publishing Limited
ISSN: 1049-2585/doi:10.1108/S1049-258520250000031001

The following contribution uses the Spanish example on human capital acquisition to propose theoretical innovations for inequality measurement that allow for Utilitarian, Prioritarian and Sufficientarian Imperatives. These imperatives demand equalization towards targets that are, unlike standard inequality measures, not necessarily a centrality parameter or distribution dependent. The author proposes Inequality Modulated Success Indices and their use is illustrated using data from the Spanish PISA Results (for the years 2009 and 2015) and for the regions of The Basque Country, Catalonia and the rest of Spain with respect to two family parenting types, Dual Parenting (representing two parents present in the household) and Single Parenting (indicating a single parent in the household), and changes in the disparity of the educational outcomes of 14-year-olds in Spain is examined. Equal opportunity sensitive measures of parental quality and student achievement are obtained by combining aggregate measures of parental quality and student achievement with measures of the extent of inequality of opportunity (IOP). The results reveal that while there has been a general improvement in the overall parenting quality confronting students and in student grade achievements, this is also coupled with diminished equality of opportunity, characterized by increased differences in circumstance conditioned achievement distributions. This is observed markedly so for single parented students. In turn, when heavy weights are applied to the equality of opportunity component, the ordering is reversed. Students in Basque and Catalan regions appear to be particularly advantaged relative to students in the rest of Spain.

The next chapter is an investigation into quantifying IOP amongst the young employees (between 10 and 25 years of age) in Cameroon, using an estimated Human Opportunity Index (HOI) in Cameroon. The authors define IOP as the differences in outcomes due to circumstances that are beyond individual controls. For this purpose, they estimate a HOI in order to quantify inequalities in opportunities among employees aged 10 to 25 years using the data from the Fourth Cameroon Household Survey (FCHS4) carried out in 2014 for the 14 Cameroonian geographical areas. Their results based on an estimated Dissimilarity index, finds that regions including North-West, East and the urban regions have relatively high levels of IOP. In contrast, a more homogeneous subgroup with a lower IOP is found in rural, North and East regions. The authors further use the Shapley-Shorrocks decomposition method to reveal that social and professional circumstances, levels of primary education and religious obedience of the household head, explain up to 51% to 79% of the overall IOP. Further analyses using Blinder-Oaxaca decomposition also reveal that 80% of the gap in their estimated Dissimilarity Index is explained by disparities in circumstances rather than by individual efforts. They conclude that effective decentralization is needed for a more inclusive employment policy that is sensitive to local labour market features.

The following chapter examines the effects of collective bargaining agreements on employees' welfare in Spanish firms. The chapter is a pioneering study on wage inequality in Spain at the company level. The authors use data from the 2018 Structure of Earnings Survey to examine the trade-off between wage inequality and mean wage levels within firms using standard regression methods. They find that while firm-level collective bargaining agreements contribute to increased intra-firm wage inequality, they also significantly enhance intra-firm average wage levels, with positive effects being consistently observed across firm types and employee skill levels. The impact of these agreements varies by firm size and the skill level of the workforce: high-skilled firms experience the most pronounced benefits in wage increases, indicating a direct correlation between workforce skill intensity and the effectiveness of collective bargaining mechanisms. Notably, they observe that the increase in mean wages tends to offset adverse effects that are associated with wage disparities, which in turn lead to improved workers' welfare within firms. The authors' results emphasize the importance of firm-level negotiations to generate equitable and prosperous labour market outcomes.

The following chapter analyses the role of friends and family in decisions made by individuals to work in the public or in the private sector, using a novel database in Spain. The authors conduct a unique survey about individual socioeconomic characteristics, parental background and participants' social networks from two prominent Spanish universities and compare the effect of peers with that of the impact of parents on the individuals' preferences. Their findings reveal that for the private sector, the influence (measured as the marginal effect) of friends is larger than the influence of parents. In contrast, the opposite is found to hold for influence in determining to work in the public sector. The chapter also identify that the effect of the horizontal channel can, however, overcome the vertical channel and that parents and friends have a larger influence on women than on men.

The next chapter provides compelling empirical evidence also from Spain on the role of IOP in shaping the dynamics of health inequality. Using a survey module conducted by the Centro de Investigaciones Sociológicas (CIS) in 2017, the authors distinguish between fair and unfair circumstances in determining health outcomes: those which are due to family background (unfair), and those related to efforts and lifestyles, and in addition, demographic variables in explaining adult health inequality. In addition, their findings highlight the importance of education in mitigating the impact of certain circumstances and serving as a transmission channel for others. Their results suggest that individuals' efforts and lifestyles alone are insufficient to counterbalance unfair circumstances beyond their control. Therefore, improving circumstances and early-life factors, or reducing their impact on health through the implementation of compensatory policies, is essential for reducing health inequality and promoting equal opportunities for inclusive development.

The volume concludes with a thorough investigation into the relationship between inequality and growth, using dynamic panel regression methods and novel Russian Federation data. The author has some robust and clear conclusions. The analysis reveals that growth is inequality increasing. In addition, using regional data, the author finds evidence of the Kuznets' inverted U curve which is in contrast with regional results from recent other countries in the world. The result however is only apparent upon accounting for potential endogeneity.

On a closer look at the case of Moscow, it reveals a pattern that sets it apart from the rest of the Russian Federation: while it starts with very high levels of inequality it eventually experiences a drastic drop.

CHAPTER 1

INTERGENERATIONAL MOBILITY IN CHILE: A YEAR-TO-YEAR ANALYSIS OF A NATIONAL COHORT OF STUDENTS

Francisco Meneses[a] and Kenzo Asahi[b]

[a]*Banco Estado de Chile, Millennium Nucleus on Intergenerational Mobility: From Modelling to Policy (MOVI), Chile*
[b]*Pontificia Universidad Católica de Chile, Millennium Nucleus on Intergenerational Mobility: From Modelling to Policy (MOVI), Centre for Sustainable Urban Development (CEDEUS), Chile*

ABSTRACT

What are the factors that affect social mobility? How are early adulthood educational and labour trajectories correlated with intergenerational mobility? This chapter presents three contributions to the intergenerational mobility literature. First, this chapter develops one of the first attempts to measure intergenerational mobility using administrative panel data sets in a developing country. A panel data set was created using a national educational test and surveys and follows students, starting in 8th grade, and analyzes their intergenerational income mobility in their late twenties. Second, this chapter uses social class and role model proxies and shows that college educational outcomes are related to initial social and educational environments. Third, a detailed analysis of academic and labour market trajectories is used, indicating that students with irregular educational and labour market trajectories show lower intergenerational income mobility. The results of this research open a new approach for analyzing life decisions and expect to provide

Opportunity, Mobility and Inequality
Research on Economic Inequality, Volume 31, 5–40

Published under exclusive licence by Emerald Publishing Limited
ISSN: 1049-2585/doi:10.1108/S1049-258520250000031002

further guidance for public policies that intend to promote social mobility among low-income individuals.

Keywords: Intergenerational mobility; education; income; economics of education; social mobility; low income; role models

I. INTRODUCTION

The question of intergenerational mobility has risen in importance in the public debate over the several past decades. Intergenerational mobility can be defined as the extent to which an individual's background influences his or her adult income (Becker & Tomes, 1979). In an unequal democratic country, intergenerational mobility is a critical counterweight that allows market economies and democratic systems to coexist (Corak, 2013). Therefore, factors that increase intergenerational mobility have gained public policy importance in a world with rising inequality. However, the research on intergenerational mobility is constrained in different developing countries that lack panel data sets (Krishna & Nolan, 2019), and by the constraints of merging tax data with other information sources in developed countries.

The empirical research on intergenerational mobility has evolved into two significant branches, helped by the availability of detailed administrative information (Iversen et al., 2019; Palomino et al., 2018). The first branch of the literature focuses on how to measure intergenerational mobility, what data to use, and how to expand the measurements in different countries.[1]

The second branch of the literature is focused on understanding the factors that promote intergenerational mobility and how these components affect different individuals. This branch of the literature centers on the dynamics that affect intergenerational mobility, the factors that promote it, the roadblocks that prevent it, and the policies that affect it. Current research has shown that intergenerational mobility is affected by different elements or channels that include family environment (ethnicity, family characteristics, neighbourhood), education (early education, school education, college education), and health (prenatal health, birth characteristics, nutrition, lifetime health) (Chetty et al., 2014; Heckman, 2006; Streib, 2011; Torche, 2011, 2015). The educational literature has shown that role models and life shocks affect educational attainment (Altmejd et al., 2020; Torche, 2010) and therefore, these variables should be incorporated into the analysis to evaluate their impact on intergenerational mobility.

The traditional methodology used to estimate intergenerational income mobility compares the long-term incomes of parents and their children. This methodology evaluates parents and children at a particular point in time. However, while some of the factors or channels that affect intergenerational mobility are fixed during life (genetics), others change over time (health or education) and depend on a plethora of factors and decisions. These current approaches to measuring the factors that affect intergenerational mobility do not consider the outcomes of adult children in terms of trajectory, where initial decisions affect subsequent ones. For example, educational investments build upon each other, and initial investments during early education or high school will increase the likelihood of achieving a college education (Chetty et al., 2011).

Therefore, analysis that does not differentiate between the timing of decisions could be distorting estimates of the factors that affect social mobility, as sometimes it is not possible to see which decisions were made first. Moreover, some connections are lost as it is not possible to analyze the interaction of choices at different moments in time. Furthermore, it could be possible that family characteristics and educational or work decisions at one particular moment in time may have a sizable effect, while the impact of the same choices later in life may be less decisive or impactful. Following the adult children over a period of years via a yearly panel data set could be useful in documenting critical decisions that affect their intergenerational mobility and could shed some light on the importance of decision dynamics and family characteristics at different moments in their lifetime.

This chapter is one of the first papers to use administrative data to measure intergenerational mobility in a developing country. Moreover, it contributes to the literature by using year-to-year control variables, taking advantage of vast and detailed administrative information, including survey data on the educational system in Chile. Using administrative data, this chapter creates a panel data set by following an entire cohort of students, starting in 8th grade, through high school, higher education and their participation in the labour market in Chile. The panel includes data from two national mandatory educational tests, a voluntary test, and wages of students in adulthood. This data also includes information on the educational trajectories for all students and the early labour market outcomes for over 72% of the sample. It also provides detailed information on other potential factors, including educational performance.

The results show that students in the lowest income quartile in 8th grade have a 9% probability of rising to the top income decile. However, these students could face many difficulties in economic mobility as they have low college enrollment and graduation rates. This chapter analyzes the correlation between educational outcomes and intergenerational mobility, using academic tests, and proxies of social class and role models as controls. These results find that social class and school environments are correlated with higher ranking positions and indicate that previous research, which does not consider school environments and social class, could be overestimating the importance of academic outcomes on intergenerational mobility. In addition, the use of educational and labour market trajectories shows that different educational trajectories, which could seem similar looking only at educational outcomes, are correlated with different intergenerational income mobility results. Individuals with irregular educational and work trajectories – gap years in education or unemployment periods – present lower intergenerational mobility.

II. BACKGROUND LITERATURE

The literature on intergenerational mobility has been re-invigorated during recent decades, as it has become a topic of public debate and policy, introducing new causal techniques and administrative data sets. One branch of the literature has focused on measuring intergenerational mobility; while a second branch focuses on analyzing its causes, estimating the effect of education, neighbourhoods, nutrition, health, and labour markets on it during different parts of the lifecycle.[2]

When measuring intergenerational mobility, transition matrices are one of the most basic tools. This methodology separates the adult children and parents into groups and analyzes if and how adult children move from their parents' group to another. Transition matrices are useful as they are not affected by changes in the variance of the outcome variable, allowing for the comparison of results without having to standardize the data.[3] Using administrative data sets, another approach was developed by Dahl and DeLeire (2008) and later Chetty et al. (2014). Chetty et al. (2014), using tax records in the United States, ranks parents according to their income and ranks children according to theirs. Then a rank-rank regression is performed, where the rank-rank coefficient is the outcome of interest and is not affected by changes in the variance or level of income.[4]

A. Education

When analyzing intergenerational mobility, education is one of the variables that has been proven, on both theoretical and empirical grounds, to promote it. Both causal and correlational empirical studies have concluded that education has a strong effect on intergenerational mobility (Chetty et al., 2011; Pekkarinen et al., 2009; Torche, 2011). There is an extensive array of literature that analyses educational investments, measuring the effect that they have on social mobility in developed and developing countries. As human capital investments are endogenous to family characteristics, different scholars have used various strategies to identify the causal effect of education on intergenerational mobility (Björklund & Jäntti, 2009). Various aspects of parental education transmit advantages to children (higher income, time allocation to family, and maternal education redistributes income to children). At the pre-school level, Chetty et al. (2011) analyze the effect of Project Star, a randomized policy in the USA, finding that better educational environments (smaller class sizes, experienced teachers, and classmates with higher test scores) are associated with positive labour market outcomes and college attendance.

National policy interventions have been a useful way to measure the effect of primary and secondary education on intergenerational mobility, as they can be evaluated as natural experiments. For example, increases in mandatory education or enrollment capacity have improved educational and intergenerational mobility, proving this causal relationship (Maurin & McNally, 2008; Oreopoulos et al., 2006; Perkins, 1965). Moreover, formal education may not be the only factor that increases labour market outcomes, but also the acquisition of soft skills such as self-efficacy and self-esteem (Krishna, 2013).

There are a battery of studies that have analyzed the positive effects of higher education on intergenerational mobility. The reduction of restrictions for college education after the 1968 student movement in France promoted social mobility (Maurin & McNally, 2008). Using national surveys, Palomino et al. (2018) and Torche (2011) analyze the effect of higher education on social mobility in the US, confirming a positive correlation, but also recognizing the different effects that it has for students from different income groups. College affirmative action programs have a positive impact on increasing the educational attainment of students by enrolling them in programs that can lead to higher expected wages (Badge et al., 2016; Gallegos et al., 2019). To quantify the role of higher education institutions, Chetty et al. (2017) estimate the effect of colleges on social mobility, finding positive effects. However, although groundbreaking in the use of new administrative data, as noted by the authors, their estimations are not causal. This is related to the fact that college education is a choice at the end of the educational pipeline, which obscures previous educational choices that could bias their estimations. Other variables, such as prior education, academic performance, role models, and others may affect the decision to attend college. Therefore, there is still space to further explore the relative importance of these initial variables on intergenerational mobility.[5]

The economic literature on intergenerational mobility has made great efforts to analyze the correlation of ethnicity, geographical areas, college education or educational tracks on intergenerational mobility. However, other factors such as social class and educational environments – usually analyzed by the sociological and educational literature – have lack the same level of attention. The omission of these factors is relevant as students' educational decision are usually affected by their social origin and educational environment. Social reproduction theory stresses that social backgrounds and conditions determine educational attainments (Bourdieu, 1986). Social hierarchies harm educational mobility (Jacoby & Mansuri, 2015), but also performance in simple ability and effort tasks once hierarchies are made known (Hoff & Pandey, 2004). Students from higher social classes have more strategies and tools to succeed in college, compared to lower-class students, generating unequal outcomes (Yee, 2016). Social class has been identified as a factor affecting children's behaviours as early as four years old Streib (2011); it also impacts the behaviour of students in classrooms and teachers (Rist, 1970), students' perspectives about future work (Hoxby & Turner, 2015), the choice of universities (Hoxby & Avery, 2012), and access to high paying jobs (Ashley et al., 2015; Marmaros & Sacerdote, 2022; Rivera, 2011, 2016). Experimental and non-experimental research on role models (Mani & Riley, 2019; Nguyen, 2008), information (Hastings et al., 2015; Hoxby & Turner, 2013), and aspirations have been able to show the important educational consequences of these decisions (i.e. dropping out of high school or pursuing a low-profitable degree), particularly for low-income students (Zirkel, 2002). These studies show that decisions, social class, and role models at different points in life affect individuals' lifetime outcomes.

Overall, the literature has found a causal link between education, from early education to college, and social mobility worldwide. However, these educational decisions are also affected by individuals' social origins. Additionally, the literature uses point-to-point analyses without an analysis of student trajectories. As noted by the same authors, the reviewed papers did not address trajectories but only the outcomes of two points in time, and it could be the case that when the decisions are made, and how they are made, affect intergenerational mobility.

B. Other Factors

While this chapter focuses on the educational channels that promote intergenerational mobility, other important factors also affect it, such as geography, neighbourhoods, maternal nutrition, children's health, infrastructure investments, labour markets, etc. Given the bigger geographical and health divides, some of these factors may be particularly important in the developing world.

There has been a reinforcement of the importance of analyzing geography and neighbourhoods in the literature in developed countries. Previous research demonstrated the importance of family factors in intergenerational mobility over other factors such as neighbourhood (Björklund & Jäntti, 2009). In the developing world, there is an essential rural–urban divide of opportunities (Iversen et al., 2019).[6] These differences are, in fact, very relevant for the developing world and should not be overlooked. Recent research studies have strengthened the theory that neighbourhoods of residence are a relevant factor impacting social mobility in the developed world (Ananat et al., 2011; Chetty et al., 2014). New research that supports this argument uses randomized residential voucher programs in the USA that show the relevance of living in neighbourhoods with low poverty rates (Bergman et al., 2019; Chetty et al., 2016). These authors have obtained data on child and parental income, commuting zones, and other characteristics but lack important data on inter-neighbourhood factors like educational trajectories and other neighborhood-related services that are not controlled for. Our article includes details on the educational trajectories and deepens the analysis beyond geographical location to guide policymakers. Although this chapter tries to comprehensively understand educational trajectories, certain factors on other dimensions are not included. For example, this chapter does not include variables such as student health or early nutrition, as this panel data set has little information available on these topics.

C. Brief background on Chile

While there is a fast-growing field of research on intergenerational mobility in developed and developing countries such as India, China, and Brazil, research on this topic is much less developed in Chile (for a review, see Behrman (2019); Iversen et al. (2019); Torche (2019)). The analysis of intergenerational mobility in Chile is nascent, with only a few studies dedicated to the topic. Torche (2005) analyzed occupational mobility in Chile, finding that there is fluidity except for richer groups, which show low downward mobility. Using synthetic parents methodology and the 2006 CASEN survey, Nuñez and Miranda (2010) estimate intergenerational income mobility in Chile, finding a high IGE estimate of over .54. This indicates that there is a low intergenerational income mobility in Chile compared to the developed world (0.12 for Denmark, 0.35 for the USA, and 0.47 for France (OECD, 2018)). This low intergenerational income mobility is somewhat correlated with education. Zimmerman (2019) shows that students from elite high schools who attend top universities have a very high probability of having a very good job compared to their college peers who did not attend elite high schools.

Chile is one of the wealthiest countries in Latin America, having had significant GDP growth since 1980 (Corsetti & Schmidt-Hebbel, 1999; Schmidt-Hebbel, 2006) and reduced poverty (Contreras, 2003; Olavarria-Gambi, 2003), with a current GDP per capita of US $15,300 in 2019 (Bank, 2020). However, this growth has not been equally distributed, and Chile ranks amongst the most unequal countries in the world, with a Gini coefficient of 0.44 (Milanovic, 2016). Economic growth has been used on public policies to improve education and health that have not yet translated into income equality. Chile has shown essential improvements in all levels of education, increasing the overall enrollment rate during the last 25 years (SIES, 2014). Early childhood net enrollment rates for children between four and five years old have reached 90% (Desarrollo Social, 2015). The gross primary and secondary education enrollment rates reached 104.1% and 99.6%, respectively, in 2015. The net primary and secondary education enrollment rates reached 93% and 74%, respectively, that year. The significant increase in coverage has been sustained with increased public expenditure in education and the use of public and private schools.[7]

Despite this success in enrollment, challenges remain regarding quality, equity, and access to preschool. The Chilean school system is ranked the third lowest in the Programme for International Student Assessment (PISA) among OECD countries. It is above the average in the correlation between parental socioeconomic status and test scores (OECD, 2016). For example, on average, students in private schools performed significantly better than public school students. Moreover, students in the top 20% of socioeconomic status outperform their peers in the bottom 20%, with a gap equal to 3.5 years of schooling (OECD, 2016). At the same time, the early childhood care enrollment rate remains low compared to the OECD average, particularly for children age three or younger (OECD, 2016).

Enrollment in tertiary education expansion has been explosive, increasing the net enrollment rate from 12.8% in 1990 to 37.4% in 2015, and is still increasing (Social, 2015)[8]; this growth has been promoted mainly through financial aid in the form of loans and scholarships and by the expansion of private sector colleges (SIES, 2014). However, the increase in higher education has not been homogeneous. While the highest income quintile has a net enrollment rate of over 53%, students from the lowest income one have a rate of 33%. Moreover, not all students have seen the same positive income effects from higher education, as some earn the same or less than what they would earn with just a high school education (Bucarey et al., 2018; Urzúa, 2012). While nutrition and health are essential factors for intergenerational mobility in other developing countries (Krishna & Nolan, 2019), they may have a much lower impact in Chile, as undernutrition has stopped being a problem and the public health system has advanced towards a system of guarantees, that offers health provisions for the population (Missoni, 2010).

III. METHODOLOGICAL FRAMEWORK

A. Data Set

Due to a lack of investment and institutional stability, developing countries have faced historical challenges in creating nationally representative longitudinal surveys that capture long-term trends (Krishna & Nolan, 2019). However, many countries have devoted essential resources to their educational system, giving tests and surveys to representative samples of the student population or, in some cases, a whole cohort of students and their families. Some countries, such as Chile, have full primary and middle school education coverage. This chapter takes advantage of the high school coverage in middle school education in Chile. It creates a data set that merges national administrative data sets and national surveys to comprehensively analyze students' educational and work trajectories. The data sets are listed in Table 1. The first data sets include school enrollment and test scores in 8th grade and high school, higher education enrollment, and higher education graduation. The first administrative data set includes all the students in the country, even those at private and public institutions. The second administrative data set comes from Chile's Ministry of Labor and consists of the wages tracked by the Department of Unemployment Insurance of the Ministry of Labor; we use this to obtain our cohort members' salaries between 2007 and 2018. The administrative surveys are the national mandatory SIMCE test and the national voluntary college selection test provided by the Ministry of Education and DEMRE (Department for the Educational Testing, Measurement, and Records of the University of Chile). Lastly, the wages of individuals in the public sector were downloaded from the Ministry of the Interior's transparency web page.

All these data sets allowed us to follow the students from 2004 to 2018, as described in Fig. 1. The data sets collected can be organized into the next group of variables:

Family Income and Education: These are the initial condition variables of these students. Family income is available for all the sample and parental educational level for over 84% of students. Parents recorded their family income level as one of 15 income brackets and their educational level using twelve different categories.

Academic Outcomes: The students' academic outcomes are high-school dropout, high school repetition, high school change, high school quality, and higher education enrollment and graduation. These variables are available for all students in the sample as the study relies on administrative data sets. These are the variables that are analyzed on a year-to-year basis. The national mandatory SIMCE test scores are also available for each student's initial year academic performance.

School Social Class: The school social class proxy is the occupation of their fellow students' parents when they are in high school. Other authors, such as Torche (2005) adapted the occupational social class structure developed by Erikson, Goldthorpe, and Portocarrero (EGP) for Chile (Erikson et al., 1979). The College Selection Test survey asks students about their parents' occupations. Although not all students answer this survey (due to attrition and school repetition), we can obtain measures at the school level that consider most graduating students similar to that of Canales (2016). This chapter follows Canales (2016), who used

Table 1. Summary of Main Variables 1.

	Mean	sd	Count	Min	Max	Source
Academic Variables						
Years of Education	15.0	3.2	249373	8	21	Ministry Education
SIMCE Test Score 2004	253.2	47.1	249372	111.0	398.9	Ministry Education
SIMCE Tests Score 2006	258.7	53.7	184687	106.9	412.4	Ministry Education
Higher Education Enrollment	0.7	0.5	249373	0	1	Ministry Education
Higher Education Graduate	0.4	0.5	249373	0	1	Ministry Education
College Graduate	0.2	0.4	249373	0	1	Ministry Education
Vocational 2-year Graduate	0.06	0.2	249373	0	1	Ministry Education
Vocational 4-year Graduate	0.1	0.3	249373	0	1	Ministry Education
Sciences & Eng. Graduate	0.2	0.4	249373	0	1	Ministry Education
Income and Demographics						
Child Wage (US)	834.6	615.6	181885	0	5390.5	Ministry of Labor
Child Wage Rank	0.5	0.3	181885	0.000005	1.0	Ministry of Labor
Top 10 percent Income	0.10	0.3	181885	0	1	Ministry of Labor
Parental Income	530.8	708.7	249373	82.0	3770.5	SIMCE 2004
Parental Income Rank.	0.5	0.3	249373	0.000004	1	SIMCE 2004
Parental Education Level	2.0	1.1	224006	1	8	SIMCE 2004
Female	0.5	0.5	249373	0	1	SIMCE 2004
S. Class and Role Models						
Manager Parent	0.02	0.1	249373	0	1	College Selection Test
Manager Parents in 12th Grade	0.02	0.06	249373	0	1	College Selection Test
Role Models 12th Grade	0.2	0.14	249373	0	1	Ministry of Education

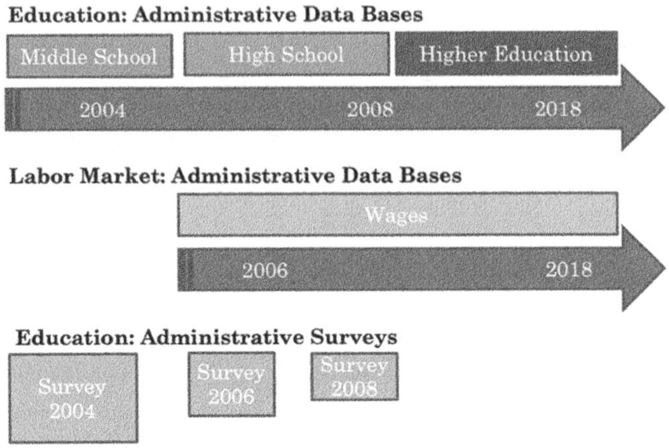

Fig. 1. Data Sets Used and Merged.

the college selection test survey and an adaptation of Torche (2005) to classify the social classes of the parents of students taking the College Selection Test. Specifically, the highest-level occupations are used as a proxy of the highest social class of individuals. In this survey, parents are classified according to 12 occupations, with the highest being: high-level managers in firms, government managers, high-level diplomats, high-level judges, or armed forces officials. In this chapter, we will focus only on this highest occupational category to generate a school-level variable indicating the proportion of high-class individuals in the schools.

School role models: Previous years of financial aid and college enrollment have been used in the Chilean literature as proxies of role models (Altmejd et al., 2020; Barrios Fernández, 2019; Blanco & Meneses, 2013), as younger students tend to mimic the patterns of financial aid and college enrollment of students from older generations in their schools. Following these previous examples, the areas of study of students and their college-major decisions will be used as proxies of role models. The main idea is that younger students in a school will tend to study the same professions and attend the same institutions as older generations of students from the same high school. In particular, this chapter will use the proportion of one older cohort of students who major in science, social science, or engineering, degrees that have been shown to lead to high wages in the labour market (Hastings et al., 2015).

Neighbourhood: Neighbourhoods are defined as the municipality of residence of the student. Previous literature has linked the neighbourhood of individuals and intergenerational mobility (Chetty et al., 2014). Hence, this variable will be included as a control.

Table 1 summarizes the main variables of this study. This presents the student wages, parental income, and educational outcomes. Parental wages are available for 249 thousand students.[9] Maternal education is obtained from the SIMCE survey; information is available for 230 thousand students. There is wage information for 181 thousand students for whom their income rank is calculated. Parental education is measured in eight different levels. The social class variable, e.g., the proportion of parents who are high-level managers, is only 2% of the sample. The role models variable, the high school indicator variable that estimates the proportion of students from older generations who studied sciences, social sciences, or engineering, shows that, on average, 20% of older students got these degrees. It is relevant to mention that students who drop out of high school or college generally appear again in the wage database; therefore, they are not a source of attrition for this database.

B. Ranking Calculations

The ranking of children and parents is calculated to pursue a rank-rank analysis. First, the 249 thousand parents are sorted according to their income and are given a value of 0 to 100, with 100 being the parent with the highest income and 0 the lowest income. Second, the children's ranking is calculated excluding the individuals with missing data.[10] The remaining 181 thousand students are sorted according to their average wage in 2016, 2017, and 2018 and then are ranked between 0 and 100. This methodology differs slightly from Chetty et al., 2014 as they replace individuals with no income with zeros. Other papers for Chile, such as Nuñez and Miranda (2010), also exclude individuals with no income and those earning below the minimum wage. For this particular data set, replacing data with zeros will generate extremely low estimates, implying high social intergenerational mobility, which would not be consistent with previous results or methodological approaches for Chile. National surveys show that for this population cohort, a significant proportion of people are not employed, educated, or trained (NEET). Appendix 1 analyzes the missing data and how it relates to gender, parental income, NEET, and informal employment. In the following sections, the consistency of this wage data will be tested using national surveys.

C. Methodology and Econometric Formulation

Once parental income rank and child wage rank are calculated, we proceed to estimate the intergenerational income mobility of students and include different control variables. The first step is running the regression on equation (1), obtaining estimates using rank-rank regressions as in Chetty et al. (2014).

$$ChildRank = \beta_0 + \beta_1 ParentalRank + \in \tag{1}$$

A second approach uses the traditional method of including educational outcomes in equation (2) but also includes social class and role model controls at the high school level. This regression intends to show that the original school environment of the students is correlated with intergenerational mobility, which could otherwise be attributed to educational outcomes.

$$\begin{aligned} ChildRank = \beta_0 + \beta_1 ParentalRank + \beta_2 Academic + \beta_3 RoleModels \\ + \beta_4 SocialClass + \in \end{aligned} \tag{2}$$

Then, the main analysis of this chapter estimates the intergenerational mobility of students using a rank-rank regression specification incorporating year-to-year control variables. Equation (3) controls for all possible work and educational trajectories. First, all possible educational and work profiles of the students are created to analyze students' trajectories, generating over 33 thousand different profiles. This method aims to identify the differentiated impact of different educational and work trajectories. Then, the profiles with more than 10 students are kept, leaving 592 profiles and replacing the other ones with a constant.

$$ChildRank = \beta_0 ParentalRank + \sum_{j=2}^{593} \beta_j * Trajectory_{j-1} + \in \quad (3)$$

IV. RESULTS

A. Intergenerational Mobility Estimation: Comparison with National Surveys

This section will compare the results of the novel panel data set with national surveys used in Chile. Table 2 shows the descriptive statistics of the wages of individuals from the CASEN 2017 survey and the wages of the panel data set. The results show that the wages of the Panel Data set are 7% higher and have a lower standard deviation than the survey. The panel data set identifies individuals with higher wages, with a higher maximum which is three times as high as the one from the CASEN survey. This is a problem of the CASEN survey, that historically has not been able to survey higher-income individuals in the population (Programme, 2017). Using their wages, the rankings of the individuals are calculated for both data sets.

As a next step, OLS regressions on equation (1) using the administrative panel data set show the relationship between child wage rank and parental income rank. Table 3 shows these regressions. Column (1) compares the results with the entire sample, finding a coefficient of 0.2, a low estimation compared to other countries in the literature, slightly above that of Scandinavian nations but lower than the USA (Chetty et al., 2014). These results would be out of the norm, as previous evidence has shown that Chile had less intergenerational mobility than the USA (Nuñez & Miranda, 2010). Columns (2)–(5) show the same calculations but for individuals originally from different income quartiles. The results seem

Table 2. Comparison Between National Survey CASEN and Panel Data.

	(1)	(2)	(3)	(4)	(5)	(6)	(7)	(8)	(9)
Source	Mean	SD	10%	25%	50%	75%	90%	Min	Max
CASEN Survey	504,936	473,738	185,000	274,167	380,000	600,000	950,000	500	1,150,000
Panel Data	539,484	394,111	170,206	288,925	431,250	688,915	1,022,850	0	3,493,000
Difference	7%	−17%	−8%	5%	13%	15%	8%		

Notes: Casen Survey Individuals 27 years old in 2017.
Panel Data Set, average wage 2016, 2017 and part of 2018.

Table 3. OLS Regressions: Adult Wages and Income Quartiles.

	(1)	(2)	(3)	(4)	(5)
VARIABLES	Full Sample	Q1	Q2	Q3	Q4
Parental Income Rank	0.204***	0.179***	0.0455***	0.184***	0.729***
Constant	0.404***	0.415***	0.475***	0.396***	−0.0303*
Observations	181,885	46,062	47,315	45,549	41,094
R-squared	0.041	0.005	0.000	0.008	0.032

Note: *** $p<0.01$, ** $p<0.05$, * $p<0.1$.

puzzling, showing high mobility for quartiles Q1, Q2, and Q3. However, the coefficient seems high (0.729) for higher-income families. This means there is high mobility amongst the lower-income groups but a high transmission of income for the higher-income groups. Previous work has mentioned that the rank-rank slope has the advantage of having a linear relationship (Chetty et al., 2014); however, it does not seem to be the case in Chile, and this assumption should likely be tested in other highly-unequal developing countries.

To review the administrative data set's validity and the missing data's possible problems, we replicate the analysis using the national CASEN survey from 2017. The CASEN survey is a nationally representative household survey used to guide social policy in Chile. It is also the source of information that previous studies used to estimate intergenerational mobility in Chile (Nuñez & Miranda, 2010; OECD, 2018). Synthetic parents are created using the educational levels from the survey, and the parental household income is used if the individuals did not answer the survey.[11] The results show a very similar overall pattern of mobility (0.208 for CASEN, and 0.204 for the administrative data). The similarity of the results obtained using the CASEN 2017 survey and the administrative data suggest that the administrative data provides consistent results, even with the missing data due to informality. Once we start to look in more detail, the results for income quartiles (1) to (3) are different, reversing the estimations. Q1 and Q3 have low estimates in the CASEN survey (0.037 and 0.005), while Q2 has a high estimate (0.209). The result for the highest income group, Q4, is high at (0.597); however, lower than the estimate from using the administrative data. This could be a weakness of the survey.[12] These differences per income quartiles could be due to the synthetic fathers' assumption, which does not allow dividing the population into smaller groups, while the administrative panel data set has detailed information on parental income.

Administrative data sets used to measure intergenerational mobility are particularly susceptible to two biases: life cycle bias and transitional income bias (Mazumder, 2016). Life cycle bias refers to income increasing during one's lifetime. Students graduating from higher education could have very volatile wages early in their careers and high wage increases afterward. Transitional income bias refers to the fact that using wages during a short period of time could capture a momentary shock in an individual's income. Both factors increase the estimation of intergenerational mobility. To attenuate transitional income bias, in Table 4 we use the average of three years of wages of students (2016, 2017, and part of 2018).

Table 4. OLS Regressions: Casen Survey 2017. Individuals 25–30 Years Old.

	(1)	(2)	(3)	(4)	(5)
VARIABLES	Full Sample	Q1	Q2	Q3	Q4
Parental Income Rank	0.208***	0.0375***	0.209***	0.00542	0.597***
Constant	0.401***	0.448***	0.377***	0.506***	0.0773***
Observations	1,658,524	368,017	401,238	425,028	464,241
R-squared	0.045	0.000	0.003	0.000	0.028

Notes: Observations represent the expanded population.
*** $p<0.01$, ** $p<0.05$, * $p<0.1$.

To analyze the problem of the life cycle bias, we use the CASEN survey. Fig. 2 compares the rank-rank income relationships estimated using the administrative data sets and the CASEN 2017 survey. In Fig. 2, the line represents the average child rank for each percentile of parental rank and different age groups. It is possible to see that the curves tend to have similar behaviour. However, the curves do not seem to have small changes when there are changes in the years of the analyzed sample. This would mean that the estimations will be different for different age groups.

Table 5 shows the rank-rank regressions using the CASEN survey for individuals from different age groups to analyze the presence of life cycle bias. It is possible to see that the full sample size obtains a coefficient of 0.238, while for the 25–30-year-old group, the coefficient estimated is 0.21. Moreover, the estimated coefficient increases for older age groups, consistent with the literature (OECD, 2018). Students are analyzed at 27 years old, which is the maximum available age

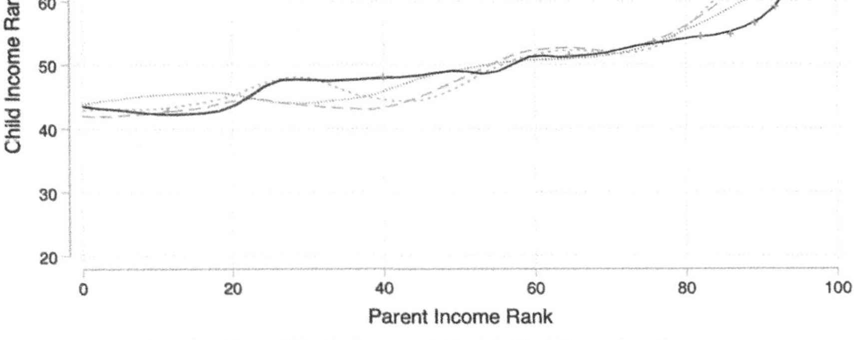

Fig. 2. Intergenerational Income Mobility in Chile.

Table 5. OLS Regressions: Casen Survey 2017.

	(1)	(2)	(3)	(4)	(5)
VARIABLES	Full Sample (25–40)	25–30	30–35	35–40	30–40
Parental Income Rank	0.238***	0.208***	0.268***	0.262	0.251***
Constant	0.369***	0.401***	0.355***	0.364***	0.388***
Observations	3,740,295	1,658,524	1,345,105	1,222,955	2,338,712
R-squared	0.06	0.0429	0.076	0.072	0.059

Notes: Observations represent the expanded population.
*** $p<0.01$, ** $p<0.05$, * $p<0.1$.

in the administrative data set. Hence, although the CASEN survey analyses individuals from different cohorts, and this survey does not follow the same cohort over time, it is possible to expect that the administrative data will present downward biased results compared to the long-term estimate. Therefore, the results of this paper using administrative data should not be considered the long-term rank-rank intergenerational income mobility but rather the early life estimate.

Fig. 3 compares rank-rank results in Chile, Italy, and Spain. The graph shows the average adult-child income rank for each parental income rank percentile. This chapter analyzes these three countries' use of administrative data to calculate intergenerational mobility. The results show similar income mobility between Chile and Spain, with high mobility for individuals in the lowest 80% of the population and high 'stickiness' or transmission of income in the upper part of the distribution. In particular, the Chilean income distribution shows very low

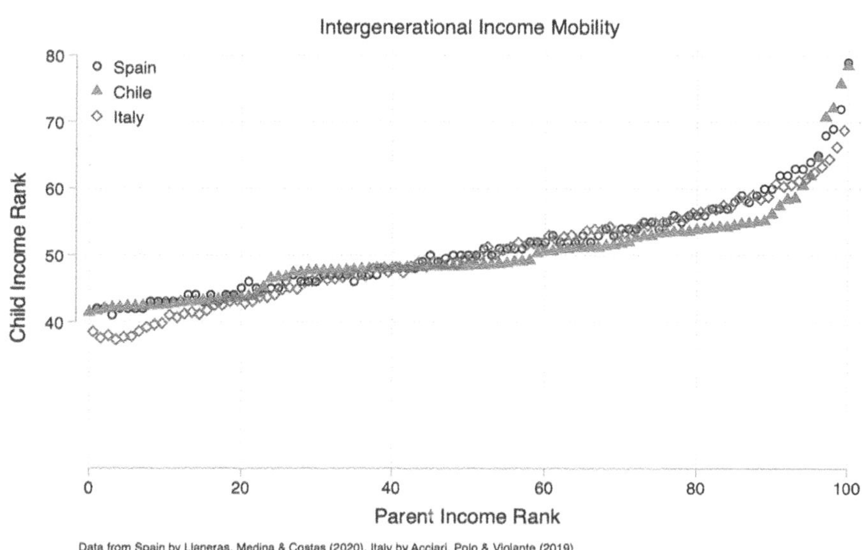

Fig. 3. Intergenerational Income Mobility in Three Countries.

mobility (or a high slope) for individuals whose parents were in the top 10% of the distribution. As explained by Bratberg (2014), it is possible that a single indicator (or a linear one) is not able to fully transmit the complexity of social mobility in countries with low mobility in the extremes. Therefore, it could be possible that only looking at the rank-rank coefficient could not be enough to understand intergenerational mobility in Chile. Other estimates (like the IGE explained in the introductory section) could provide more information.

It is also relevant to note that the data from Chile and Spain do not show stickiness at the bottom of the distribution, while the results from Italy present a slope change. This is likely due to a failure of the data on parental and child income (taxes for Spain and unemployment insurance in Chile) and not the country itself. Both studies have data limitations; the Spanish data set lacks information on the 40% of children who did not declare income, while the current paper lacks data for 27% of the children who either do not work or do not work in the formal sector. Missing data is a problem for research using administrative data sets; Appendix 2 (Table 8 and Fig. 16) compares the estimates and missing data from different countries.

B. Climbing the Mobility Ladder

Transition matrices analyze how students succeed or not in the mobility ladder by analyzing the income mobility of parents and children. Table 6 shows the transition matrix of students, dividing them into four income quartiles for parents and children. The parental quartile shows where the students started, and the child adult income quartile shows the final income of the child.[13] The transition matrix shows that there is 'stickiness' at both extremes. Individuals in the lowest income quartile have a 29% probability of remaining in that quartile, and a 16% probability of reaching the top quartile, while high-income individuals have a 42% probability of continuing in the same quartile. Note that previous estimates from the literature have shown even more mobility in Chile. Using the CASEN Panel Survey, the OECD (2018) found that low-income individuals had a 25% probability of remaining in the low-income quartile and a 23% probability of entering the top one.[14] Analyzing occupations, Torche (2005) has found income fluidity in Chile but downward rigidity for higher occupational groups. Although these results are also similar to a paper using administrative data in Scandinavian countries (Bratberg, 2014), it is important to mention that these income quartiles hide important variations that make the IGE or rank-rank coefficients differ.

Table 6. Income Transition Matrix.

		Child Adult Income			
		q1	q2	q3	q4
Parental Income	q1	29%	30%	25%	16%
	q2	24%	26%	26%	23%
	q3	24%	26%	25%	25%
	q4	20%	17%	21%	42%

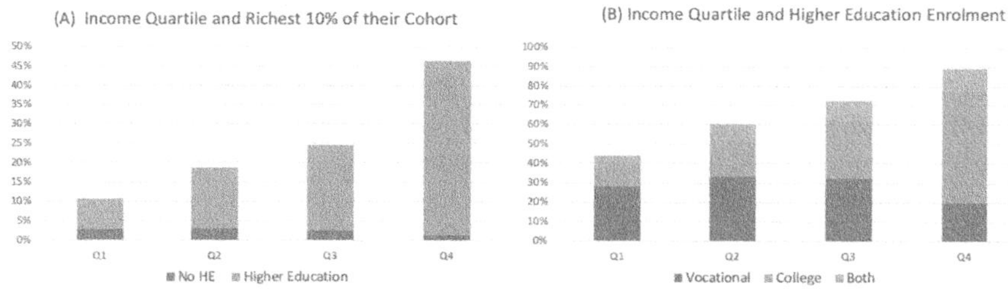

Fig. 4. Higher Education Enrollment, Top 10% in Wages and Income Quartiles.

While the transition matrix analyzed the movement between quartile groups, it could be useful to investigate the individuals from all income groups who reach the top 10% of their cohort measured in wages. Fig. 4 (left) shows this proportion of students. It is possible to see that 40% of the students in the top 10% are from the fourth income quartile and have tertiary education. It seems that proportionally, higher education is correlated with high-income students reaching the top ten percent, something that will be reviewed later.

In Chile, while children in all income groups had important gains in educational achievement, access to higher education is still stratified. Fig. 4 (right) shows that, while 89% of the students in the highest income quartile had enrolled in higher education, only 44% of students in the lowest income quartile did. Moreover, while the majority of low-income students access vocational education, higher-income students were much more likely to enroll in college. Additionally, while the difference in higher education access is significant, the proportion of low-income students who reach the highest 10% income group of their cohort is even lower, compared to individuals from the highest income quartile.

Fig. 5 (left) shows that of students who reach the richest 10%, most of them graduated from college. Fig. 5 (right) shows that low-income students graduate at a lower rate. Therefore, we have identified our first factors correlated with intergenerational mobility roadblocks; low-income students have lower higher educational enrollment, college enrollment, and graduation rates.

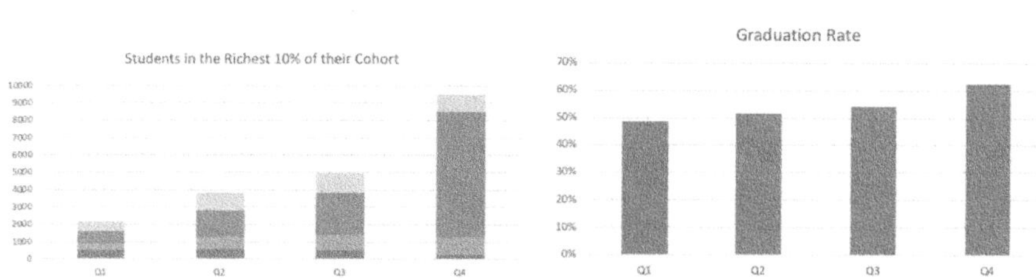

Income quartiles calculated from parental survey in 2004.

Fig. 5. Higher Education Enrollment Type, Graduation Rates and Income Quartiles.

Even after graduating from college, low-income students face several challenges. One is that they tend to enroll in majors that are rarely found in the richest 10% (Appendix 3). In Chile, students choose their college major before enrolling in college and have almost no possibility to change later. Thus, this is a factor that is associated with their high school environment, not their higher education environment. Low-income students will tend to study degrees and programs with lower profitability, even when having College Selection Test scores that allow them to attend other programs.

C. Academic Outcomes, Social Class, and Role Models

Role models in school have been proven to be a relevant factor in educational decisions (Altmejd et al., 2020; Barrios Fernández, 2019; Blanco & Meneses, 2013), and there are similar arguments about the social class of origin as well (Bourdieu, 1986). This subsection will analyze the correlation of academic outcomes, role models, and social class on intergenerational income mobility. First, the maximum educational level attained by each student will be used as a control variable as in other papers in the literature (Chetty et al., 2017). Second, a social class and role model proxy will be created at the high school level. The first indicator measures the proportion of older classmates in each school who graduated successfully from high-wage majors (engineering, the sciences, and social sciences). The proxy for social class will be the proportion of fellow students whose parents are high-level managers. Meanwhile, the student's academic quality is controlled for by using the 2004 SIMCE test scores.

Table 6 shows the results considering five different specifications. Column (1) includes the students' academic outcomes, showing that increased educational achievement is correlated with upward intergenerational mobility. In particular college graduation is associated with a 0.235 rank increase. Columns (2) and (3) include social class controls and the SIMCE test scores. The results show that the inclusion of social class and role models proxies have a positive and significant coefficient and furthermore, reduce the college coefficient. Column (4) includes a municipality dummy variable, to control for neighbourhood environments. The proxies of social class and role models are correlated with higher students' income rankings, even when controlling for the SIMCE test scores at the student and school levels. The results for the 8th-grade SIMCE test score show that higher test scores increase the probability of upward intergenerational mobility. The proxies of social class and role models continue to be significant after the municipality and quality controls are included. Column (5) includes the SIMCE test score at the school level and the interaction between the social class proxy and college education. The interaction effect between social class and college is positive and significant, meaning that being enrolled in a higher-class school is associated with higher intergenerational mobility once the students attend college, similar to the results of Zimmerman (2019). The results also show that the inclusion of the social class and role model proxies increased the adj-R-squared, increasing the explanatory power of the model, over the model in column (1). This increase in the adj-R-squared or explanatory power leads to the conclusion that regressions that include only parental income ranking and educational outcomes could be lacking other important social components -such as social class – that should be included in future research. Appendix 5 (Table 14) shows the OLS results including Standard Deviations.

Fig. 6 shows a pattern similar compared to Table 7, column (5), where students from higher-class schools who attend college have a higher curve compared to those who went to college but went to regular high schools. These results suggest that students attending higher-class high schools tend to have less intergenerational downward mobility, a higher slope, and a higher rank level.

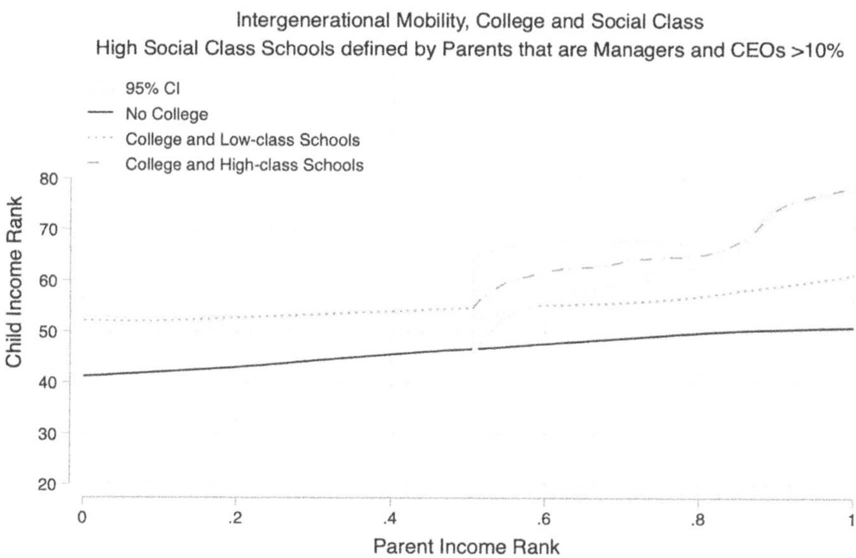

Fig. 6. Intergenerational Income Mobility, College and Social Class Proxy. *** $p<0.01$, ** $p<0.05$, * $p<0.1$

Table 7. OLS Results: Academic Outcomes, Role Models and Social Class.

VARIABLES	(1)	(2)	(3)	(4)	(5)
Parental Income Rank	0.0802***	0.0468***	0.0418***	0.0109***	0.0143***
Middle School	−0.0843***	−0.0754***	−0.0710***	−0.0663***	−0.0661***
9th Grade Drop-out	−0.0819***	−0.0723***	−0.0694***	−0.0684***	−0.0680***
10th Grade Drop-out	−0.0733***	−0.0628***	−0.0608***	−0.0603***	−0.0598***
11th Grade Drop-out	−0.0565***	−0.0454***	−0.0454***	−0.0444***	−0.0438***
HE Freshman Drop-out	0.0480***	0.0462***	0.0421***	0.0299***	0.0303***

(*Continued*)

Table 7. *(Continued)*

VARIABLES	(1)	(2)	(3)	(4)	(5)
HE Sophomore Drop-out	0.0298***	0.0276***	0.0239***	0.0172***	0.0175***
HE Junior Drop-out	0.0400***	0.0369***	0.0325***	0.0271***	0.0274***
HE Senior+more Drop-out	−0.0188***	−0.0265***	−0.0347***	−0.0358***	−0.0345***
Vocational Graduate	0.113***	0.104***	0.0971***	0.0981***	0.0987***
College Graduate	0.235***	0.204***	0.188***	0.195***	0.192***
Role Models Proxy		0.128***	0.0870***	0.114***	0.123***
Social Class Proxy		0.337***	0.324***	0.256***	0.119***
SIMCE Test Score 2004			0.000417***	0.000427***	0.000449***
SIMCE Test School					−0.000129***
Social Class & College					0.189***
Municipality	no	no	no	yes	yes
Constant	0.400***	0.395***	0.307***	0.367***	0.391***
Observations	181,885	181,885	181,884	181,884	181,884
Adj-R-squared	0.151	0.158	0.161	0.182	0.182

Notes: Standard errors in parentheses.
*** $p<0.01$, ** $p<0.05$, * $p<0.1$.

Overall, the results in Table 7 also show that the inclusion of the proxies for role models, social class, and SIMCE test scores reduces the college graduation coefficient's magnitude and increases the adjusted-R squared. The results also show that social class of origin and school environments are related to changes in intergenerational mobility, particularly higher-income ranking for the students, and lower mobility (as higher-income students attend higher-class schools). Therefore, it is possible that previous studies that did not include factors such as social class or high school environment, (like Torche (2011); Palomino et al. (2018); Chetty et al. (2017)) could be overestimating the impact of college on intergenerational mobility as they did not control for previous school and social class environments.

D. Year-to-Year Analysis

Besides test scores, educational environments, and social class, students' educational and work trajectories could also influence their intergenerational mobility. This section will perform a year-to-year analysis of their actual educational and work trajectories. To analyze the student trajectories, the regression includes 592 possible profiles. These profiles were chosen as they each represent 10 or more students.

The OLS regressions are performed with students in middle school as the base of the analysis (Appendix 4, Table 13). Fig. 7 shows the 40 most common student

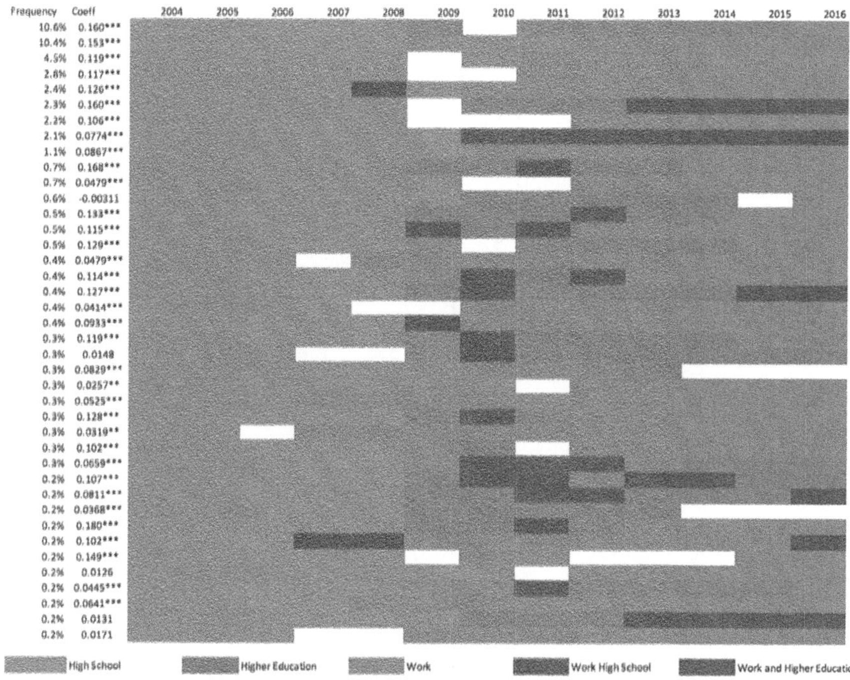

Fig. 7. Most Frequent Profiles: Coefficient for Joint Trajectories.
*** $p<0.01$, ** $p<0.05$, * $p<0.1$.

profiles. There is a great diversity of possible education and work profiles. It's possible to see that in seven of the categories, students have a gap year before they enter higher education or start working. However, these profiles are not the most profitable ones in terms of intergenerational mobility. Fig. 8 shows the 40 profiles that provide the highest returns in terms of income rank in their cohort. Note that the majority of these profiles do not have gap years, start and end higher education soon, and include steady work trajectories. The top trajectories have the characteristic of direct high-school to higher education transitions, direct higher-education to work transitions, and a steady work pattern. This means that gap years are negatively correlated with higher income mobility. Moreover, the majority of these profiles include a mixture of working while attending high school and working while attending higher education. Therefore, it could be possible that there are positive externalities to working and studying at the same time. However, it's possible that these success profiles correspond to different types of individuals.

Fig. 9 shows the top 20 profiles, that generate the most income mobility, for students in the top income quartile in 8th grade. Fig. 9 shows that 19 of these profiles include higher education, and 16 include a steady and stable work profile, with no gap years. For higher-income students, then, higher education seems to be associated with upward social mobility. Moreover, it's possible to see that most

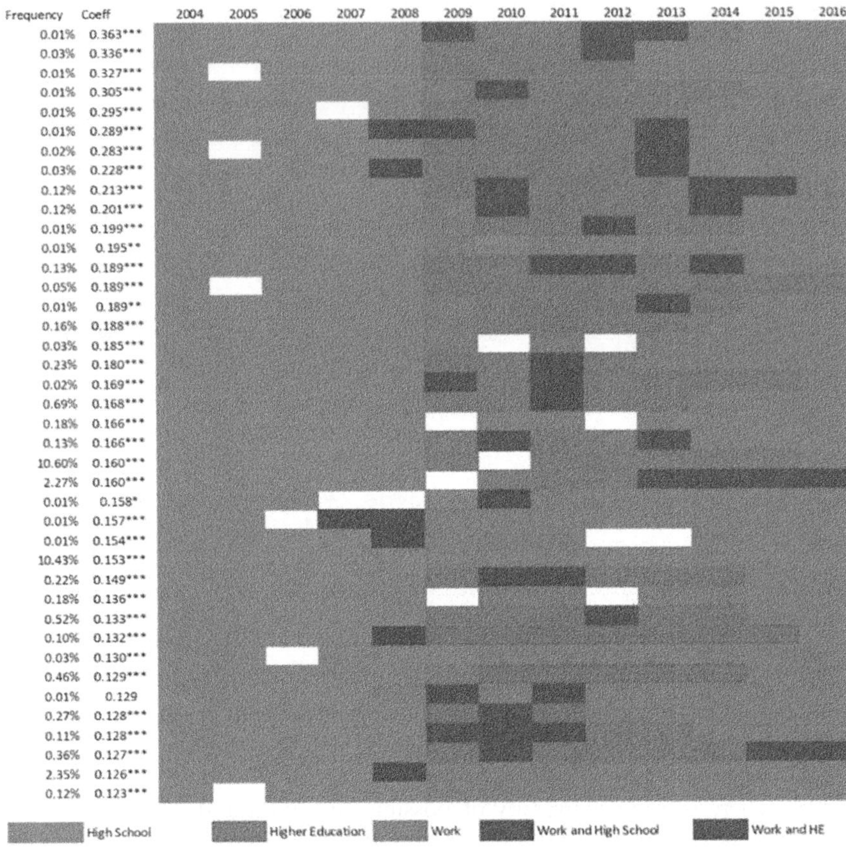

Fig. 8. Top 40 Profiles: Coefficient for Joint Trajectories.

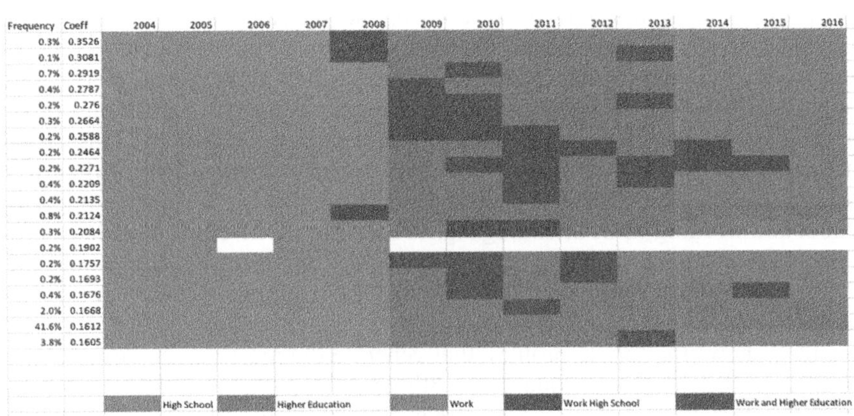

Fig. 9. Top Quartile Income Families: Top 20 Profiles: Coefficient for Joint Trajectories.

of these profiles include a steady high school education and only three include high school and work. However, many include higher education and work at the same time. Overall, these profiles seem very 'traditional' in the sense that students graduate high school on time, attend higher education, and then work, without gap years.

Fig. 10 shows the top profiles, for individuals in the bottom income quartile in 8th grade. The results are extremely different compared to their high-income counterparts. Only 3 out of the 20 profiles include higher education. Eighteen out of the 20 profiles include steady work patterns after high school and higher education. Most of these profiles do not include gap years, showing that stable labour market participation is associated with upward mobility.

The analysis then shows that while, for high-income students, upward mobility is achieved mainly through higher education, for lower-income students, higher mobility is achieved mainly through the labour market and in particular, a stable work pattern, without gap years.

These results would point out in the same direction as the findings from the previous section, which found that higher education was more effective to promote mobility amongst individuals from upper-class schools. Moreover, from a policy perspective, the conclusions to promote social mobility for different types of individuals could be different. While for high-income individuals, a stable higher education seems key, for low-income individuals, fast labour market integration and labour stability are crucial.

Fig. 11 shows the education and work trajectories that have the lowest returns in terms of rank. In general, these profiles have students not finishing high school or finishing it in an irregular pattern. These are the students that have failed in the educational system and in the labour market; having problems finishing high school and keeping a stable work. Further research should focus on the social variables and shocks that these students are facing, and propose policies that would help these individuals to effectively attend high school and successfully integrate themselves into the labour force.

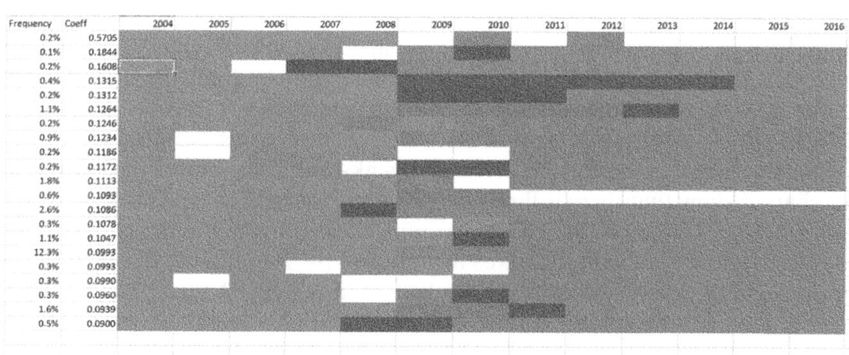

Fig. 10. Bottom Quartile Income Families: Top 20 Profiles: Coefficient for Joint Trajectories.

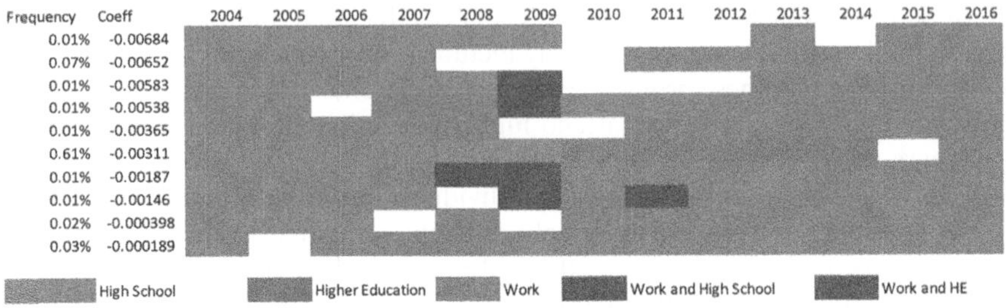

Fig. 11. Bottom 10 Profiles: Coefficient for Joint Trajectories.

The results of this subsection show that while higher education is important, the profile of education and work are also relevant in achieving upward intergenerational mobility. Profiles of students who are able to maintain a steady educational and work profile, with no gap years, are correlated with the highest increases in intergenerational income mobility. Although previous studies have shown that higher education stop-out (taking a gap year or changing programs) is not necessarily correlated with lower graduation rates (Blanco, 2018), these trajectories seem to have intergenerational mobility effects.

V. CONCLUSIONS

This chapter is one of the first attempts to estimate intergenerational mobility in a developing country using administrative data sets, tackling data limitations as well as the emergence of results that generate new puzzles.

The analysis using administrative data and the national CASEN survey found that the administrative data sets and the CASEN 2017 survey generate similar results for individuals of the same age group, with a rank-rank coefficient of 0.20. The IGE estimates for Chile were found between 0.43 and 0.53 (Nuñez & Miranda, 2010), while the rank mobility estimates found are between 0.20 and 0.26 for different age groups. This big difference in intergenerational mobility estimates between this paper and previous papers could be explained by changes in the level of income and income variance of the children, the assumptions in the creation of synthetic fathers, and particular characteristics of Chilean society.

Overall, using transition matrices and rank-rank regressions, the results of this chapter show that there is fluid intergenerational mobility in Chile. However, there is 'stickiness' for higher-income groups, presenting high rank-rank correlations (0.79) compared with the lower-income groups. These results are in line with previous intergenerational mobility results for Chile (OECD, 2018; Torche, 2005) that present a mobile society with a rigid upper class.

The results of this chapter showed the strengths of detailed administrative data sets. Using OLS regressions, the association between academic outcomes and intergenerational mobility is tested. Taking advantage of detailed individual and school-level information, this chapter analyzed the inclusion of academic quality, social class, role model proxies, and municipality controls. The results showed an association between these controls and intergenerational mobility, increasing their explanatory power, and reducing the estimated association with college education. These results highlight the importance of neighbourhood and school environments. Moreover, it suggests that previous papers that do not include environmental or school controls could be overestimating the correlation between college and intergenerational mobility.

The year-to-year analysis of educational and labour market trajectories showed there are many possible educational and work trajectories that students could have, however not all of the trajectories that include pursuing higher education are as effective. In particular, trajectories that include higher education but also include a gap year are associated with lower mobility. While trajectories that included direct high school to higher education transitions and direct higher education to work transitions were related to higher intergenerational mobility.

Moreover, the year-to-year analysis showed that lower-income students on average find better results by integrating directly into the labour market than by pursuing the higher-education strategy, while the higher-education strategy could provide for a higher variance. The higher variance but lower average effect could explain in part why an important proportion of students from the lowest quintile reaching the highest income decile have a college education and also explain why so few low-income students get to the highest income decile. Higher education seems to be providing a risky path for low-income students towards social mobility.

The utilization of administrative panel data sets and year-to-year analysis allows for new research, as complex questions can be answered, specifically about the life trajectories that individuals take. From a policy perspective, these year-to-year analyses shed light on the negative effects of slow or failed transitions between high school, higher education, and work, as well as gap years. Further research needs to be done in this arena to analyze the causes and long-term consequences of these slow transitions that are initially associated with lower intergenerational income mobility.

NOTES

1. This element of the literature is useful as it explains the macro trends at the country level, brings up the topic of intergenerational mobility, and informs the public. The deployment of various sources of information has produced diverse methodologies for analyzing the information and estimating social mobility, further contributing to the academic debate.
2. This second branch is nurtured by the methodological developments of the first, taking advantage of the empirical innovations and data set developments.
3. Intergenerational Elasticity (IGE) is the standard measurement in the economic literature used to relate parental income with child's income and is usually estimated over the logs of income (log-log). However, the IGE has estimation problems as income variance changes over different cohorts. The differences in the income variance of the child's cohort will affect the estimations, making them not bounded between 0 and 1.
4. The lack of intergenerational surveys in some countries has motivated the development of new methodologies using cross-section surveys, retrospective questions, or synthetic connections. However, retrospective questions are problematic, as children have a difficult time recalling their parents' income (Chetty et al., 2014). Another approach is proposed by Björklund and Jäntti (1997), using parental education and occupation as an instrument to predict income. This methodology consists of estimating an earning

equation using parental cohorts. Then these estimated coefficients are used to predict parental income in the sample of children who reported retrospective parental information. Using the predicted parental wages, then IGE can be calculated. This methodology is known as the two-sample two-stage least squares (TSTSLS) or two-sample instrumental variable (TSIV) (Ñunez and Miranda, 2010). This methodology and subsequent variations of 'synthetic fathers' has allowed for the expansion of the literature in developing countries that did not have the money, time or institutional capacity to perform longitudinal surveys, but have the capacity to perform cross-sectional ones (Nayaran et al., 2018; OECD, 2018).

5. While there is consensus that on average higher education promotes social mobility, it is also true that for some groups of students, this is not always the case. In some countries, higher education could be reinforcing inequality (Haveman & Smeeding, 2006). The expansion of higher education in Britain disproportionately benefited higher income groups, increasing inequality (Machin, 2007). Using a sociological approach, and following more than 50 students over six years, Armstrong and Hamilton (2013) find that college education tends to maintain initial inequalities. For India, Iversen et al. (2019) note that there is a disconnect between educational mobility and occupational mobility as other characteristics (gender, identity, or location) may be making it harder to transform educational gains into labor market ones. Bucarey et al. (2018) find that students who enrolled in college in Chile and were at the margin of the financial aid cutoff do not obtain higher wages when compared to their counterparts who did not enroll in college. These authors attribute this effect to low-quality institutions and under-prepared students who do not graduate from college.

6. In the developing world, the low availability of services or state capacity in rural areas may affect intergenerational mobility.

7. At the secondary level, although the gross enrollment rate reaches 99.6%, the net enrollment rate only reaches 73.6%, suggesting a pronounced overage in this education level, due to important dropout and stop-out rates.

8. The tertiary education system, including both university and vocational education, had 245,000 enrolled students in 1990, and is currently nearly 1.3 million students.

9. According to Chile's CASEN survey, there were 283,695 individuals of 26 years of age in 2017. The SIMCE test was planned for 280,753 students, and 249,373 parents answered the income question in the parental survey.

10. The parents of the missing children are not excluded from the calculation, results are robust to this assumption.

11. The usage of the effective wages is necessary to have enough data to perform the regressions for each quartile group.

12. All individuals with available data are included, including those making less than the minimum wage.

13. Average between year 2016, 2017 and 2018.

14. These results found by the OECD show high mobility for Chile, similar to countries such as Denmark, Portugal, or Great Britain (OECD, 2018).

ACKNOWLEDGEMENTS

We would like to thank the support of Anirudh Krishna, Marcos Rangel, Christian Blanco, Harlan Down-Stepper, Emily Rains and the DevLab, GRW seminars at Duke, The Chilean Ministry of Labor and the Chilean Ministry of Education. Millennium Nucleus on Intergenerational Mobility: From Modeling to Policy (MMOVI), Santiago, Chile: Banco del Estado de Chile.

K.A. acknowledges and thanks the Chilean Agencia Nacional de Investigación y Desarrollo (ANID) for funding through the Millennium Nucleus on Intergenerational Mobility: From Modelling to Policy (MOVI) [NCS2021072], the Centre for Sustainable Urban Development (CEDEUS) [ANID FONDAP 1522A0002], and the Fondecyt Regular program [1231755].

REFERENCES

Acciari, P., Polo, A., & Violante, G. L. (2022). And yet it moves: Intergenerational mobility in Italy. *American Economic Journal: Applied Economics*, *14*(3), 118–163.

Altmejd, A., Barrios-Fernandez, A., Drlje, M., & Neilson, C. (2020). Siblings' spillover effects on college and major choice: Evidence from Chile.

Ananat, E., Gassman-Pines, A., & Gibson-Davis, C. (2011). The effects of local employment losses on children's educational achievement.

Armstrong, E., & Hamilton, L. (2013). *Paying for the party*. Harvard University Press.

Ashley, L., Duberley, J., Sommerlad, H., & Scholarios, D. (2015). *A qualitative evaluation of non-educational barriers to the elite professions*. Social Mobility and Child Poverty Commission London.

Bank, W. (2020). Poverty and shared prosperity 2020: Reversals of fortune. The World Bank.

Barrios Fernández, A. (2019). Should I stay or should I go? Neighbors. *Effects on University Enrollment. Neighbors' Effects on University Enrollment*.

Becker, G., &Tomes, N. (1979). An equilibrium theory of the distribution of income and intergenerational mobility. *Journal of Political Economy*, *87*(6), 1153–1189.

Behrman, J. (2019). *Human capital and social mobility in low-and middle-income countries*. WIDER Working Paper.

Bergman, P., Chetty, R., DeLuca, S., Hendren, N., Katz, L., & Palmer, C. (2019). *Creating moves to opportunity: Experimental evidence on barriers to neighborhood choice*. National Bureau of Economic Research.

Björklund, A., & Jäntti, M. (1997). Intergenerational income mobility in Sweden compared to the United States. *The American Economic Review*, *87*(5), 1009–1018.

Björklund, A., & Jäntti, M. (2009). Intergenerational income mobility and the role of family background. In W. Salverda, B. Nolan, & T. M. Smeeding (Eds.), *Oxford handbook of economic inequality* (Vol. 491, p. 521).

Blanco, C., M. F. P. R. (2018). Más allá de la deserción: trayectorias académicas en la educación superior en chile. *Calidad en la educación*, *49*(49), 137–187.

Blanco, C., & Meneses, F. (2013). Impacto de la ayuda financiera en la matrícula técnica y universitaria. *Sociedad Hoy*, *24*, 107–117.

Bourdieu, P. (1986). The forms of capital. In J. Richardson (Ed.), *Handbook of theory and research for the sociology of education* (Vol. 241, pp. 46–58). Greenwood.

Bratberg, E., R. K. M. E. V. K. (2014). Intergenerational earnings mobility and divorce. *Journal of Population Economics*, *27*(96), 1107–1126.

Bratberg, E., Davis, J., Mazumder, B., Nybom, M., Schnitzlein, D. D., & Vaage, K. (2017). A comparison of intergenerational mobility curves in Germany, Norway, Sweden, and the US. *The Scandinavian Journal of Economics*, *119*(1), 72–101.

Bucarey, A., Contreras, D., & Muñoz, P. (2018). Labor market returns to student loans. Series Documentos de Trabajo No. 464, Mayo, pp. 1–48.

Canales, A. (2016). Diferencias socioeconómicas en la postulación a las universidades chilenas: El rol de factores académicos y no académicos. *Calidad En La Educación*, *44*, 129–157.

Chetty, R., Friedman, J., Hilger, N., Saez, E., Schanzenbach, D., & Yagan, D. (2011). How does your kindergarten classroom affect your earnings? *Evidence from Project STAR. The Quarterly Journal of Economics*, *126*(4), 1593–1660.

Chetty, R., Friedman, J., Saez, E., Turner, N., & Yagan, D. (2017). *Mobility report cards: The role of colleges in intergenerational mobility*. NBER Working Paper. Working Paper No. 23618.

Chetty, R., Hendren, N., & Katz, L. (2016). The effects of exposure to better neighborhoods on children: New evidence from the moving to opportunity experiment. *American Economic Review*, *106*(4), 855–902.

Chetty, R., Hendren, N., Kline, P., & Saez, E. (2014). Where is the land of opportunity? the geography of intergenerational mobility in the United States. *The Quarterly Journal of Economics*, *129*(4), 1553–1623.

Contreras, D. (2003). Poverty and inequality in a rapid growth economy: Chile 1990-96. *Journal of Development Studies*, *39*(3), 181–200.

Corak, M. (2013). Income inequality, equality of opportunity, and intergenerational mobility. *Journal of Economic Perspectives*, *27*(3), 79–102.

Corsetti, G., & Schmidt-Hebbel, K. (1999). *Pension reform and growth*. The World Bank.

Dahl, M., & DeLeire, T. (2008). *The association between children's earnings and fathers' lifetime earnings: Estimates using administrative data*. University of Wisconsin-Madison, Institute for Research on Poverty.

Desarrollo Social, M. (2015). *CASEN*. Informe de Desarrollo Social 2015, Ministerio de Desarrollo Social.

Deutscher, N., & Mazumder, B. (2020). Intergenerational mobility across Australia and the stability of regional estimates. *Labour Economics*, *66*, 101861.

Erikson, R., Goldthorpe, J., & Portocarero, L. (1979). Intergenerational class mobility in three western European societies: England, France and Sweden. *The British Journal of Sociology*, *30*(4), 415–441.

Gallegos, S., Meneses, F., & Contreras, D. (2019). *Rescuing low-income, high ability students*. Working Paper.

Hastings, J., Neilson, C., & Zimmerman, S. (2015). *The effects of earnings disclosure on college enrollment decisions*. National Bureau of Economic Research.

Haveman, R., & Smeeding, T. (2006). The role of higher education in social mobility. *The Future of Children*, *16*, 125–150.

Heckman, J. (2006). Skill formation and the economics of investing in disadvantaged children. *Science*, *312*(5782), 1900–1902.

Heidrich, S. (2017). Intergenerational mobility in Sweden: A regional perspective. *Journal of Population Economics*, *30*(4), 1241–1280.

Heller, O. (2017). Intergenerational income mobility in Israel. In *Yad-Hanadiv Conference on Social Mobility and Equality in Israel, Jerusalem Israel, June*, volume *15*.

Hoff, K., & Pandey, P. (2004). *Belief systems and durable inequalities: An experimental investigation of Indian caste*. The World Bank.

Hoxby, C., & Avery, C. (2012). *The missing" one-offs": The hidden supply of high-achieving, low-income students*. National Bureau of Economic Research.

Hoxby, C., & Turner, S. (2013). Expanding college opportunities for high achieving, low-income students. *Stanford Institute for Economic Policy Research Discussion Paper*, *12*, 014.

Hoxby, C., & Turner, S. (2015). What high-achieving low-income students know about college. *American Economic Review*, *105*(5), 514–517.

Iversen, V., Krishna, A., & Sen, K. (2019). Beyond poverty escapes – social mobility in developing countries: A review article. *The World Bank Research Observer*, *34*(2), 239–273.

Jacoby, H., & Mansuri, G. (2015). Crossing boundaries: How social hierarchy impedes economic mobility. *Journal of Economic Behavior Organization*, *117*, 135–154.

Krishna, A. (2013). Making it in India: Examining social mobility in three walks of life. *Economic and Political Weekly*, 38–49.

Krishna, A., & Nolan, S. (2019). Synthetic fathers and real consequences: Social mobility research in transition. *The Journal of Development Studies*, *55*(4), 737–742.

Machin, S. (2007). Education expansion and intergenerational mobility in Britain. In L. Woessmann & P. E. Peterson (Eds.), *Schools and the equal opportunity problem* (Vol. 7, pp. 1–63). The MIT Press.

Mani, A., & Riley, E. (2019). Social networks, role models, peer effects, and aspirations. In *WIDER Working Paper 2019/120*. UNU-WIDER, Helsinki.

Marmaros, D., & Sacerdote, B. (2002). Peer and social networks in job search. *European Economic Review*, *46*(4–5), 870–879.

Maurin, E., & McNally, S. (2008). Vive la revolution! long-term educational returns of 1968 to the angry students. *Journal of Labor Economics*, *26*(1), 1–33.

Mazumder, B. (2016). Estimating the intergenerational elasticity and rank association in the United States: Overcoming the current limitations of tax data. *Research in Labor Economics*, *43*, 83–129.

Milanovic, B. (2016). *Global inequality: A new approach for the age of globalization*. Harvard University Press.

Missoni, E. S. G. (2010). Towards universal health coverage: The Chilean experience. *World Health Report*, *97*(96), 119–124.

Nguyen, T. (2008). *Information, role models and perceived returns to education: Experimental evidence from Madagascar*. Unpublished Manuscript, 6.

Nuñez, J., & Miranda, L. (2010). Intergenerational income mobility in a less developed, high-inequality context: The case of Chile. *The BE Journal of Economic Analysis Policy*, *10*(1), 1–17.

OECD. (2016). *Education at a Glance 2016*. OECD Publishing.

OECD. (2018). *Broken social elevator?: How to promote social mobility*. Organization for Economic Development.

Olavarria-Gambi, M. (2003). Poverty reduction in Chile: Has economic growth been enough? *Journal of Human Development*, *4*(1), 103–123.

Oreopoulos, P., Page, M., & Stevens, A. (2006). The intergenerational effects of compulsory schooling. *Journal of Labor Economics*, *24*(4), 729–760.

Palomino, J., Marrero, G., & Rodríguez, J. (2018). One size doesn't fit all: A quantile analysis of intergenerational income mobility in the us (1980–2010). *The Journal of Economic Inequality*, *16*(3), 347–367.

Pekkarinen, T., Uusitalo, R., & Kerr, S. (2009). School tracking and intergenerational income mobility: Evidence from the Finnish comprehensive school reform. *Journal of Public Economics*, *93*(7–8), 965–973.

Perkins, H. (1965). Classroom behavior and underachievement. *American Educational Research Journal*, *2*(1), 1–12.

Programme, U. N. D. (2017). *Desiguales. Orígenes, cambios y desafíos de la brecha social en Chile*, volume *00*.

Rist, R. (1970). Student social class and teacher expectations: The self-fulfilling prophecy in ghetto education. *Harvard Educational Review*, *40*(3), 411–451.

Rivera, L. (2011). Ivies, extracurriculars, and exclusion: Elite employers' use of educational credentials. *Research in Social Stratification and Mobility*, *29*(1), 71–90.

Rivera, L. (2016). *Pedigree: How elite students get elite jobs*. Princeton University Press.

Schmidt-Hebbel, K. (2006). Chile's economic growth. *Cuadernos de Economía*, *43*(127), 5–48.

SIES. (2014). *Panorama de la Educación Superior en Chile*. Technical report, División de Educación Superior, Ministerio de Educación.

Social, O. (2015). Ministerio desarrollo social (2016). *Encuesta de Caracterización Socioeconómica CASEN*.

Streib, J. (2011). Class reproduction by four year olds. *Qualitative Sociology*, *34*(2), 337.

Torche, F. (2005). Unequal but fluid: Social mobility in Chile in comparative perspective. *American Sociological Review*, *70*(3), 422–450.

Torche, F. (2010). Economic crisis and inequality of educational opportunity in Latin America. *Sociology of Education*, *83*(2), 85–110.

Torche, F. (2011). Is a college degree still the great equalizer? Intergenerational mobility across levels of schooling in the United States. *American Journal of Sociology*, *117*(3), 763–807.

Torche, F. (2015). Analyses of intergenerational mobility: An interdisciplinary review. *The Annals of the American Academy of Political and Social Science*, *657*(1), 37–62.

Torche, F. (2019). Educational mobility in developing countries. *WIDER Working Paper Series wp-2019-88*, World Institute for Development Economic Research (UNU-WIDER).

Urzúa, S. (2012). La rentabilidad de la educación superior en chile:¿ educaci´on superior para todos? centro de estudios públicos. *Estudios Públicos*, *2012*(125), 2–52.

Yee, A. (2016). The unwritten rules of engagement: Social class differences in undergraduates' academic strategies. *The Journal of Higher Education*, *87*(6), 831–858.

Zimmerman, S. (2019). Elite colleges and upward mobility to top jobs and top incomes. *American Economic Review*, *109*(1), 1–47.

Zirkel, S. (2002). Is there a place for me? Role models and academic identity among white students and students of color. *Teachers College Record*, *104*(2), 357–376.

APPENDIX 1

This chapter has 27% of missing data. As a first approach, the table below in Fig. 12 shows the proportion of students with missing data. We see a pattern of missing data for females and high-income males. This pattern of missing data gets reduced slightly when we consider higher education as a control, as a small proportion of individuals continue studying and do not work.

The missing data has two sources, individuals that are not working, in Education or Training (NEET) and individuals in the informal sector. To analyze informality and NEET we use the National CASEN survey and re-created the methodology of synthetic fathers. Then we classified students according to the expected income of their fathers. The table below in Fig. 13 shows the proportion of informal workers in four income quartiles. It's possible to see that they distribute evenly across income groups.

The table in Fig. 14 shows the NEET for individuals in four income quartiles. The results show a very high proportion of low-income females' NEET (32%) and a low proportion of high-income males (8%). This profile seems different from the administrative data, as we have a low proportion of NEET low-income males and more high-income males without data.

	No Wage		
	Total	Female	Male
Q1	26%	33%	18%
Q2	24%	31%	18%
Q3	25%	30%	20%
Q4	33%	35%	31%
Total	27%	32%	22%

	No Wage & No Higher Education		
	Total	Female	Male
Q1	26%	34%	17%
Q2	24%	31%	17%
Q3	24%	29%	19%
Q4	29%	31%	26%
Total	25%	31%	20%

Fig. 12. No Wage and No Higher Education Levels Compared Across Gender.

	Male	Female	
q1	11%	10%	11%
q2	11%	12%	12%
q3	10%	7%	9%
q4	10%	11%	11%
Total	11%	9%	10%

Fig. 13. Informal Workers in Chile.

	Male	Female	
q1	20%	32%	26%
q2	12%	28%	20%
q3	17%	31%	25%
q4	8%	27%	16%
Total	13%	27%	20%

Fig. 14. Not Working, in Education or Training.

Lastly, using CASEN 2017 it's possible to analyze if the wages of individuals are similar to their total income. The figure below in Fig. 15 shows the wages and total income of individuals and their ages. It's possible to see that the wages are an excellent proxy of their income between 25 and 32 years of age.

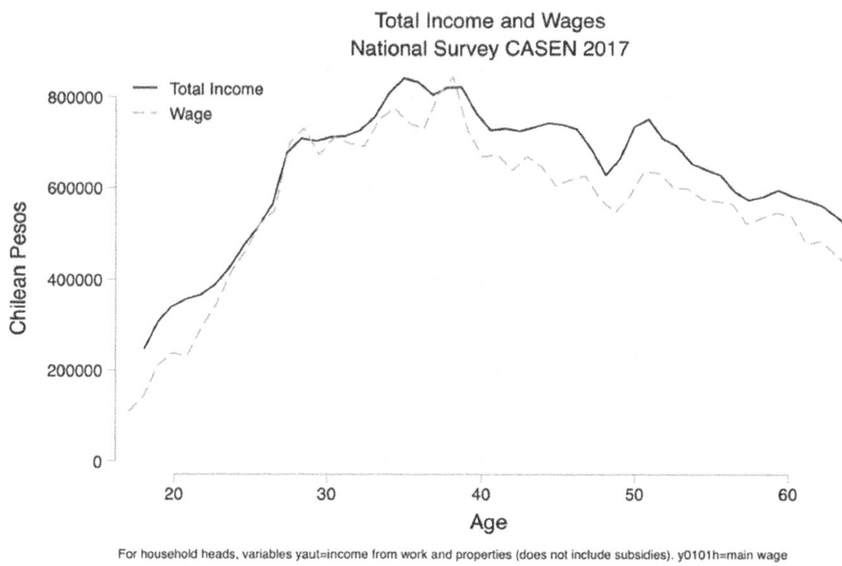

Fig. 15. Total Income Versus Wages (CASEN, 2017).

APPENDIX 2

Table 8. Intergenerational Mobility Estimates Using Administrative Data.

Results from other countries				
Country	IGE	Rank-Rank	Missing Data	Authors
Australia	0.185	0.215	15–20%	Deutscher and Mazumder (2020)
Chile	0.43	0.21	27%	Authors' own work
Italy	0.25	0.25	65%	Acciari et al. (2022)
Israel	0.28	0.251	18.3%	Heller (2017)
Norway	0.194	0.223	4%	Bratberg et al. (2017)
Spain		0.235	40%	Costas et al. (2020)
Sweden	.216	0.183	5%	Heidrich (2017)
United States	0.344	0.341	15–50%	Chetty et al. (2014)

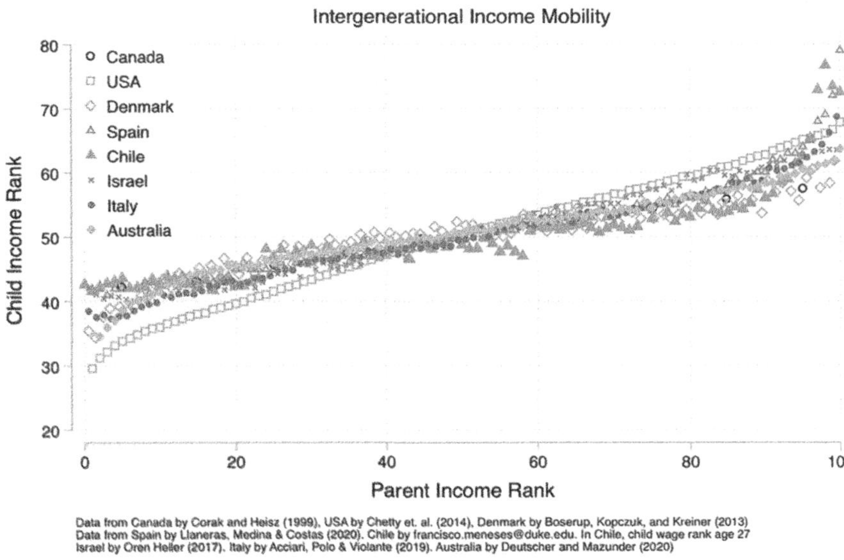

Fig. 16. Intergenerational Mobility Rank-Rank Comparison.

APPENDIX 3

Even after graduating from college, low-income students face several challenges. Table 7 shows the areas of study defined by the OECD and the probability of these students reaching the top 10%. There are areas of study that, even after graduation, provide a very low chance for the student to get to the richest 10%. For low-income students, being an engineer provides over 30% probability of reaching the richest 10%, while there is no possibility if the student studied humanities. An important roadblock that students face is choosing the area of study. In Chile, students select their college major before enrolling in college and have almost no possibility to change later.

The effect on intergenerational mobility of the area of study reinforces the impact of role models. It has been shown that role models affect the area and major of study of students in Chile (Altmejd et al., 2020; Barrios Fernández, 2019). Therefore, role models seem important for students to climb the mobility ladder, as they will help students choose the most profitable career paths.

Table 8 shows the students that reach the top 10%, by their parental income and sex. The results show that male students have a 60% probability of getting to the top 10%, while female students have only a 40% probability. However, these probabilities are not homogeneous among all income groups. High-income females compose 45% of the individuals of their income group that reach the top 10%, while for low-income individuals that reach the top, females are only 32%. Table 10 displays the areas of study.

EDUCATIONAL MOBILITY

Moving towards education, Table 9 shows the average years of education for children and their mothers for their original income quartile. The results show that children in all income groups increase their average years of education by 3.6 years or more compared to their mothers, with the lowest income group increasing the most, 5.5 years of average education. These results would confirm that in Chile there have been important increases in educational investment and mobility, benefiting all income groups as displayed in Table 11.

Table 9. Areas of Study of Students, and Proportion That Reaches Richest 10%.

	q1	q2	q3	q4
Agriculture	17%	19%	14%	30%
Sciences	29%	39%	40%	45%
Social Sciences	23%	29%	27%	45%
Education	15%	16%	14%	19%
Humanities	0%	7%	7%	15%
Engineering	31%	36%	39%	56%
Health	23%	27%	32%	40%
Services	12%	12%	16%	20%

Table 10. Areas of Study of Students, and Proportion of Total Graduates.

	q1	q2	q3	q4
Agriculture	2%	1%	2%	2%
Sciences	4%	5%	5%	4%
Social Sciences	22%	21%	22%	31%
Education	33%	31%	28%	16%
Humanities	2%	2%	3%	5%
Engineering	13%	14%	15%	18%
Health	20%	22%	22%	22%
Services	4%	3%	3%	2%
Total	100%	100%	100%	100%

Table 11. Original Income Quartile.

	Original Income Quartile			
	q1	q2	q3	q4
Childs' Education	13.4	14.5	15.4	17.2
Maternal Education	7.9	9.4	10.7	13.5
Difference	5.5	5	4.7	3.6

Table 12 shows the matrix of intergenerational educational mobility, comparing maternal education and the education of the adult child at age 26. The matrix shows the different categories of education (primary, high school, vocational, college, and graduate). The matrix shows that there is upward educational mobility for the children of mothers with primary, high school, and vocational education. There is a high correlation between the educational level of the children of mothers with college and graduate education and their mothers.

The descriptive results of this subsection start to describe the intergenerational mobility environment of this cohort in Chile. These last results also confirm the stickiness and downward mobility of female students. As the educational level has increased in this generation, there is high upward educational mobility in all groups.

Table 12. Educational Mobility Matrix.

	Maternal Education				
Child Education	Primary	High School	Vocational	College	Graduate
Primary	2%	0%	0%	0%	1%
High School	51%	24%	9%	4%	2%
Vocational	30%	33%	22%	11%	7%
College	17%	41%	66%	78%	80%
Graduate	0%	1%	4%	6%	11%

APPENDIX 4

Table 13. Summary of Main Regression Results.

	Equation (1)	Equation (3)
VARIABLES		
Parental Income Rank	0.204***	0.106***
592 Trajectories	no	yes
Constant	0.404***	0.08***
Observations	181,885	181,884
Adj R-squared	0.041	0.242

*** $p < 0.01$, ** $p < 0.05$, * $p < 0.1$.

APPENDIX 5

Table 14. Individuals Not Working, in Education or Training.

	(1)	(2)	(3)	(4)	(5)
VARIABLES	Full Sample	Full Sample	Full Sample	Full Sample	Full Sample
Parental Income Rank 2004	0.0796***	0.0461***	0.0411***	0.0103***	0.0136***
	(0.00242)	(0.00256)	(0.00256)	(0.00265)	(0.00273)
Middle School	−0.0847***	−0.0759***	−0.0713***	−0.0665***	−0.0663***
	(0.00687)	(0.00686)	(0.00685)	(0.00683)	(0.00683)
9th Grade Drop-out	−0.0822***	−0.0726***	−0.0696***	−0.0686***	−0.0683***
	(0.00505)	(0.00506)	(0.00505)	(0.00501)	(0.00501)
10th Grade Drop-out	−0.0735***	−0.0631***	−0.0611***	−0.0605***	−0.0600***
	(0.00390)	(0.00392)	(0.00392)	(0.00388)	(0.00388)
11th Grade Drop-out	−0.0568***	−0.0458***	−0.0456***	−0.0446***	−0.0440***
	(0.00383)	(0.00385)	(0.00384)	(0.00381)	(0.00381)
HE Freshman	0.0479***	0.0461***	0.0420***	0.0299***	0.0303***
	(0.00639)	(0.00636)	(0.00635)	(0.00630)	(0.00629)
HE Sophomore	0.0299***	0.0277***	0.0239***	0.0172***	0.0175***
	(0.00466)	(0.00464)	(0.00463)	(0.00459)	(0.00459)
HE Junior	0.0402***	0.0370***	0.0326***	0.0271***	0.0275***
	(0.00403)	(0.00401)	(0.00401)	(0.00397)	(0.00397)
HE Senior + more	−0.0188***	−0.0264***	−0.0346***	−0.0358***	−0.0344***
	(0.00186)	(0.00189)	(0.00191)	(0.00190)	(0.00191)
Vocational Graduate	0.113***	0.104***	0.0972***	0.0982***	0.0988***
	(0.00195)	(0.00200)	(0.00202)	(0.00200)	(0.00200)
College Graduate	0.235***	0.204***	0.188***	0.195***	0.192***
	(0.00203)	(0.00225)	(0.00233)	(0.00232)	(0.00239)
Role Models Proxy		0.128***	0.0874***	0.114***	0.123***
		(0.00638)	(0.00657)	(0.00677)	(0.00695)
Social Class Proxy		0.338***	0.324***	0.257***	0.119***
		(0.0122)	(0.0122)	(0.0137)	(0.0254)
SIMCE Test Score 2004			0.000418***	0.000427***	0.000449***
			(1.66e-05)	(1.65e-05)	(1.73e-05)
SIMCE Test School					−0.000127***
					(3.39e-05)
Social Class & College					0.188***
					(0.0270)
Municipality	no	no	no	yes	yes
Constant	0.400***	0.395***	0.307***	0.367***	0.391***
	(0.00153)	(0.00166)	(0.00386)	(0.0132)	(0.0147)
Observations	181,885	181,885	181,884	181,884	181,884
R-squared	0.151	0.158	0.161	0.182	0.182

Notes: Standard errors in parentheses.
*** $p<0.01$, ** $p<0.05$, * $p<0.1$.

CHAPTER 2

FOCUSED INEQUALITY AND WELLBEING MEASUREMENT FOR PUBLIC POLICY INITIATIVES: EQUALIZING OPPORTUNITY AND LEVELLING UP, A SPANISH EXAMPLE

Gordon J. Anderson

University of Toronto, Canada

ABSTRACT

Beyond just equalizing opportunities, 'levelling up', 'inclusive growth' and 'no child left behind' policy initiatives require inequality measurement from a different perspective than conventional measures provide. Whereas standard inequality measures quantify normalized aggregate distance from some centrality parameter or distribution, these imperatives demand equalization towards targets that are not necessarily a centrality parameter or distribution dependent upon the underlying egalitarian philosophy. Here, Inequality Modulated Success Indices are proposed in the face of Utilitarian, Prioritarian and Sufficientarian Imperatives. The techniques meet the challenges of both continuously measured and ordered categorical environments and are exemplified in a study of human capital acquisition in Spain over the 2009–2015 period. When such considerations are introduced in the final analysis, wellbeing improvement is no longer universally observed across the three imperatives.

Opportunity, Mobility and Inequality
Research on Economic Inequality, Volume 31, 41–63

Published under exclusive licence by Emerald Publishing Limited
ISSN: 1049-2585/doi:10.1108/S1049-258520250000031003

Whilst, under a First Order wellbeing indicator, Utilitarians and Egalitarians see an improvement in wellbeing whereas Prioritarians do not, under a second order indicator Utilitarians see an improvement whereas both Egalitarians and Prioritarians see a deterioration.

Keywords: Inequality of opportunity; human capital acquisition; levelling up; inclusive growth; utilitarianism; prioritarianism; sufficientarianism

INTRODUCTION

Much has been said and written in the public discourse about levelling up and equalizing the chances of the disadvantaged, the United Kingdom Government now has a Minister responsible for 'Levelling Up'[1] and the No Child Left Behind act in the United States (Klein 2015) which can in turn be interpreted as a levelling up priority, are cases in point. There has been a growing consensus that excessive unequalness between a society's constituents is detrimental to its overall wellbeing which has seen increasing use of inequality sensitive wellbeing comparison instruments in the last 50 years. Most inequality tempered wellbeing indices modulate average wellbeing levels with measures of overall inequality. Examples abound, Sen (1976) proposed scaling down the Per Capita National Product by one minus the Gini coefficient. Based upon the Atkinson (1970) family of inequality indices, the Human Development index (UNDP, 2019) modulates the level of wellbeing in health, education and income dimensions by the extent of overall inequality in each dimension, then aggregates the three resultant modulated measures.

An inherent presumption in these approaches is that all inequality is normatively 'bad', yet it can be argued that some inequalities contribute positively to overall societal wellbeing and should not be so considered. For example, in meritocratic incentive driven societies, securing an efficient allocation of resources that maximizes the feasible social good requires differentiated, and thus inherently unequal, reward structures for differentiated contributions to that social good (Autor, 2014). Furthermore, if agents in a society facing the same set of options but choose differently as a matter of free and unhindered choice, Revealed Preference Theory (Samuelson, 1948) suggests that, since each could have chosen the others path but didn't, each is in its preferred position, so why should such differences be considered detrimental to aggregate wellbeing? Indeed, such inequalities could be deemed to be justifiable and aggregate wellbeing enhancing and should probably not be a component of the wellbeing modulation calculus which suggests that standard inequality measures could be exaggerating the impact of inequality on wellbeing which may be exemplified as follows.

Let x be a measure of an agents contribution to the social good with $f(x)$ the pdf of a societies agent contributions so that per capita or average contribution is $E_f(x) = \mu$ and G, the societies overall Gini coefficient of contribution inequality is $G = \frac{1}{\mu}\int_0^\infty\int_0^\infty f(x)f(x)|x-y|\,dydx$. Suppose, within the society, agents are arbitrarily assigned, without any agency, to K identifiable groups, indexed $k = 1,\ldots, K$ with resultant respective population proportions w_k and contribution distributions $f_k(x)$ with $E_{f_k}(x) = \mu_k$ so that $f(x) = \sum_{k=1}^{K} f_k(x) w_k$ and $\mu = \sum_{k=1}^{K} \mu_k w_k$. Within a group, agents can freely choose their efforts in contributing x and are where they have freely chosen to be within $f_k(x)$, then the corresponding G_k will reflect the variation of those freely chosen efforts and so it is acceptably different from 0 in a normative sense. However, between group differences, reflecting differences over which agents had no choice, are normatively unacceptable. Following Anderson and Thomas (2019), G, the societal Gini coefficient of inequality in contribution may be decomposed into three non-negative terms, i.e.:

$$G = \sum_{k=1}^{K} w_k^2 \frac{\mu_k}{\mu} G_k + \frac{1}{\mu} \sum_{k=2}^{K} \sum_{j=1}^{k} w_k w_j \left| \mu_k - \mu_j \right| + \frac{2}{\mu} \sum_{k=2}^{K} \sum_{j=1}^{k-1} w_k w_j \int_0^{\infty} f_k(y) \int_y^{\infty} f_j(x)(x-y)\, dx dy$$

where G_k is the Gini coefficient of inequality in contribution the *kth* group.

The first term represents that part of the Gini coefficient relating to normatively acceptable inequalities which should not be included in the modulation of overall wellbeing, whereas the second and third terms represent normatively unacceptable differences which should be part of the wellbeing modulation calculus. This decomposition highlights the distinction between Ex Post Equality of Opportunity (defined by equality of chances) and Ex Ante in Equality of Opportunity (defined by equality of circumstance-group averages).[2] When all groups are distributionally identical, the overall Gini is simply a population weighted sum of the within group Ginis' which are identical. When all groups have the same mean outcome the middle term disappears but the third term remains, a reflection of distributional differences that result in Ex Post inequality of opportunity (in effect an illustration of why subgroup equality of average success is only a necessary condition of Ex Post Equality of Opportunity and not a good indicator of it). In effect Ex Post Equality of Opportunity encompasses Ex Ante Equality of Opportunity with the former requiring both second and third terms to be zero and the latter requiring just the second term to be zero.

Obviously, this begs questions as to whether such justifiable differences can be identified and distinguished from unjustifiable differences which are really questions of whether observed differentiated reward structures truly reflect differentiated contributions to the social good or whether different choices have been made in a genuinely unhindered fashion. Even if they can, the question still remains as to how to measure the extent of inequality inherent in them. An Egalitarian position would have it that some aggregation of distances from a centrality measure would be appropriate whereas a Prioritarian position with concerns for levelling upward (as opposed to levelling downward), would prefer an aggregation of distances from some 'preferred' position as an inequality measure.

Here inequality tempered wellbeing measures are proposed which modulate overall wellbeing with measures focussed on 'bad' inequalities under the presumption that all other inequalities are not necessarily bad. These measures are exemplified in an examination of student success through the lens of an Equal Opportunity paradigm concerned with the dependence of student achievements on parental and regional circumstances in Spain over the period 2009–2015. Whilst somewhat specific, it is illustrative of a much broader family of potential applications of 'good' versus 'bad' inequality considerations. The analysis is based upon the premise that, in elevating the stock of embodied human capital, student achievements are overall wellbeing enhancing. When unhindered by circumstances beyond individual control, differences in student grades, indicate the varying degrees to which individuals have successfully augmented their stock of human capital, are necessary for the efficient allocation of resources and thus can be considered 'good' for societies overall wellbeing. Measures of overall levels of student success such as average or median grades provide indices of societal wellbeing in this dimension. However, when these are achieved at the expense of some inequality in opportunity, such measures need modulating to reflect the impact of such socially undesirable inequalities. In this framework, potential for inequality of opportunity is engendered by the circumstance of being born into a particular group defined by family type and regional location, but groups so defined can be heterogeneous with respect to the quality of their parental endowments (i.e. the quality of circumstance groupings can be more or less similar). When these circumstance groups are less similar in quality, the more will the exigencies of circumstance impact student outcomes so that when comparing societies, some accommodation of the extent to which circumstances vary in quality need to be made.

Some background to the analysis of Equality of Opportunity is discussed in Section 1. Section 2 develops methods for measuring the extent to which equality of opportunity prevails and outlines the incorporation of such measures into an overall measure of societal wellbeing. These methods facilitate examination of progress towards a 'level playing field' whether it be under an Egalitarian or a Prioritarian imperative. A bi-product is a technique for examining the notion of Universal Convergence, the situation in which all circumstance groups are progressing towards the common goal. Using Pisa results in Reading and Science over the 2009–2015 period, the techniques are exemplified in an analysis of the extent to which human capital has been augmented and equal opportunity in its acquisition has prevailed in Regions of Spain. Section 3 outlines some background to the Spanish application, the results are reported in Section 4 and some conclusions are drawn in Section 5. To anticipate the results, while there has been an improvement over the period both in terms of the overall parenting quality and overall student grade achievements, this has been modulated by diminished equality of opportunity especially with respect to single parented students. There has not been universal convergence, indeed in some situations the orderings are reversed when Prioritarian as opposed to Egalitarian views are adopted.

2. EQUAL OPPORTUNITY AND THE EGALITARIAN PROJECT

Arrow et al. (2000) dubbed the amalgam of policies for ensuring economic security and equality of opportunity for all the Egalitarian Project, arguing that it had faltered due in part to the lack of consensus as to what constitutes 'a level playing field' and how it should be measured. Roemer (2006) averred that public education was the institution through which the Projects policy objectives of enhanced human resource stocks and level playing fields could be achieved and measurement should proceed in that context. Recently a Sufficientarianism[3] doctrine emerged from political philosophy (Alcantud et al., 2022; Bossert et al., 2021, 2022) which grants special status to an outcome threshold defining 'sufficient' or 'good enough' and prioritizes the proportion of the population who have at least a sufficient level of the good. Other than ensuring that such a proportion does not diminish, it is less concerned with the extent to which people have more than enough and is more concerned with progress of people who don't possess at least a sufficient level of the good in question. The basic idea is to designate a sufficient level and record the proportion of the population that enjoys at least a sufficient level of the good (essentially the survival function value of the outcome one below is sufficient level) which is the measure of the extent to which sufficiency has been achieved. This measure is then modulated with an insufficiency measure of the extent to which agents in the population failed to attain the sufficient level. This can be computed as one plus the Sufficient Level SF Value minus the average of the SF values below the sufficient level. The Insufficiency Modulated Sufficiency Measure is then simply some weighted average of the two measures. However, Atkinson (2012) and Sen (2009), each contended that the ultimate level playing field, however construed, is seldom attainable and argued that the policy objective should be to foster progress towards the optimal state. Thus, assessing the Egalitarian Projects' progress is an empirical challenge, requiring measurement of the net accretion of human resources which can be modulated by the prevailing lack of equal opportunity in its acquisition.

The Equal Opportunity paradigm encapsulates the idea that individual achievement should be the result of personal choice and effort and not be hostage to the fortune of the uncontrollable circumstances. Because choices and efforts differ, achievement variation is inevitable amongst individuals confronting similar circumstances, but, in the overall calculus of success, inequalities engendered by differences in choices and efforts should be of lesser concern than those resulting from differences in circumstances beyond individual control. Distinguishing between the former and the latter and modulating measures of aggregate success with respect to the latter but not the former, is the empirical challenge.

The Equal Opportunity literature has been somewhat at odds as to how inequality measurement should be approached, whether it be differences in achievement chances of circumstance groups (Bourguignon et al., 2007; Checchi & Peragine, 2010; Ferreira & Gignoux, 2011; Peragine, 2002) or differences in the achievement chances of groups with common efforts (Aaberge et al., 2011; Checchi & Peragine, 2010). While Fleurbaey and Peragine (2013) have shown the two positions to be incompatible, the fact remains that, however inequality of opportunity is construed, a collection of conditional achievement distributions need to be similar for a level playing field to prevail and the policy objective should be to get the collection of distributions to converge to a common shape or form i.e. the issue is one of distributional convergence.

Expressing the Egalitarian Equal Opportunity imperative in terms of the commonality of a collection of conditional achievement distributions has a 'distributional veil of ignorance' flavour (Harsanyi, 1953, 1955) in the sense that knowledge of the actual allocation of outcome chances is less important than that all conditioning typologies confront the same allocation. In this case, the basic Egalitarian policy objective should be to level the playing field by securing the same distribution of chances to all types, whatever that distribution may be. This could result in levelling downwards, levelling upwards or a mixture of both. An alternative, 'Prioritarian' view proffered by Rawls (1971) (see Buchak, 2017 and references therein), has it that benefitting the worse off is of greater importance than giving the same benefit to the more advantaged.[4] In this context, 'levelling upwards' becomes an additional priority with a social aspiration for all to have similar chances as the most favourably endowed group. In both cases, overall outcome levels matter and wellbeing measures should be able to reflect these joint societal aspirations for more and more equality be it an Egalitarian or a Prioritarian Imperative.

Having grouped individuals into appropriate types, the immediate empirical issue is one of comparing a collection of type conditional outcome distributions with a view to measuring their progress towards commonality. In essence, much like the issue faced in economic growth and convergence literatures (Galor 2011), attention should be focussed on whether or not the various group conditioned outcome distributions are converging to a common distribution over time, perhaps with Prioritarian caveats on the nature of the common distribution and the 'upward' nature of the convergence process. Typically, the extent of inequality of opportunity is evaluated by examining differences in locational summary statistics of circumstance groups[5] with objects like Generalized Gini coefficients or coefficients of variation of the group means or medians being the norm. However, Carneiro et al. (2003), in critiquing general difference in means comparisons in treatment effects models, effectively argue that such comparisons are uninformative as to general mass relocation. Such methods lose important information about outcome state differences which can only be countervailed by comparing complete outcome distributions. Moreover, outcomes of interest are often ordered categories or achievement groupings without cardinal measure, witness the proliferation of health, wellness, life satisfactions and grade range based studies (Kahneman & Krueger, 2006). Given concerns expressed in Schroder and Yitzhaki (2017) and Bond and Lang (2019), arbitrary Cantril (1967) scaling of categories is not a solution here since the scale dependency of most comparison measures presents the possibility of contradictory orderings based upon equally valid alternative scaling processes. When success is a multidimensional outcome, these problems are intensified given the arbitrary nature of dimensional aggregation.

3. ON EVALUATING THE PROGRESS OF THE EGALITARIAN PROJECT

Formally, the canonical Equal Opportunity model (Ferreira & Peragine, 2015) considers a population over which $f_t(x)$ $\{p_t(x)\}$, the continuous {discrete} distribution of an S-dimensioned vector (In the application $S = 2$) of universally desired individual achievements or rewards x *in period t* is defined (with higher x being preferred to lower) and classifies the population into K mutually exclusive and exhaustive circumstance or effort groups or classes indexed $k = 1,\ldots, K$. If outcome variables X are described by the group conditioned outcome distributions $f_{k,t}(x)$ $\{p_{k,t}\}$ appropriate for each respective member of the K groups in period t, then, given category k's proportion of the population is w_k $\left(\sum_{k=1}^{K} w_k = 1\right)$,[6] the overall population distribution is given by:

$$f_t(x) = \sum_{k=1}^{K} w_{k,t} f_{k,t}(x) \left\{= \sum_{k=1}^{K} w_{k,t} p_{k,t}\right\} \quad [1]$$

Given space concerns, the following discussion will be pursued in terms of continuous univariate distributions,[7] with discrete environments dealt with by analogy. Three issues need to be addressed, the extent of distributional differences, ranking and ordering distributions, developing inequality of opportunity sensitive wellbeing measures.

3.1. Evaluating Distributional Differences

A necessary condition[8] for the transcendentally optimal Equal Opportunity state to obtain in period t requires that $f_{k,t}(x) = f_t(x)\ \forall\ x$ *and all* $k = 1, \ldots, K$, it is this set of distributional equalities that both Atkinson and Sen contend will seldom prevail. Suppose $f_{k,t^*}(x)$ are the outcome distributions appropriate for the members of the K circumstance classes at some later period t^*, then the question Sen and Atkinson pose is how to assess whether the collection $f_{k,t^*}(x) k = 1,\ldots, K$ is closer to some Optimal Target Distribution $f_{t^*}^{O}(x)$ than is the collection $f_{k,t}(x) k = 1, \ldots, K$ close to $f_t^{O}(x)$ and what the nature of the Optimal Distribution should be. A pure Egalitarian view would have the optimal distribution being the 'average' distribution wherever it is, whereas a Prioritarian or 'Levelling Upward' view would have some other pre-specified preferred distribution in mind such as the outcome distribution of the most favourably endowed group. Of course, if all distributions had converged to $f_{t^*}^{O}(x)$, it would be the average distribution. The issues become ones of convergence to a target distribution, the extent to which greater proximity is achieved in subsequent as opposed to former periods and exactly how should the target distribution be defined?

Typically, the extent of inequality of opportunity has been evaluated by examining differences in the μ_k's or μ_k/μ's where $\mu_k = \int x f_k(x)\,dx$, $k = 1,\ldots, K$ *and* $\mu = \sum_{k=1}^{K} w_k \mu_k$ (see for example, Bourguignonet al., 2007; Checchi & Peragine, 2010; Ferreira & Gignoux, 2011) in which case the target distribution is simply a weighted (or unweighted) average of distributions with common means. However, Carneiro et al. (2003), in critiquing general difference in means comparisons, have effectively argued that such summary statistic comparisons are uninformative as to general mass relocation. They lose important information about outcome state differences which can only be countervailed by comparing outcome distributions across their entire support. For example, suppose groups had identical conditional means while conditional variances $(\sigma_k^2 = \int (x-\mu_k)^2 f_k(x)dx,\ k=1,\ldots,K)$ were very different, then while mean comparisons would record equality of opportunity, different circumstance types would have very different chances of 'good' and 'not so good' outcomes contrary to the equal opportunity ideal.[9]

Anderson et al. (2021) proposed several asymptotically normal Multilateral Distributional Inequality measures analogous to the basic Range, Coefficient of Variation and Gini Coefficients used for measuring differences in collections of numbers. Unlike the basic statistics, the distributional inequality measures can be readily employed in multilateral, multidimensional, continuous, discrete and ordered categorical environments. Two of the measures, the Distributional Coefficient of Variation statistic *DCV* (a distributional analogue of a coefficient of variation) and the Distributional Gini Coefficient *DisGini* (a distributional analogue of a Gini coefficient) are useful in the present context. Both are based upon extensions to, and applications of, Ginis' Transvariation measure GT (Gini, 1916, 1959) which, for two distributions $f_i(x)$ *and* $f_j(x)$, is given by:

$$GT_{i,j} = \frac{1}{2}\int_0^\infty \left| f_i(x) - f_j(x) \right| dx = \frac{1}{2}\int_0^\infty [\max\left(f_i(x), f_j(x)\right) - min\left(f_i(x), f_j(x)\right)]dx \quad [2]$$

[2] will take the value 0 when the two distributions are identical and 1 when they have mutually exclusive support. $GT_{i,j} = 1 - OV_{i,j}$ where $OV_{i,j} = \int \min\left(f_i(x), f_j(x)\right)dx$ is the overlap measure of the degree to which two distributions have common mass location (Anderson et al., 2012).

3.1.1. Analyzing Convergence to a Common Distribution

The DCV statistic is based upon a weighted aggregation of the respective group and overall ($f(x)$) distributional transvariations. Denoting the overlap of $f(x)$ and the kth distribution $f_k(x)$ as $OV_{ko}\left(= \int \min\left(f_k(x), f(x)\right)dx\right)$, *DCV*, the weighted average of the group and target distribution transvariations, is given by:

$$DCV = \frac{1}{\left(1-\sum_{=1}^{K} w_k^2\right)} \sum_{k=1}^{K} w_k GT_{ko} = \frac{1}{\left(1-\sum_{=1}^{K} w_k^2\right)} \sum_{k=1}^{K} w_k\left(1 - OV_{ko}\right) \quad [3]$$

If $DCV_t > DCV_{t+c}$ *for* $c > 0$ convergence can be established.

3.1.2. The Notion of Uniform Convergence

Effectively [3] is a weighted aggregation of the extent to which subgroup distributions differ from the 'average' or target distribution. This in turn suggests a new notion of Uniform or Multilateral Convergence. Denoting the ith subgroup/overall distribution transformation in period 't' as $GT_{i,O,t}$ for $i = 1, \ldots, K$ if $GT_{i,O,t} > GT_{i,O,t+c}$ *for all* $i = 1, \ldots, K$ then convergence is uniform in that all subgroups have become closer to the overall or average distribution over the period. This may be examined by testing the joint hypothesis H_0: $GT_{i,O,t} \geq GT_{i,O,t+c}$ *for all* $i = 1, \ldots, K$ against H_1: $GT_{i,O,t} < GT_{i,O,t+c}$ *for* some $i = 1, \ldots, K$ which may be effected using Stoline and Ury (1979) maximum modulus distribution tables.

Anderson et al. (2020) defined DCV in terms of the 'average' distribution but there is no reason why some other 'ideal' distribution could not be substituted, perhaps to reflect some policy objective like minimizing distance from the ideal distribution. For example, under a Prioritarian imperative levelling upwards (rather than downwards) would be a policy goal and emulating the outcome distribution of those circumstantially best endowed would be the target distribution.

3.1.3. General Distributional Differences

[3] only measures distributional distance from some target distribution and does not reflect the full extent of distributional differences in the population of groups which are only captured by *DisGini*, the Distributional Gini coefficient which is given by:

$$DisGini = \frac{1}{(1-\sum_{k=1}^{K} w_k^2)} \sum_{i=1}^{K}\sum_{j=1}^{K} w_i w_j (1-OV_{ij}) = \frac{1}{(1-\sum_{k=1}^{K} w_k^2)} \sum_{i=1}^{K}\sum_{j=1}^{K} w_i w_j (GT_{ij}) \quad [4]$$

Unweighted versions of both [3] and [4] can be obtained by setting $w_k = 1/K$ for all k.

3.2. Ranking and Ordering Distributions

Anderson et al. (2020) and, following Gravel et al. (2020), Anderson and Leo (2020), have provided methods for ranking and ordering collections of distributions defined over both cardinal and ordered categorical spaces with respect to some family of value functions. Based upon stochastic dominance concepts, the upper and lower boundaries of the collection of distributions and their integrals can be determined, and measures of each distributions proximity to those boundaries used as an ordering instrument which reflects the properties of the value function and provides an unambiguous ordering in certain situations.

Suppose *U(x)* represents a family of Value Functions of x, where for some s:

$$(-1)^{i-1} d^i U(x) / dx^i > 0 \; i = 1, \ldots, s,$$

where $E(U(x))$ is the focus of interest. Then for a collection of K distribution functions $F_k(x)$ indexed $k = 1, \ldots, K$ let $F_k^s(x) = \int_0^x F_k^{s-1}(z)dz$ *where* $F_k^0(x) = f_k(x)$, let $UE(F_1^s(x), F_2^s(x), .F_K^s(x)) = \max_x(F_1^s(x), F_2^s(x), .F_K^s(x))$,

and let

$$LE(F_1^s(x), F_2^s(x), \ldots F_K^s(x)) = \min_x(F_1^s(x), F_2^s(x), \ldots F_K^s(x))$$

then $UD_s(x)$, an sth order Utopia - Dystopia index of the value $E(U(x))$, is given by:

$$UD_s(f_k)=\frac{\int_0^{\infty}(UE(x)-F_k^s(x))dx}{\int_0^{\infty}(UE(x)-LE(x))dx} \quad for\ k=1,\dots,K\ and\ s=1,2,\dots \qquad [4]$$

[4] does not work in ordered categorical environments without cardinal measure, however following the insights in Gravel et al. (2020), Anderson and Leo (2020) proposed analogous indices for such ordered categorical situations. Integration can be mimicked by successively cumulating probabilities, and the value function construed in terms of a greater chance of a better outcome. For C ordered outcome categories, denote the corresponding probabilities p_{ck}: $c = 1, \dots, C$, for groups $k = 1, \dots. K$ and consider the ith order cumulated sequence $F_{ck}^i=\sum_{j=1}^{c}F_{ck}^{i-1}$ where $F_{ck}^0=p_{ck}$. Defining $UE_c^i,(LE_c^i)$ respectively as $\max_k\left(F_{ck}^i,\ k=1,\dots,K\right),\left(\min_k\left(F_{ck}^i,\ k=1,\dots,K\right)\right)$, the ordered categorical equivalent of [4] is given by:

$$UDC_k^s=\frac{\sum_{c=1}^{C}\left(UE_c^i-F_{ck}^i\right)}{\sum_{c=1}^{C}\left(UE_c^i-LE_c^i\right)} \qquad [5]$$

To facilitate interpretation and comparability, analysts usually seek indices that possess certain properties (see for example Gravel et al., 2020; Sen, 1987, 1995). Continuity with respect to x is a standard requirement, which, in the ordered categorical case (Parental Education level), is not a continuously measured variate, however in such cases indices are piecewise continuous in the variable p. To facilitate analysis in ordered categorical environments, scales are frequently and somewhat arbitrarily associated with categories (Bond & Lang 2019), the Scale Independence property secures independence from arbitrary monotonic translations of the wellbeing function, however [5] is scale independent by construction. Coherency (indices should reflect the preference ordering) will be satisfied when indices are monotonic increasing in category ordering. [5] is Normalized (bounded on the unit interval) by construction. Anderson and Leo (2020) formally demonstrate that [5] possess all of these properties. [4] and [5] also work well in multivariate environments (Anderson & Leo, 2020) and avoid arbitrary dimension weighting problems associated with indices such as the Human Development Index.

3.3. Inequality of Opportunity Sensitive Wellbeing Indices

Sen (1976), with the intention of modifying the National Income measure of aggregate wellbeing to account for the extent of inequality in a society, proposed reducing the level of average per capita income μ, by some function of the extent to which inequality is prevalent, specifically, he proposed $\mu(1-G)$ where G is the Gini coefficient of income inequality[10] and $(1-G)$ may be construed as an inequality penalty factor. More generally, a family of inequality sensitive wellbeing indices which can accommodate more or less aggressive reduction of income could be $\mu^{\alpha}(1-G)^{1-\alpha}$ with $0 \leq \alpha \leq 1$ where the importance of per capita income is reflected in the magnitude of α and the importance of inequality by $(1-\alpha)$. To reflect Sen's original intent of modifying the per capita national income level, this could be reorganized as $\mu(1-G)^{\frac{(1-\alpha)}{\alpha}}$. In the present context, a problem with this formulation is that G reflects all inequalities i.e. those that have arisen as a consequence of choice and effort as well as those that are a result of the force of circumstance. This can be rectified by replacing G with a measure of inequality of opportunity.

Letting A_k, D_k, w_k, $k = 1, \ldots, K$ be respectively the Human Capital Embodiment or Academic Achievement Index, Inequality of Opportunity Penalty factor, and weighting proportion for the kth group. Average wellbeing achievement is given by $\bar{A} = \sum_{k=1}^{K} A_k w_k$, if inequality of opportunity were of no consequence, as an aggregation of subgroup achievements, $\bar{A}$ provides an index of achievement in a society. The Inequality of Opportunity Penalty factor is based upon the idea that achievement is more valued when it has been attained on a level playing field, less so when opportunities to achieve are unequal. When IO_k corresponds to a measure of the extent to which the kth group experiences inequality of opportunity, $D_k = 1 - IO_k$ provides a measure of distance from the equal opportunity-level playing field state applicable to the kth group. Let $0 \leq 1 - \alpha < 1$ be the weight attached to the equal opportunity imperative in a society (so that $\alpha = 1$ implies equality of opportunity is ignored, $\alpha = 0$ implies equality of opportunity is all that matters) and consider a measure of a societal wellbeing achievement is given by AW, where:

$$AW = \sum_{k=1}^{K} A_k D_k^{\frac{1-\alpha}{\alpha}} w_k \qquad [6]$$

In the event that achievements are not cardinally measured, set $A_k = UDC_k^i$ *for some i.*

3.4. Compensating for the Extent to Which Circumstances Differ in Quality

It is possible that the quality of circumstances may vary over time so that being born into a particular circumstance at one point in time has different consequences for the unborn child than it being born into that same circumstance at another point in time because the quality of that circumstance has changed. For example, suppose circumstance groups are defined by family type (single parent versus dual parent) and region (urban versus rural) and the pattern of human capital acquisition changes across groups over time, then the unborn child faces varying degrees of equality of opportunity if levels of parental human capital vary across circumstances. It is possible to modulate [6] to account for the extent to which inequality of opportunity at birth has been overcome. One way to do this would be to set $1 - \alpha$ equal to a measure of the extent to which circumstances genuinely differ in quality, for example the Disgini or Distributional Coefficient of variation for circumstance quality distributions. Indeed, it is possible to modify $1 - \alpha$ on a circumstance group basis making it large for groups with poor circumstance quality and small for superior group circumstance quality.

4. BACKGROUND TO THE APPLICATION

To exemplify the application of these new techniques and approaches, changes in the disparity of the educational outcomes of 14-year-olds in Spain is examined. It has long been recognized that growing divergences between constituencies within an entity can be a catalyst for the deterioration of its cohesion (Milanovic, 2011) and, with substantive regional disparities in many dimensions, especially with respect to education (McGowan & Millán, 2019), Spain is a case in point. Catalonia and the Basque Country are two of the wealthiest regions of Spain with strong regional identities (Rhune, 2009; Shubert, 2003) which have fuelled conflict between the Center and those regions regarding administrative autonomy and fostered secessionist movements in both regions over the years. While the overall structure of its education system is centrally determined, Spain's regions possess considerable budgetary and organizational autonomy in their educational investments (McGowan & Millán, 2019). It is thus of interest to see if these regional disparities have found expression in corresponding differences in educational outcomes.

The quality of a child's family background, in terms of its parental educational and wealth status (or parental quality), single parent versus dual parent status and its regional location, has long been recognized as a determinant of its educational success (see references and chapters in Arrow et al., 2000, Morgan et al., 2006). *In the data set to hand, no income data is available so educational status will be deemed a proxy for education and wealth status. For simplicity,* family type (single vs two parent family) and regional location (Basque, Catalan and the Rest of Spain) have been designated as the identified circumstances that a 14-year-old person confronts. To be clear it is the parental type that is being held responsible for the child's outcomes and ideally it would be sensible to order parental type by parent quality but data limitations preclude this. Given the paucity of observations on single parented students in Basque and Catalan regions, those groups were amalgamated so that five circumstance classes are identified namely, Dual Parented Basque, Dual Parented Catalan, Dual Parented Rest of Spain, Single Parented Basque or Catalan and Single Parented Rest of Spain. Couched in these terms the question being asked is: Does a young person randomly selected from a given circumstance class have the same chances of success as a similarly randomly selected person from another circumstance class. Success is measured in terms of their joint achievements in Science and Reading in the Pisa Tests of 2009 and 2015.

The first question to be addressed is whether or not there are differences in circumstances confronting young people across regional and family type divides and, if there are, can those differences be ordered in some sense and are they diminishing or increasing over time. Alternatively put, the question is, does a child randomly drawn from a given circumstance class face the same distribution of parental quality as a child randomly selected from an alternative circumstance class and, if not, can one set of circumstances be deemed preferable to another are those distributions converging or diverging? In essence this is a matter of whether or not the unborn child faces the same opportunities for access to parental endowments across regional and parenting type divides. This can be addressed by establishing the extent to which parental quality distributions differ across the circumstance classes and, if they do, can they be ordered in some fashion? If no such differences can be established, then distributional inequalities in student outcomes can be attributable to family type and regionally administered educational policies.

A similar approach can be taken to student performance. The extent to which student outcome distributions differ across their respective circumstance groups is a reflection of the lack of equality of opportunity in the embodiment of human capital. Ordering those distributions will provide a measure of the extent to which circumstance groups are disadvantaged. Student wellbeing in the dimension of human capital acquisition can be quantified by some overall measure of performance modulated by the extent to which the acquisition was impeded by a lack of equal opportunity.

5. THE RESULTS

The analysis is based upon Spanish Pisa Results for in Reading and Science for the years 2009 and 2015 for the Regions of The Basque Country, Catalonia and the Rest of Spain with respect to two family parenting types, Dual Parenting (denoted DP and representing two parents present in the household) and Single Parenting (denoted SP indicating a single parent in the household). To be clear it is the parental type that is being held responsible for the child's outcome. And the results should be interpreted accordingly. Clearly defining circumstance groups by parenting type and regional location is a gross simplification Forced by data limitations but to help interpret the results Parental quality within circumstance type will be examined.

Student science and reading achievements were analyzed in terms of the joint distribution of their Pisa scores $p_{i,j,k}$, $i, j = 1, \ldots, 10$ $k = 1, \ldots, K$ where $p_{i,j,k}$ is the joint probability that a randomly selected student from the kth circumstance group is in the ith science grade decile and the jth reading grade decile. The 'quality' of the parental circumstances confronting a randomly selected student is assessed in terms of the parental educational attainment distribution he/she faces having been born into that regional and parenting type determined group. Parental Education Level (PEL) is an ordered categorical variable, with PEL1: Primary level of education or lower. PEL2: Lower secondary level. PEL3: Upper secondary level. PEL4: Post-secondary, non-tertiary education. PEL5: First Stage Tertiary education. PEL6 Second Stage Tertiary Education and Above. The highest parental PEL attainment in the household was considered as an indicator and its ordered categorical probability density function and cumulative distribution

	Basque DP	Catalan DP	Rest of Spain DP	Basque/Catalan SP	Rest of Spain SP	Total
2009	1990	614	8,558	151	376	11,689
2015	1291	658	12,354	67	345	14,715

Fig. 1. Research Sample Sizes.

across the sample from each circumstance group computed. The shortage of SP observations in the Basque and Catalan regions forced the amalgamation of those categories resulting in a five-category analysis with respective sample sizes, shown below in Fig. 1.

5.1. Parental Endowments

Table 1 presents the first order Utopia – Dystopia rankings of ordered categorical parental quality in the circumstance groups for the two observation years. In 2009 Students of DP families in the Basque region have unambiguously the best parental endowment followed by Catelonian DP's, and DP's in the Rest of Spain, children of SP's in the Basque/Catalan region then follow, with children of SP's in the Rest of Spain enjoying the least favourable parental quality unambiguously. In 2015, a similar ordering applies except that the Single Parent Rest of Spain group moves above the corresponding Basque/Catalan group. Table 2 reports Distributional Ginis and Distributional Coefficients of Variation for each observation year all of which indicate significant variation in parental quality across the circumstance groupings in all comparison types in both years. Unweighted

Table 1. Parental Background.

Subgroup CDF's and 1st Order Utopia – Dystopia Ranks:

2009	U-D1 Rank	PEL1	PEL2	PEL3	PEL4	PEL5	PEL6
Basque two parent	1.0000	0.0327	0.1161	0.1402	0.3633	0.5146	1.0000
Catelonia two parent	0.6853	0.0684	0.2329	0.2590	0.4723	0.6401	1.0000
Rest of Spain two parent	0.5973	0.0833	0.2572	0.2794	0.5323	0.6620	1.0000
Basque/Catalan single parent	0.3250	0.1126	0.3046	0.3642	0.6887	0.7815	1.0000
Rest of Spain single parent	0.0000	0.2048	0.4521	0.5000	0.7713	0.8457	1.0000
Overall		0.0782	0.2388	0.2628	0.5101	0.6432	1.0000

Note: Mean U-D1 0.5215, coefficient of Variation U-D1 0.7252.

2015	U-D1 Rank	PEL1	PEL2	PEL3	PEL4	PEL5	PEL6
Basque two parent	1.0000	0.0225	0.1154	0.1789	0.2905	0.4756	1.0000
Catelonia two parent	0.8876	0.0532	0.1702	0.2264	0.3161	0.5106	1.0000
Rest of Spain two parent	0.6807	0.0684	0.2319	0.3041	0.4274	0.6012	1.0000
Basque/Catalan single parent	0.0000	0.1343	0.4328	0.5672	0.7910	0.8806	1.0000
Rest of Spain single parent	0.1061	0.1188	0.4116	0.5188	0.7246	0.8493	1.0000
Overall		0.0652	0.2241	0.2959	0.4190	0.5932	1.0000

Note: Mean U-D1 0.5349, Coefficient of Variation U-D1 0.8526.

Table 2. Overall Parental Education Level Cumulative Densities.

	Distributional Gini		Distributional Coefficient of Variation			
	Unweighted	Weighted	From the Overall		From the Best	
			Unweighted	Weighted	Unweighted	Weighted
2009 Stat	0.1667	0.1658	0.1309	0.0556	0.2079	0.1495
Std Error	0.0008	0.0009	0.0028	0.0069	0.0032	0.0025
2015 Stat	0.2055	0.1641	0.1835	0.0318	0.2272	0.1303
Std Error	0.0007	0.0005	0.0028	0.0046	0.0029	0.0019

	≤ PEL1	≤ PEL2	≤ PEL3	≤ PEL4	≤ PEL5	≤ PEL6
Overall 2009	0.0782	0.2388	0.2628	0.5101	0.6432	1.0000
Overall 2015	0.0652	0.2241	0.2959	0.4190	0.5932	1.0000
3rd Order Comparison	0.0130	0.0407	0.0353	0.1210	0.2567	0.3924
2 Parent 2009	0.0735	0.2307	0.2534	0.4988	0.6345	1.0000
2 Parent 2015	0.0636	0.2186	0.2892	0.4099	0.5857	1.0000
3rd Order Comparison	0.0099	0.0319	0.0181	0.0932	0.2171	0.3410
Single Parent 2009	0.1784	0.4099	0.4611	0.7476	0.8273	1.0000
Single Parent 2015	0.1214	0.4150	0.5267	0.7354	0.8544	1.0000
3rd Order Comparison	0.0570	0.1089	0.0952	0.0937	0.0651	0.0365
2009 SP-DP 1st Order Comp.	0.1049	0.1792	0.2077	0.2488	0.1928	0.0000
2015 SP-DP 1st Order Comp.	0.0578	0.1964	0.2375	0.3255	0.2687	0.0000

versions indicate greater diversity than weighted versions indicating greater divergence from the average distribution in low weighted groups which are the SP groups.

The unweighted versions of the indices show an increase in diversity over the observation period whereas the weighted versions show a diminution, indicating some convergence in high weighted groups (essentially dual parenting groups) with divergence in groups with low weight (single parent groups). Direct stochastic dominance comparisons of overall distributions reveal DP distributions dominate the corresponding SP distributions at the first order comparison so that it can be reasonably construed that dual parented students enjoy better circumstances than their single parented counterparts in both observation periods. As for intertemporal comparisons, 2015 distributions dominate 2009 distributions at the third order comparison both overall and in the respective parenting types, suggesting some overall intertemporal improvement in the parenting quality that students have enjoyed over the observation period.

5.2. Student Achievements

Table 3 reports Distributional Gini and Distributional Coefficients of Variation for circumstance conditioned student grade distributions. Much like the parental quality results, these indicate significant variation in student achievement distributions across the circumstance groupings in all comparison types in both years. Unweighted versions indicate greater diversity than weighted versions indicating

Table 3. Between Group Distributional Variation.

	Distributional Gini		Distributional Coefficient of Variation			
	Unweighted	Weighted	About the Overall Distribution		About the Best Distribution	
			Unweighted	Weighted	Unweighted	Weighted
2009	0.1568	0.1464	0.1481	0.0500	0.1858	0.1533
	(0.0008)	(0.0009)	(0.0032)	(0.0025)	(0.0034)	(0.0057)
2015	0.2010	0.1474	0.1840	0.0329	0.2256	0.1481
	(0.0007)	(0.0005)	(0.0029)	(0.0019)	(0.0031)	(0.0055)

greater divergence from the average distribution in low weighted groups which are the single parented groups. The unweighted versions of the Distributional Coefficient of Variation indices show an increase in diversity over the observation period whereas the weighted versions show a diminution, indicating some convergence in high weighted groups (essentially dual parenting groups) with divergence in groups with low weight (essentially the single parent groups).

When the Utopia-Dystopia indices for achievements are viewed in Table 4 in 2009 the ordering of success is Catalan Dual, Basque Dual, Rest of Spain Dual, Basque/Catalan single followed by Rest of Spain single whereas in 2015 Basque Dual Parented students appear to fall back somewhat and are overtaken by the Dual Parented Students in the rest of Spain. Differences in the individual group transvariations suggest convergence is not universal (no difference was

Table 4. Utopia-Dystopia Achievement Indices and Transvariations.

	2009				2015			
	UD1	UD2	Transv	Transv	UD1	UD2	Transv	Transv
			Average	Best			Average	Best
Basque Dual parent	0.9104	0.9585	0.0883	0.1408	0.6543	0.6563	0.0886	0.1700
Catalan Dual Parent	0.9657	0.9883	0.1455	0.0000	0.9771	0.9967	0.1425	0.0000
Rest Dual Parent	0.6752	0.7091	0.0229	0.1578	0.8682	0.9059	0.0136	0.1476
Basque/Catalan Single.	0.2652	0.3000	0.2607	0.3346	0.3396	0.4260	0.4492	0.5135
Rest of Spain Single.	0.0082	0.0007	0.2227	0.2961	0.1128	0.0006	0.2260	0.2968

	Universal Convergence Analysis:			
	Convergence to the average		Convergence to the best	
	Stoline-Ury statistic	~ $\|t\|$ test*	Stoline-Ury statistic	~ $\|t\|$ test[a]
Basque Dual parent	−0.0003	0.0025	−0.0292	0.2161
Catalan Dual Parent	0.0030	0.0180	0.0000	0.0000
Rest Dual Parent	0.0093	0.1804	0.0102	0.1208
Basque/Catalan Single.	−0.1885	0.6068	−0.1789	0.5673
Rest of Spain Single.	−0.0033	0.0157	−0.0007	0.0032

[a] 1% critical value for the Stoline-Ury test is 3.5.

significantly different) with for Rest of Spain Dual Parented Students with divergence for Single Parented Basque and Catalan students with all other groups showing very little change.

5.3. Equality of Opportunity Sensitive Measures of Wellbeing

Ultimately the value of a nations schooling program hinges upon the success of its students and the homogeneity with which it is delivered across its jurisdictions. It is to be hoped that regional disparities in resources do not affect student outcomes which should depend in a very basic way on student's choices and efforts. In this application, wellbeing is measured in terms of the success of students in their jointly distributed Science and Reading scores. The circumstances they confront are the nature of the parenting they received and the region they were born into. [6] can be used to evaluate student wellbeing in the context of the quality of parental endowments the unborn face in terms of its level and variation. It can also be used to evaluate societal wellbeing in the context of its embodiment of Human Capital.

A first order Utopia-Dystopia index was the basis of the level which was modulated with respect to Inequality of Opportunity using circumstance specific/overall transvariations and alternatively an overall distributional coefficient of variation. Both weighted and unweighted versions of the index were employed together with a variety of alpha values representing the relative importance of level versus equality of opportunity.

Inequality of opportunity was measured in the context of proximity to the societal average distribution and in addition, to reflect the aspiration for levelling upward, it was measured in the context of proximity to the best distribution. In the case of the wellbeing of the unborn child (Table 5), with the exception of two cases (when overall Distributional Coefficient of Variation was employed and Inequality of Opportunity most heavily weighted) an improvement in wellbeing was recorded over the 2009–2015 period. In essence the overall quality of parents has increased over the period as has the variation in overall quality, but it is only when that variation in overall quality is most heavily weighted that the quality of circumstance faced by the unborn child appears to have diminished.

The same pattern of outcomes prevails when Societal Wellbeing is evaluated in the context of its acquisition and embodiment of human capital (Table 6). Overall levels of human capital acquisition have improved over the period, it is only when inequality of opportunity is most heavily weighted and an overall inequality of opportunity applied to each circumstance group does the overall wellbeing measure appear to diminish.

Finally, a data determined value for $\frac{1-\alpha}{\alpha}$ is posited which varies with the quality of the circumstance confronted by the student. Here WB, the wellbeing index is of the form:

$$WB = \sum_{k=1}^{K} w_k UDI_k \left(1 - IO_k\right)^{(1-QC_k)}$$

Table 5. $\sum_{k=1}^{K} w_k UD1_k \left(1 - IO_k\right)^{\frac{1-\alpha}{\alpha}}$ An Equality of Opportunity Sensitive Measure of Access to Parental Quality (All Indices Refer to Parental Quality, α Chosen by Investigator).

Proximity to the Average Distribution:

		Alpha =				
		1	0.95	0.90	0.75	0.1
$IO_k = GT_{ko}$, w_k = population proportion	2009	0.6477	0.6456	0.6433	0.6346	0.4169
	2015	0.7014	0.7003	0.6990	0.6942	0.5704
$IO_k = GT_{ko}$, w_k = 1/K for all k	2009	0.5215	0.5187	0.5156	0.5041	0.2466
	2015	0.5349	0.5320	0.5287	0.5168	0.2518
$IO_k = DCV$, w_k = population proportion	2009	0.6477	0.6429	0.6377	0.6181	0.1833
	2015	0.7014	0.6940	0.6858	0.6556	0.1131
$IO_k = DCV$ w_k = 1/K for all k	2009	0.5215	0.5177	0.5134	0.4977	0.1475
	2015	0.5349	0.5292	0.5230	0.4999	0.0863

Proximity to the 'Best' Distribution:

		Alpha =				
		1	0.95	0.90	0.75	0.1
$IO_k = GT_{ko}$, w_k = population proportion	2009	0.6477	0.6431	0.6379	0.6190	0.2611
	2015	0.7014	0.6968	0.6917	0.6728	0.2615
$IO_k = GT_{ko}$, $w_k = 1/K$ for all k	2009	0.5215	0.5180	0.5141	0.4998	0.2611
	2015	0.5349	0.5326	0.5301	0.5208	0.3340
$IO_k = DCV$, w_k = population proportion	2009	0.6477	0.6398	0.6312	0.5993	0.0795
	2015	0.7014	0.6920	0.6816	0.6437	0.0690
$IO_k = DCV$ $w_k = 1/K$ for all k	2009	0.5215	0.5151	0.5082	0.4825	0.0640
	2015	0.5349	0.5277	0.5198	0.4909	0.0526

Table 6. Equality of Opportunity Sensitive Measures of Student Human Capital Acquisition: $\sum_{k=1}^{K} w_k UD1_k \left(1 - IO_k\right)^{\frac{1-\alpha}{\alpha}}$ (All Indices Refer to Student Achievement, α Chosen by Investigator).

Proximity to the Average Distribution:

Quality of Education		Alpha =				
		1	0.95	0.90	0.75	0.1
$IO_k = GT_{ko}$, w_k = population proportion	2009	0.7038	0.7019	0.6999	0.6923	0.4811
	2015	0.8342	0.8329	0.8316	0.8265	0.6808
$IO_k = GT_{ko}$, $w_k = 1/K$ for all k	2009	0.5649	0.5614	0.5576	0.5433	0.2393
	2015	0.5904	0.5856	0.5805	0.5618	0.2619
$IO_k = DCV$, w_k = population proportion	2009	0.7038	0.6978	0.6913	0.6672	0.1664
	2015	0.8342	0.8253	0.8156	0.7795	0.1339
$IO_k = DCV$ $w_k = 1/K$ for all k	2009	0.5649	0.5602	0.5550	0.5355	0.1336
	2015	0.5904	0.5841	0.5772	0.5517	0.0947

Table 6. *(Continued)*

Proximity to the 'Best' Distribution:						
Quality of Education		Alpha =				
		1	0.95	0.90	0.75	0.1
$IO_k = GT_{ko}$, w_k = population proportion	2009	0.7038	0.6980	0.6917	0.6681	0.1958
	2015	0.8342	0.8274	0.8200	0.7923	0.2277
$IO_k = GT_{ko}$, $w_k = 1/K$ for all k	2009	0.5649	0.5611	0.5569	0.5415	0.2698
	2015	0.5904	0.5847	0.5786	0.5565	0.2622
$IO_k = DCV$, w_k = population proportion	2009	0.7038	0.6962	0.6879	0.6571	0.1106
	2015	0.8342	0.8230	0.8108	0.7660	0.0836
$IO_k = DCV$ $w_k = 1/K$ for all k	2009	0.5649	0.5588	0.5522	0.5275	0.0888
	2015	0.5904	0.5825	0.5739	0.5422	0.0591

Where w_k is the weight attached to the kth circumstance group (in the representative agent example here it is set to $1/K$), UDI_k is a Utopia-Dystopia index recording the kth circumstance groups achievement, IO_k is a measure of distributional difference (transvariation) between the kth student outcome distribution and some target distribution (the average distribution in the case of egalitarian social preferences, the 'best' or highest ranked distribution in the case of Prioritarian preferences) and $0 \leq QC_k \leq 1$ is an index reflecting the quality of parental circumstance confronted by a student in circumstance group k.

In the case of both unmodulated indices shown above in Table 7 above (Utilitarian Social Preferences), student performance in 2015 is better than in 2009. Modulation with respect to differences from the average, reflecting egalitarian preferences sees a reduction in the gap in the first order case and a reversal of the ordering in the second order case. Modulation with respect to differences from the 'best' distribution, reflecting a Prioritarian view of the world, sees better outcomes in 2009 than in 2015 a result of the increasing distance between poorly endowed student outcome distributions and the outcome distributions of the best endowed.

Table 7. Subgroup Specific Inequality Modulated Wellbeing Indices.

First Order Utopia-Dystopia Index:			
	Inequality Modulation Group Un-modulated,	Inequality Modulation Group Transvariation from Average	Transvariation from Best
2009	0.5649	0.5442	0.5427
2015	0.5904	0.5512	0.5408

Second Order Utopia-Dystopia Index:			
	Inequality Modulation Group Unmodulated,	Inequality Modulation Group Transvariation from Average	Transvariation from Best
2009	0.5913	0.5694	0.5674
2015	0.5971	0.5546	0.5443

6. CONCLUSIONS

The success of the Egalitarian Project depends in part on the overall elevation of level of human capital and in part on ensuring that all have an equal opportunity for doing so and assessment of the projects success requires measures that incorporate both aspects. Here, treating parenting type and regional location as circumstances beyond a students' control, such measures have been proposed and implemented in a study of Student performance in Reading and Science in Spanish regions over the period 2009–2015. Aggregate measures of parental quality and student achievement have been combined with measures of the extent of inequality of opportunity to produce equal opportunity sensitive measures of parental quality and student achievement. Generally, there has been an improvement over the period both in terms of the overall parenting quality confronting students and in student grade achievements but this has been modulated somewhat by diminished equality of opportunity characterized by increased differences in circumstance conditioned achievement distributions especially with respect to single parented students. However, only when the equality of opportunity component gets heavy weight is the ordering reversed. Students in Basque and Catalan regions appear to be particularly advantaged relative to students in the rest of Spain. In the final analysis when the weighting factor is governed by the quality of the circumstances while under a First Order wellbeing indicator Utilitarians and Egalitarians see an improvement in wellbeing whereas Prioritarians do not, under a second order indicator Utilitarians see and improvement whereas both Egalitarians and Prioritarians see a deterioration.

NOTES

1. In the UK, the Department for Levelling Up, Housing and Communities was formed in 2006 and its first minister (Secretary of State) was David Milliband.

2. Ex Ante Equality of Opportunity is usually examined by seeking equality of conditional means (Bjorklund et al., 2012), Ex Poste Equality of Opportunity has been examined by seeking the absence of stochastic dominance between distributions (Checchi & Peragine, 2010). While each approach is simply implemented neither secure equality of chances which is the essence of Ex Poste Equality of Opportunity though each are compatible with levelling up (Brunori et al., 2023).

3. The foundational work on Sufficientarianism (Frankfurt 1987) only focused on those who had enough, Crisp (2003) added a refinement that drew attention to those who were not at the sufficient outcome level. Recently, Sufficientarian measures have been axiomatically developed and codified in Alcantud et al. (2021) and Bossert et al. (2021, 2022).

4. Moreno-Ternero and Roemer (2008) found the Egalitarian and Priority positions to be at odds whereas Buchak (2017) offers an intermediate Relative Prioritarianism position.

5. See for example, Weymark (2003), Bourguignon et al. (2007), Checchi and Peragine (2010), Ferreira and Gignoux (2011), and Lefranc Pistolesi and Trannoy (2008, 2009).

6. To weight or not to weight? that is the question, and it is clearly of consequence for the policy maker. Weighted versions of these indices reflect the overall inequality in the society, downplaying the distributional differences and wellbeing levels associated with lowly populated groups and emphasising differences in heavily populated groups. On the other hand, unweighted versions compare distributions directly as in a representative agent version of the society, giving equal status to differences experienced by minorities and majorities alike.

7. In the following application achievement measures are multivariate and some are ordered categorical. Unlike quantifying distributional differences using conditional moments, when x is a vector, multilateral comparisons of multivariate distributions are straight forward. Suppose the distributions are tri-variate $f(x,y,z)$, then simply write [1] as:

$$GT_{i,j} = \int_0^\infty \int_0^\infty \int_0^\infty \frac{|f_i(x,y,z) - f_j(x,y,z)|}{2} dxdydz \left(= \sum_x \sum_y \sum_z |p_i(x,y,z) - p_j(x,y,z)| \right)$$

And substitute into [3] or [4] as appropriate, again with unweighted versions following as before. Comparing multivariate distributions in such a fashion provides a very natural way of combining the various outcome dimensions avoiding the invidious and arbitrary weighting problems involved in aggregation across dimensions.

8. It is only necessary because there is no reason to believe that $f_i(x)$ is the same as some policy target distribution $f_{i*}(x)$.

9. Recent literature (see Brunori et al., 2019) has widely shown that ad-hoc type creations often lead to Asymptotically biased IOp estimates in terms of mean differences, however the same arguments do not apply when basic distributional differences are considered. Though small samples remain a concern for estimate reliability.

10. An illuminating discussion of Prioritarian versus Egalitarian views in the context of such a wellbeing index can be found in Fleurbaey (2015).

REFERENCES

Aaberge, R., Mogstad, M., & Peragine, V. (2011). Measuring long-term inequality of opportunity. *Journal of Public Economics*, *95*(3–4), 193–204.

Alcantud, J. C. R., Mariotti, M., & Veneziani, R. (2022). Sufficientarianism. *Theoretical Economics*, *17*, 1529–1567.

Anderson, G., & Leo, T. W. (2020). *Searching for complete, unambiguous, multilateral orderings of states defined on cardinal and/or ordinal variable spaces*. Mimeo University of Toronto.

Anderson, G., Linton, O., Pittau, M. G., Whang, Y.-J., & Zelli, R. (2021). On unit free assessment of multilateral distributional variation. *The Econometrics Journal*, *24*(3), 502–518.

Anderson, G., Linton, O., & Whang, Y.-J. (2012). Nonparametric estimation and inference about the overlap of two distributions. *Journal of Econometrics*, *171*(1), 1–23.

Anderson, G., Post, T., & Whang Y.-J. (2020). Somewhere between Utopia and Dystopia: Choosing from multiple incomparable prospects. *Journal of Business and Economic Statistics*, *38*(3), 502–515.

Anderson, G., & Thomas, J. (2019). Measuring multi-group polarization, segmentation and ambiguity: Increasingly unequal yet similar constituent Canadian income distributions. *Social Indicators Research*, *145*, 1001–1032.

Arrow, K., Bowles, S., & Durlauf, S. (Eds.) (2000) *Meritocracy and economic inequality*. Princeton University Press.

Atkinson, A. B. (1970). On the measurement of inequality. *Journal of Economic Theory*, *2*(3), 244–263.

Atkinson, A. B. (2012). Public economics after the idea of justice. *Journal of Human Development and Capabilities*, *13*(4), 521–536.

Autor, D. H. (2014). Skills, education, and the rise of earnings inequality among the "other 99 percent". *Science*, *344*, 843–851.

Bjorklund, A., Jantti, M., & Roemer, J. E. (2012). Equality of opportunity and the distribution of long-run income in Sweden. *Social Choice and Welfare*, *39*, 675–696.

Bond, T. N., & Lang, K. (2019). The sad truth about happiness scales. *Journal of Political Economy*, *127*(4), 1629–1640.

Bossert, W., Cato, S., & Kamaga, K. (2021). Critical-level sufficientarianism. *The Journal of Political Philosophy*,*30*(4), 434–461.

Bossert, W., Cato, S., & Kamaga, K. (2022). Thresholds, critical levels, and generalized sufficientarian principles. *Economic Theory*, *75*, 1099–1139.

Bourguignon, F., Ferreira, F. H. G., & Menendez, M. (2007). Inequality of opportunity in Brazil. *Review of Income and Wealth*, *53*(4), 585–618.
Brunori, P., Ferreira, F. H., & Salas-Rojo, P. (2023). *Inherited inequality: A general framework and an application to South Africa*. International Inequalities Institute Working Paper 107.
Brunori, P., Peragine, V., & Serlenga, L. (2019). Upward and downward bias when measuring inequality of opportunity. *Social Choice and Welfare*, *52*, 635–661.
Buchak, L. (2017). Taking risks behind the veil of ignorance. *Ethics*, *127*(3), 610–644.
Cantril, H. (1965). *The pattern of human concerns*. New Brunswick, NJ: Rutgers University Press.
Carneiro, P., Hansen, K. T., & Heckman, J. J. (2003). Lawrence R. Klein Lecture estimating distributions of treatment effects with an application to the returns to schooling and measurement of the effects of uncertainty on college choice. *International Economic Review*, *44*, 361–422.
Checchi, D., & Peragine, V. (2010). Inequality of opportunity in Italy. *Journal of Economic Inequality*, *8*(4), 429–450.
Ferreira, F. H. G., & Gignoux, J. (2011). The measurement of inequality of opportunity: Theory and an application to Latin America. *Review of Income and Wealth*, *57*(4), 622–657.
Ferreira, F. H. G., & Peragine, V. (2015). Individual responsibility and equality of opportunity. In M. D. Adler & M. Fluerbaey (Eds.), *Chapter 25 in the Oxford handbook of wellbeing and public policy*. Oxford University Press.
Fleurbaey, M. (2015). Equality versus priority: How relevant is the distinction?*Economics and Philosophy*, *31*, 203–217.
Fleurbaey, M., & Peragine, V. (2013). Ex Ante versus ex post equality of opportunity. *Economica*, *80*, 118–130.
Galor, O. (2011). *Unified growth theory*. Princeton University Press.
Gini, C. (1916). Il concetto di transvariazione e le sue prime applicazioni.*Giornale degli Economisti e Rivista di Statistica*.
Gravel, N., Magdalou, B., & Moyes, P. (2020). Ranking distributions of an ordinal variable. *Economic Theory*. https://doi.org/10.1007/s00199-019-01241-4
Harsanyi, J. C. (1953). Cardinal utility in welfare economics and in the theory of risk-taking. *Journal of Political Economy*, *61*(5), 434–435.
Harsanyi, J. C. (1955). Cardinal welfare, individualistic ethics, and interpersonal comparisons of utility. *Journal of Political Economy*, *63*(4), 309–321.
Kahneman, D., & Krueger, A. B. (2006). Developments in the measurement of subjective well-being. *Journal of Economic Perspectives*, *20*, 3–24.
Klein, A. (2015, April 10). No child left behind: An overview. *Education Week*. https://www.edweek.org/policy-politics/no-child-left-behind-an-overview/2015/04
Lefranc, A., Pistolesi, N., & Trannoy, A. (2008). Inequality of opportunities vs. inequality of outcomes. *Review of Income and Wealth*, *54*, 513–546.
Lefranc, A., Pistolesi, N., & Trannoy, A. (2009). Equality of opportunity and luck: Definitions and testable conditions, with an application to income in France. *Journal of Public Economics*, *93*, 1189–1207.
McGowan, M. A., & Millán, J. A. S. (2019). *Reducing regional disparities for inclusive growth in Spain*. [OECD Economics Department Working Papers No. 1549].
Milanovic, B. (2011). *The haves and the have-nots: A brief and idiosyncratic history of global inequality*. Basic Books.
Moreno-Ternero, J. D., & Roemer, J. E. (2008, July). The veil of ignorance violates priority. *Economics & Philosophy*, *24*(2), 233–257.
Morgan, S. J., Grusky, S. B., & Fields, G. S. (2006). Mobility and inequality: Frontiers of Research in Sociology and Economics. Stanford University Press.
Rawls, J. (1999/1971). *A theory of justice*. Oxford University Press (revised edition).
Roemer, J. E. (2006). *Democracy, education, and equity; Graz Schumpeter Lectures*. Cambridge University Press.
Rhune, D. F. (2009). *The rise of regionalism: Causes of regional mobilization in Western Europe*. Routledge.
Samuelson, P. A. (1948). Consumption theory in terms of revealed preference. *Economica*, *15*,243–253.
Schroder, C., & Yitzhaki, S. (2017). Revisiting the evidence for cardinal treatment of ordinal variables. *European Economic Review*, *92*, 337–358.

Sen, A. K. (1976). Real national income. *Review of Economic Studies*, *43*, 19–39.
Sen, A. K. (1987). *Choice, welfare and measurement*. MIT Press.
Sen, A. K. (1995). *Inequality re-examined*. Harvard University Press.
Sen, A. K. (2009). *The idea of justice*. Harvard University Press.
Shubert, A. (2003). *A social history of modern Spain*. Routledge.
Stoline, M. R., & Ury, H. K. (1979). Tables of the studentized maximum modulus distribution and an application to multiple comparisons among means. *Technometrics*, *21*, 87–93.
UNDP. (2019). HUMAN DEVELOPMENT REPORT Beyond income, beyond averages, beyond today: Inequalities in human development in the 21st century. Technical notes.
Weymark, J. A. (2003). Generalized gini indices of equality of opportunity. *Journal of Economic Inequality*, *1.1*, 5–24.

CHAPTER 3

NON-LINEAR DECOMPOSITION OF INEQUALITY OF OPPORTUNITY AMONG THE YOUNG ON THE LABOUR MARKET IN CAMEROON: EVIDENCES FROM SPATIAL COMPARATIVE ANALYSIS

Romus Noufelie[a,b,c], Cosmas Bernard Meka'a[c,d,e] and Astride Claudel Njiepue Nouffeussie[c,e,f,g]

[a]*Faculty of Economics and Management, University of Ngaoundéré, Ngaoundéré, Cameroun*
[b]*Laboratory of the Economic Analysis (LEA), University of Nagoundéré, Ngaoundéré, Cameroun*
[c]*Microeconomics of Development Laboratory, Douala, Cameroun*
[d]*Faculty of Economics and Management, University of Bertoua, Bertoua, Cameroun*
[e]*Research Center on Innovation, Institutions and Inclusive Development, Yaoundé, Cameroun*
[f]*Faculty of Economics and Applied Management, University of Douala, Douala, Cameroun*
[g]*Association Française d'Economie du Développement, Paris, France*

ABSTRACT

The aim of this study is to investigate the determinants of Inequalities of Opportunity (IOP) among the young in Cameroonian labour market. IOP are the differences in outcomes which are explained by the circumstance factors, meaning that the variables which are beyond individual controls. For this purpose, this study performs the Human Opportunity Index (HOI) in order to quantify the IOP among employee over 10- to 25-year-olds. Using the data from the Fourth Cameroon Household Survey (FCHS4) carried out in 2014 by

Opportunity, Mobility and Inequality
Research on Economic Inequality, Volume 31, 65–90

Published under exclusive licence by Emerald Publishing Limited
ISSN: 1049-2585/doi:10.1108/S1049-258520250000031004

Statistical National Institute, IOP is quantified for each of 14 Cameroonian's geographical areas. Based on the Dissimilarity index (D-Index) value, two main trends are outlined: a spatial subgroup including North-West, East and the urban regions which is characterized by a higher D-Index; meaning that IOP is relatively significant. In contrast, a more homogeneous subgroup with a lower IOP is found in rural, North and East regions. Moreover, regarding on the one hand the Shapley-Shorrock's decomposition method, it appears that the mayor circumstances contributing to the D-index are socio-professional category, primary education and religious obedience of the household head which explain from 51% to 79% the overall IOP. While on the other hand, the Blinder-Oaxaca decomposition shows that 80% of the gap in D-Index is explained by disparities in circumstances, rather than individual efforts. Finally, our conclusions argue in favour of effective decentralization, for a more inclusive employment policy that takes into account local labour market features.

Keywords: Decomposition; D-Index; inequality of opportunity; HOI; labour market; young

1. INTRODUCTION

Although the issue of inequality is relatively old, it has emerged as the most relevant concern of the 21st century, given its impact on growth. Indeed, Kuznets (1955) argued that there is a positive correlation between inequality and long-term growth. Particularly, author observed that at the first economic development stage, the inequality levels are high, characterizing a 'curse' situation, but at a second stage, that would be mitigated after that the development level will reach a threshold accordingly to a best distribution policy of previous economic gain accumulated ('trickle down' effect). At the third stage, inequality level would be significantly reduced in the long term. These three-development stage referring to U-shaped curve describing inequality-economic development nexus (Kuznets, 1955). Therefore, any policy aimed at reducing inequality might be detrimental to development in the short term.

However, this theory has been largely contradicted and it has been replaced by the theory of cumulative causality theory developed by Myrdal (1965). The latter supports that inequalities are detrimental for economic growth. Therefore, author recommended to policymakers to fight this scourge in all its aspect (Alesina & Rodrik, 1994). Moreover, neither Kuznets (1955) nor Myrdal (1965) ignored to consider the spatial inequality concern in their studies. It's the main contribution from Lewis's investigation. Lewis (1954) as others authors supported that, inequalities featured the first stage of the development process, but author added that, spatial gaps could be addressed if migration flows from rural to industrial sectors are high.

As a result, the fight against inequality now seems to be high on the international agenda. The recent 2030 United Nation's agenda on Sustainable Development points the reduce inequality objective in the core of goal 10 (SDG10). Furthermore, understanding labour market participation is a crucial aspect of this goal (Naidu & Yuchtman, 2013). Moreover, access to the labour market and especially for young people, is considered as the main channel through which inequalities of opportunity (IOP) affect economic development, especially in developing countries (Anyanwu, 2014; Hussain & Awad, 2022; Thieme, 2010). However, inequalities do not manifest themselves in the same way and they vary over time, space, between or within people groups (World Bank, 2006).

Regarding their manifestations' side, the labour market has been recognized as an appropriate field for analyzing inequalities in developing countries. Indeed, the economic crises in 1990s have not been damageable for the labour market and the socio-economic inequalities in Africa; which is likely widen by coronavirus pandemic (Covid-19) (Fambon et al., 2018). According to World Bank (2014), almost 70% of Africa's population is under 30 years old, but they remain the most vulnerable. While Africa should benefit from this potential[1] labour force, the expected role of youth in the development process is still controversial (Hussain & Awad, 2022), with record levels of inequality (Thorbecke, 2013).

Moreover, inequality concern has a theoretical basis, with an abound literature following the political philosophy development. In fact, recent approaches share the idea that inequalities are not always bad since supported by classical theoretical. In this way, it is mentioned that this approach breaks with the Welfares theory supported by Fambon et al.[2] (2018), Harsanyi (1955) and Stiglitz (1982). On the other hand, Rawls (1971) develops the theory of justice, from which the inequality analyses considered whether they depend on the responsibility (effort) or not (circumstance) of individuals. This path taken by several authors in sub-Saharan Africa in recent years in order to explain labour market inequalities (Assaad et al., 2019; Dimova & Karim, 2019; Hussain & Awad, 2022). Overall, race, gender, place of birth, age and family characteristics are the main circumstantial factors highlighted. In these studies, some were interested in young people or underemployed people subgroups (Talla et al., 2017).

In Cameroon in particular, Statistical National Institute (SNI, fore after) revealed that getting job concern for the young people does not make exception and the analysis of inequalities regarding the opportunities approach is fairly documented (SNI, 2010). The parametric approach based on equal opportunity theory has allowed Fotso et al. (2019) and Talla (2017) to deep the debate on Inequality of Opportunity (IOP) in the labour market by addressing the dimensions of wages, occupational mobility and job quality.

However, they limit their analysis to the national level, which does not allow to highlight regional specificities; and when these are taken into account, they are integrated as simple indicator variables. This contrasts with several reports that point to the existence of deep spatial and rural-urban inequalities in Cameroon (Njikam et al., 2005; SNI, 2014). Therefore, the current study extends these last empirical works which studied the IOP in Cameroon context.

Thus, the contribution of this study is threefold: first, by restricting our sample to the young employee people from 10 to 25 years old, we put forward the share of labour force which is the most affected by unemployment; and further, there is not yet been analyzed the employment access inequality from the opportunity perspective. Secondly, we have focused on the role of residence (regional, urban and rural) in order to highlight heterogeneity at a more small spatial scale, which is necessary for designing the targeted employment policies (Le Gallo, 2002; Islam, 2013). Finally, as in the previous studies, the current one uses the Human Opportunity Index (HOI) method which is an ex-ante approach of IOP and developed by de Barros et al. (2009). However, the current study uses both the Shapley's decomposition method (Shorrock, 2013) which outline the marginal contribution to IOP of each factor; and the Blinder (1973) and Oaxaca (1973) decomposition one, which highlights which of the compositional or structural effects explains the spatial differences in IOP.

For this purpose, we use the data from the Fourth Cameroon Household Survey (FCHS4) compiled in 2014 by SNI. As it limited to include all circumstances factors, the IOP value Computed represents the lower bound of its real magnitude. However, the World Bank (2009) points out that this value tells us relevant significant about the IOP extend in outcomes.

The rest of the chapter is structured as follows. The second and third sections are devoted to the literature review and the methodological framework, respectively. The fourth section is devoted to the results. The fifth one presents the discussion, and the sixth section is bequeathed to the conclusion and policy implications.

2. LITERATURE REVIEW

This section provides a conceptual analysis of inequality of opportunity and a review of the determinants of inequality of opportunity in the labour market.

2.1. Opportunity Inequality: A Conceptual Analysis

The inequality analysis has long been a hotly debated topic among policymakers, practitioners and researchers across fields. However, in contrast to the normative literature view, the issue of inequality of opportunity has remained virtually unexplored in empirical work (Roemer & Trannoy, 2016). According to the authors, the concept of equality of opportunity best unites proponents of social justice theory. But what does this concept refer to?

To answer this question, several authors have drawn in reference of the social justice theory which has firstly developed by Rawls (1971). Indeed, this theory emphasizes that IOP is a key component of social justice. This last author supports that the social responsibility to provide equal opportunities for all can be constrained by the behaviour of those same individuals. Dworkin (1981) took a different approach, distinguishing between an individual's preferences and available resources. The overall structure of his theory based on the idea that a person's feature can be split into two components: the one that is made up of factors what can be held accountable (*effort*) and others for which one cannot (*circumstance*). In the first case, inequalities are legitimate and accepted in the society member, whereas in the second case, it is unacceptable and decision-makers' actions are relevant to hold this scourge (Peragine, 2004). Furthermore, while the ethical concept of equalizing resources between individual's remains theoretical, the differences appeared among the final outcomes are the consequences from disparities among their choices. In this context, Dworkin (1981) mentions that individuals are responsible for their preferences, but not for their resources (arbitrary factors).

However, authors as Anerson (1989) and Cohen (1989) (cited in Motiram, 2018) are critical of the fact that Dworkin (1981) holds individuals responsible for choices that are beyond their control. As a result, Anerson (1989) proposed an alternative analysis for the equal distribution of resources, by supposing that individuals have equal opportunities to satisfy their preferences. Cohen (1989) has proposed a definition based on equal access to benefits that is similar to Anerson's but goes beyond individual welfare.

Acknowledging that previous studies made the relevant contributions, a third way suggested by Roemer (1998), by upbraiding their predecessors of did not give a correct and intuitive understanding of the idea to which this concept refers. Indeed, Roemer (1998) observed that the interpretation of equality of opportunity as equality of fixed opportunities (which forcing all individuals to make the same choice), is very restrictive and does not sufficiently include all sections of the population, especially the poorest one. Roemer (1998), Roemer and Trannoy (2016) proposed a most largely used definition of IOP. They suggested that the individual outcome factors should be separated from circumstances and effort. From this perspective, circumstances are factors that are exogenous and unmodifiable by individuals (gender, race, place of birth, etc.), since they affect the outcomes of individuals over whom they have no control. Furthermore, effort can also determine outcomes, but it is influenced by individual choices. Finally, Roemer suggests the development of 'equal opportunity' policies aimed at neutralizing the advantages for each percentile of the within-group effort distribution.

Finally, Fleurbaey and Peragine (2013) mention two measurement approaches of IOP: one based on ex-ante and another on ex-post analysis. The former case investigates the contribution in the resource distribution gaps to inequalities in outcomes. Van Der Gaer (1992, 2013) supported that this case is focused on inequalities in resources access. The second case, argued by Roemer (2002), focuses on inequalities in outcomes with respect to factors that are assumed to be equally distributed across individuals. However, Bourguignon et al. (2007) and Motiram (2018) point to the complementarity between these two approaches.

2.2. Determinants of Inequality of Opportunity in the Labour Market

Overall, studies of explaining factors of IOP are relatively limited. Indeed, most existing studies have addressed this concern from poverty and economic growth perspective (Anis & Hamdaoui, 2020; El-Saadani & Metwally, 2019; Krafft & Alawode, 2018; Shekhar & Ebeke, 2020). As a result, only a few papers have so far linked IOP to specific labour market indicators (Ahmed et al., 2020; Bindop, 2019; Chameni et al., 2013; CoMoschion, 2015; Fambon et al., 2018; Hussain & Awad, 2022).

Ahmed et al. (2020) use a logit model, dissimilarity index and Shapley decomposition on 2014 poverty survey data to examine IOP in the labour market in Sudan. Their estimates show that gender inequality of opportunity is the highest at 73.41%. Authors add that the gender gap in the mean probability in getting employment is 0.274 in favour of men. Using instead the HOI as a proxy for inequality of opportunity, Hussain and Awad (2022) determine how gender, age, place of residence, parental education and occupation, contribute to the likelihood of young people being outside the labour market in six sub-Saharan African. Using data from the 2014 and 2015 International Labour Organization (ILO) School-to-Work Transition Surveys, the authors show that dissimilarity has a strong impact in Madagascar and to some extent in Malawi and Uganda, while Liberia, Zambia and Congo have comparatively low dissimilarity activity index. Furthermore, findings show that factors such as gender and father's education are the factors that cause the risk gaps in inactivity opportunity.

In the same vein, the work of Pasquier-Doumer (2010) identifies in seven West African capitals the way in which of worker socio-economic relates to their chances in the labour market. Based on a log-linear model, the author reports that the position of the father directly affects the labour market position of his child. Bindop (2019) used a log-linear model on data from the first and second employment surveys carried out by INS (2005–2010) in Cameroon and highlighted the role of school and family characteristics in this dynamic of intergenerational transmission of labour market status. This approach was used by Fotso et al. (2019) or Abras et al. (2013) to show the role of IOP in job quality and socio-professional mobility in Cameroon and in SSA's labour market, respectively.

3. METHODOLOGICAL APPROACH

This section first presents the model and estimation strategy, data and variables used.

3.1. Model and Estimation Strategy

3.1.1. Computation Method for IOP

This study uses the HOI methodology to evaluate the access to employment as a function of individual and family circumstances. This approach originally proposed by de Barros et al. (2009), has been used by Krafft and Assaad (2016), Dimova and Karim (2019), Brunori et al. (2019) and Assaad et al. (2019).

The HOI (access rate) and the coverage rate are determined, representing the share of available job opportunities and the share of the population with access to opportunities, respectively. The dissimilarity index (D_index), which measures the inequality magnitude, is the percentage of opportunities that would be reallocated in order to reach to equal access. Finally, the marginal contribution of each circumstance to the IOP is analyzed using the Shapley method and Blinder-Oaxaca (BO, 1973). The calculation of *D-index* is a three-step procedure:

The first step aims to estimate the conditional likelihood by regressing the probability $p(.)$ of accessing an opportunity (Y) in each setting to a set of circumstances x_j. The following equation is estimated from the logit method:

$$Ln\left[P(I=1/x)/1-P(I=1/x)\right]=\sum\gamma x \quad (1)$$

In the second step, the predicted probabilities (ωi) in employment access in each area of residence allow to estimate the average probability $\bar{\omega}$ (coverage rate) as follow:

$$\bar{\omega} = \sum_{i=1}^{n} \pi_i \omega_i \qquad (2)$$

Let $\pi_i = \frac{1}{n}$ are n observations size, and $\omega_i = Exp\left(\gamma_0 + \sum x_i \hat{\gamma}\right) / \left[1 + Exp\left(\gamma_0 + \sum x_i \hat{\gamma}\right)\right]$

The third step goes to compute the dissimilarity index (*D-index*) using the following equation:

$$D = \frac{1}{2\bar{\omega}} \sum_{i=1}^{n} \pi_i \mid \omega_i - \bar{\omega} \mid \qquad (3)$$

D-index is the IOP of employment access in each region, compared to the national average access rate. It is a binary variable which takes the value 0 in the perfect equality in opportunity access case; and 1 in the perfect IOP one. Furthermore, *D-index* allows to perform the HOI, which refers to the number of opportunities to reallocate according to the *equal opportunity principle* (Assad et al., 2019). Therefore:

$$HOI = \bar{\omega}(1 - D) \qquad (4)$$

Whether *HOI* equal to 1, implying that job opportunity access do not link to the individual's circumstances, and therefore inequalities are '*legitimate*' or '*justified*'.

Moreover, for fully understand the IOP's behaviour and their spatial variations, it's important to decomposition IOP regarding circumstance factors.

3.1.2. Shapley Decomposition Method - Shorrock and Blinder-Oaxaca of IOP measure

The Shapley decomposition based might be of interest as it allows to decomposition IOP in subgroups. This approach is important as it take into account all permutations of the circumstance's variables. We further perform the average marginal effect of each circumstance on the total IOP. However, this procedure is computationally intensive because 2^k number of circumstances must be computed. In this way, Shapley method is advantageous over other decomposition methods, as the decomposition is order-independent, and the different components equal the total value of IOP. Ferreira and Gegnoux (2014) cautioned that the decomposition should not be considered as causal effect as it indicate only an idea on the relative contribution. This because the circumstances are probably high correlated among them.

The application of this method can be traced back first to Shorrocks (1985), who used it to perform distributional analysis of the marginal contribution of each circumstance to the inequalities (Shorrock, 2013).

Let $x \in X = \{1,2,\ldots,n\}$ be a circumstances set, described by $\theta = \{\theta_1;\theta_2,\ldots,\theta_n\}$ the order in which circumstances are removed; with $S(\theta_j,\theta) = \{\theta_k \mid k \succ j\}$ the circumstance vector remaining after the removal of θ_j circumstances. Therefore, for a specific order of removal of circumstances, the marginal contribution of a circumstance x to D-index is given by:

$$C_x^\theta = D - index(S(x,\theta) \cup \{x\}) - D - index(S(x,\theta)) \tag{5}$$

However, $C_x = \Delta_x D - index(S(x,\theta))$

Where $\Delta_x D - index(S(x,\theta)) \equiv D - index(S \cup \{x\}) - D(S)$,

Which represents, the change at the margin of the inequality of opportunity, resulting from the addition of a circumstance.

A second approach which is widely used is based on decomposition in the IOP gap, developed by on the Blinder-Oaxaca technique (BO, 1973). It is a based-counterpart analysis which allows to firstly determine the probabilities to opportunity access, and secondly the gap between subgroups in these probabilities. This method is important as the sum of the contribution from each variable, equal to aggregate contribution from all of variable. Additionally, this approach considers that whether both the circumstances are different between subgroups and they affect the outcome, IOP calculated seems most really. Finally, this approach and contrary to linear decomposition one, allows to solve limits from the path dependence (order for becoming variable in the regression equation), problem of index (reference category subgroup) and the weighting one. According to Contreras (2012), differences in IOP between two groups can be associated with differences in circumstances (composition effect) or differences in the impact of circumstances on access to employment opportunities (structure effect). Therefore:

$$(D - index)r - (D - index)s = \Bigg(\underbrace{\bar{X}_r - \bar{X}_s}_{composition\ effect}\Bigg)\hat{\beta}_r + \bar{X}_r\Bigg(\underbrace{\hat{\beta}_r - \hat{\beta}_s}_{structure\ effect}\Bigg) \tag{6}$$

$\bar{X}_r$ and $\bar{X}_s$ are the vectors of Circumstances in the region r and s respectively; $\hat{\beta}_r$ and $\hat{\beta}_s$ are the vectors of the coefficients associated with the circumstances respectively.

The first term on the right-hand side of this equation corresponds to the spatial variation in the coverage rate (scale effect), and the second term refers to the change in the spatial opportunities distribution (distribution effect).

3.2. Data and Variables

In this study, whose objective is to evaluate IOP in the labour market within and between the different areas of residence (MDR) in Cameroon, we consider the area of residence to be a rural or urban area or the region (12 regions).[3] In particular, we are interested in IOP within the labour force and by region or area of residence (rural/urban). The choice of variables is inspired by the literature on the determinants of labour market accessibility (Njikam et al., 2005) and the literature on IOP (Assaad et al., 2019; Brunori et al., 2019; Dimova & Stephan 2020; Krafft & Assaad, 2016). In this study, the opportunity variable is access to employment. Thus, among the working population aged 10-25, equality of opportunity exists when differences in access to employment are not due to circumstances, but only to individual effort.

We have as Regions: DLA (Douala); YDE (Yaoundé): ADW (Adamaoua); CEN (Centre); EAS (East); FAN (Far North); NOR (North); LIT (LIT); WES (West); NOW (North West); SOU (South); SOW (Southwest). Based on the several relevant literature existing and the data from Fourth Cameroonian survey (FCHS), variables to be used in this study are presented below in Table 1.

Table 2 shows that at the time of the survey (2014), just over a quarter (28%) of the employed population was aged between 10 and 25. This relatively high proportion may be related to the fact that by the age of 25 almost all students have completed upper secondary education and a significant number of them enter the labour market each year.

Table 1. Presentation of Variables.

Variables	Definitions
JEM	Young employment
PSCH	Social professional position of the household head
ELH	Live quality of the household head
RELHH	Religion of the household head
SEXH	Nature of household head's sex
HANDH	Household head with physical handicap
PRIMH	Household head with at most a primary school level
SECH	Household head with at most a secondary and a least primary school level
SIZE	Number of person who permanent lively in the household
AREA	Location of household

Source: Authors.

Table 2. Presentation of Variables and Descriptive Statistics.

Variables	Mean	Observation
Opportunity variables		
JEM: 1 if an employee is aged between 10 and 25 years	0.2812155	19,021
0 otherwise	(0.4496042)	
Circumstance variables		
PSCH: 1 if asset in managerial position (manager, self-employed or boss)	0.1438359	19,021
0 otherwise (labourer, skilled worker, domestic helper)	(0.350927)	
ELH: 1 if the head of household declares to be non-poor	0.0487973	46,560
0 otherwise	(0.2154462)	
RELHH: 1 if the head of household is Catholic, Protestant or Muslim	0.010567	46,560
0 otherwise (animist, no religion or other religion)	(0.1022525)	

(*Continued*)

Table 2. (*Continued*)

Variables	Mean	Observation
SEX: 1 if the individual is male	0.4890893	46,560
0 otherwise	0.4998863	
HANDH: 1 if the individual has a disability	0.0357174	46,560
0 otherwise	(0.1855865)	
PRIMH: 1 if the head of the household has at most a primary school diploma	0.1285304	46,666
0 otherwise	(0.334683)	
SECH: 1 if the head of the household has at most a secondary school diploma	0.0319933	46,666
0 otherwise	(0.1759841)	
SIZE: the logarithm of the number of people living permanently in the household	1.720046 (0.6242437)	46,560
AREA: 1 if the household is located in an urban area	0.5000644	46,560
0 otherwise (rural area)	(0.5000054)	

NB: Values in brackets are standard deviations.
Source: Authors, data from FCHS (2014).

Indeed, as Table 2 shows, the low proportion of rich household heads (5%) can be explained by the intensity of their children's participation in the labour market. There are almost equal proportions of urban and rural households. Among the people interviewed, 35% suffer from a disability that prevents them from moving in the labour market. All these factors, which cannot be influenced by working people, since their choice depends either on their parents or on their environment, could, on the other hand, determine their position on the labour market.

To deep the descriptive statistical analysis, we study in Table 2 the variable behaviour by regarding their normality's distributions. Indeed, normality can be tested through two other measures of shape: skewness and excess kurtosis which are the best method for testing normality with a substantial benefit on the analysis of the sample data. This test is based on the null statement, according to that the studied data is not statistically different than normal versus an alternate statement that the normal distribution. We use two main tests based on Skewness/kurtosis test and Shapiro-Francia (W') test.[4]

Findings show that Skewness value for young employee is 0.97, whereas the Kurtosis's value reached to 1.94. Therefore, and according to the Thumb's rule, that respectively meaning that the data are moderately skewed and the distribution has heavier tails (leptokurtic). It appears that nearly all variables have a Kurtosis value greater than 1, implying that the data are highly skewed and leptokurtic; The results from Table 3 show that for each variable, except localization and gender, *P*-value regarding the normality test join is less than 1%; implying that, we cannot validate the null hypothesis for the normal distribution. Moreover, the W' value from SF nearly to 1, therefore, the distribution is non-Gaussian.

From Table 4, findings show that the gap rural-urban to be employee is positive and statistically very significant at the 1% threshold, meaning that in the urban areas, young are most de probability to get a job, comparatively to their counterparts located in rural areas.

Table 3. Normality Analysis for the Distribution.

Variable	Skewness/Kurtosis Tests for Normality joint			Shapiro-Francia		
	Skewness	Kurtosis	Tests for Normality Joint	*W'*	*V'*	Prob for Normality
JEM	0.97	1.94	0.0000	1.00000	0.000	1.00000
PSCH	2.029869	5.120367	0.0000	1.00000	0.000	1.00000
ELH	4.188587	18.54426	0.0000	1.00000	−0.000	0.00001
RELHH	9.57313	92.64483	0.0000	1.00000	−0.000	0.00001
HANDH	5.003462	26.03464	0.0000	1.00000	−0.000	0.00001
SIZE	−0.697430	3.846251	0.0000	0.95943	970.448	0.00001
CEPH	2.219853	5.927747	0.0000	1.00000	0.000	1.00000
SECH	5.318795	29.28958	0.0000	1.00000	−0.000	0.00001
HISH	11.91354	142.9324	0.0000	1.00000	−0.000	0.00001
AREA	0.0002577	1	–	1.00000	−0.000	0.00001
SEXH	−0.043653	1.001906	–	1.00000	0.000	1.00000

Source: Authors.

Table 4. Tests for the Differences Rural–Urban in Getting Job.

Group	Mean		Std. Dev.
Urban	0.251073		0.4336549
Rural	0.3074653		0.4614665
combined	0.2812155		0.4496042
diff	0.0065229		−0.0436069
Pr($T < t$)		**0.0000**	

Source: Authors.

4. RESULTS AND COMMENTS

This paragraph presents on one hand the determinants of access to Cameroonian labour market, and the other hand, analyses of HOI index, coverage rate and dissimilarity index. Regarding the findings from probit estimation approach (Table A1 in appendix), it is arising that almost all circumstance variables presented in Table 1 are relevant for getting job, and this, irrespectively of spatial localization.

Furthermore, for analyzing the IOP in the labour market, the results of current study are presented regarding three indicators: the probability of access to a job (or the average coverage or prevalence of the job opportunity); the HOI, which is the rate of access to this opportunity (or the number of opportunities available in a region) currently allocated on the based-opportunity principle; and the D-index (dissimilarity), which measures the inequality of opportunities. This index is interpreted as the proportion of the number of opportunities that would have to be redistributed between groups of circumstances in order to ensure equal access to employment opportunities in each region.

At the national level, the results of Fig. 1 show that, in terms of circumstances that do not depend on young workers, the dissimilarity of access to employment and the inequality of opportunities vary between 29% and 30%.

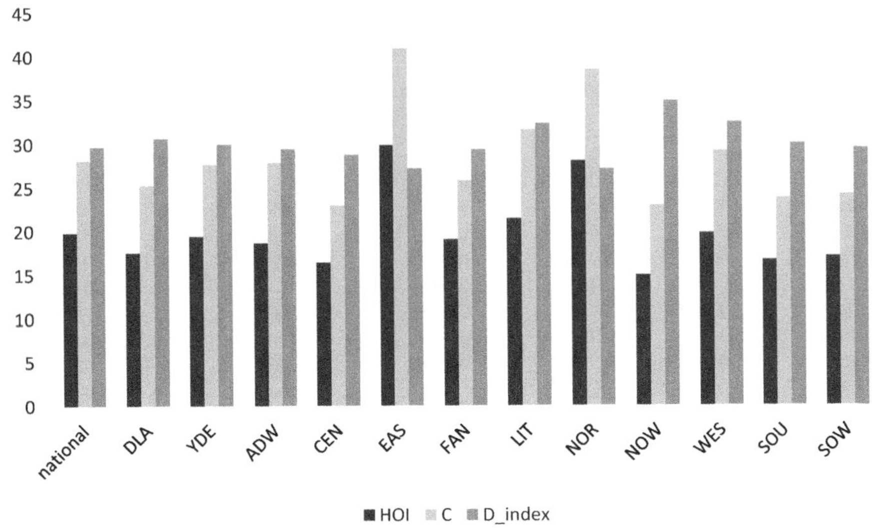

Fig. 1. Computation of HOI, Coverage (C) and D Index Per Region.
Source: Authors, data from the Fourth Cameroonian Household Survey (FCHS4, 2014).

At the national level, it is 29.63%. In the light of Ahmed et al. (2020), this proportion also represents the share of opportunities to be redistributed to the non-employed (unemployed) in order to achieve an equal redistribution of jobs, according to the principle of equal opportunity defined by Roemer (2008). This value masks enormous disparities between the 12 regions of Cameroon, where the D_index varies between 27% and 35%. The level of inequality in the regions of Yaoundé, Adamaoua, the Far North, the South and the South West is almost the same as that observed at national level, i.e. almost 29%. Moreover, the East and North regions show greater homogeneity in terms of young people's access to employment, unlike the Northwest region, where this form of inequality is more pronounced than at national level. In order to check the robustness of these results, a bootstrap estimation based on 100 replications was carried out. It turned out that the standard errors for each region are all between 1% and 2.5%, which according to Ferreira and Gignoux (2014) is relatively small to question the quality of our results.

Furthermore, when asked about the average chances of being employed, it turns out that low coverage rates (prevalence) are generally negatively associated with heterogeneity in the distribution of this employment opportunity. Indeed, the North-West region (more unequal) offers young people only a 15% chance of employment, followed by the Centre (16.4%) and South (16.65%) regions, while the East region (less unequal) offers almost 30%. In other words, the level of job distribution among young people in the East is twice as high as in the North-West. In fact, the probability of a young person aged 10–25 having access to a job opportunity is higher in the East region, with a chance rate of around 41% in 2014, compared with only 23% in the Centre and North West regions.

An analysis based on rural–urban localization shows that (Fig. 2), compared to the urban labour market, the rate of access to employment in rural areas is significantly higher (21% against 18% in urban areas). Furthermore, young rural workers have a higher probability of access to employment, 37% compared to 25% in urban areas. This result may be due to the availability of agro-pastoral activities in urban areas and to the fact that emigration, which appears to be three times lower in urban areas (3%) than in rural areas (9%), reduces competition on the labour market in the area of origin and consequently improves the employability rate in these areas.

On the other hand, we find that the disparity in access to employment is greater in rural areas (30%) than in urban areas (28%); which shows a greater heterogeneity in the distribution of jobs between young people aged 10–25 in urban areas than in rural areas. This finding confirms that of Fambon et al. (2018), who state in their analysis that most rural youth cannot afford to remain unemployed, given the ease of access to land and the development of agro-pastoral activities.

In order to answer the question of how the gap between the different sources of IOP affects the overall inequality within each region, we proceed on the one hand to the decomposition by source of opportunity according to Shapley (1953), followed by the Binder-Oaxaca technique (Blinder, 1973; Oaxaca, 1973). The answer to this question is the source decomposition of the D_index (Tables 5a, 5b and Fig. 3). From this we can see that, at national level, the IOP of young workers getting a job is the consequence of two main factors: the households head's socio-professional category of the head of the household (41%) and the possession of at most a primary school diploma (27%).

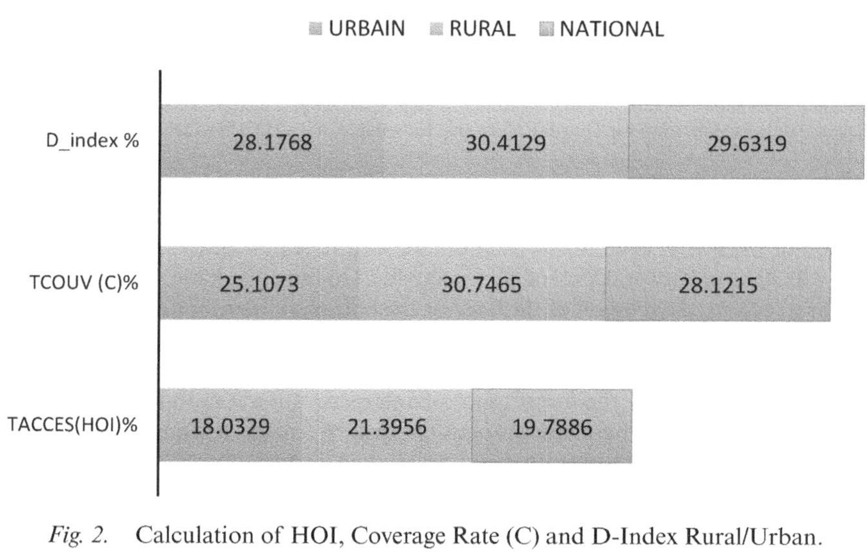

Fig. 2. Calculation of HOI, Coverage Rate (C) and D-Index Rural/Urban.
Source: Authors, data from the Fourth Cameroon Household Survey (FCHS, 2014).

Table 5. Shapley Decomposition of the IOP for Youth Access to Employment.

Table 5a

Variables	NAT	DLA	YDE	ADW	CEN	EAS	FAN
PSCH	**40.83%**	**34.08%**	**34.56%**	**45.28%**	**50.37%**	**23.79%**	**30.03%**
RELHH	1.46%	0.85%	1.19%	18.35%	0.02%	26.97%	0.00%
SEXH	−0.04%	0.91%	0.44%	−0.05%	1.08%	5.48%	1.60%
HAND	3.10%	0.26%	5.60%	3.57%	1.08%	2.48%	0.58%
ELH	9.59%	5.23%	3.26%	1.87%	6.46%	15.33%	8.02%
PRIMH	27.27%	28.79%	32.01%	21.43%	28.55%	8.84%	36.23%
SECH	6.93%	24.37%	15.96%	5.89%	6.01%	−4.38%	14.03%
HISH	1.37%	3.52%	4.44%	0.39%	0.43%	−0.87%	7.92%
SIZE	4.01%	2.00%	2.54%	1.75%	1.28%	7.32%	1.25%
AREA	3.76%	0.00%	0.00%	1.13%	4.71%	7.44%	0.28%
TOTAL	100.00	100.00%	100.00%	100.00%	100.00%	100.00%	100%
IOP	0.29226	0.29521	0.28882	0.29080	0.28711	0.290295	0.26092

Source: Authors, data from the Fourth Cameroon Household Survey (FCHS4, 2014).

Table 5b

Variables	NAT	LIT	NOR	NOW	WEST	SOU	SOW
PSCH	40.83%	25.24%	**44.48%**	**40.97%**	**45.11%**	**32.49%**	**41.65%**
RELHH	1.46%	**37.51%**	2.28%	0.04%	2.49%	−0.65%	1.23%
SEXH	−0.04%	2.40%	3.02%	1.88%	1.65%	2.75%	2.42%
HAND	3.10%	0.74%	1.85%	0.84%	1.56%	9.85%	1.11%
ELH	9.59%	9.27%	17.73%	13.65%	5.53%	4.12%	7.53%
PRIMH	27.27%	13.83%	15.55%	33.16%	28.25%	31.81%	29.38%
SECH	6.93%	3.60%	1.41%	3.53%	6.26%	8.52%	8.09%
HISH	1.37%	0.10%	−0.22%	0.84%	−0.45%	1.63%	2.35%
SIZE	4.01%	4.62%	4.81%	1.52%	3.21%	6.13%	3.59%
AREA	3.76%	1.74%	8.46%	2.96%	5.56%	1.17%	2.65%
TOTAL	100.00	100%	100%	100%	100%	100%	100.00%
IOP	0.29226	0.328815	0.267718	0.3447	0.32143	0.3000	0.29094

Source: Authors, data from the Fourth Cameroon Household Survey (FCHS4, 2014).

With the exception of the East, Littoral and Far North regions, this result remains valid in the other 09 regions, albeit at markedly different rates. The contribution of the PSCH is more important in the Centre region, and it explains almost half (50.37%) of the total level of this inequality. On the other hand, in the East and Littoral regions, the religion of the head of the household was found to be the main source of IOP for access to youth employment at 26.97% and 37.51% respectively.

Overall, the impact of parents PSCH on their offspring's occupational mobility status helps to explain the importance of intergenerational mobility highlighted by Bindop (2019) in the Cameroonian context. We reach a similar conclusion, with a stronger contribution in rural areas than in urban areas. However, our results suggest that the correlation decreases with the level of education of the head of household, which would imply that parental education leads to a decrease

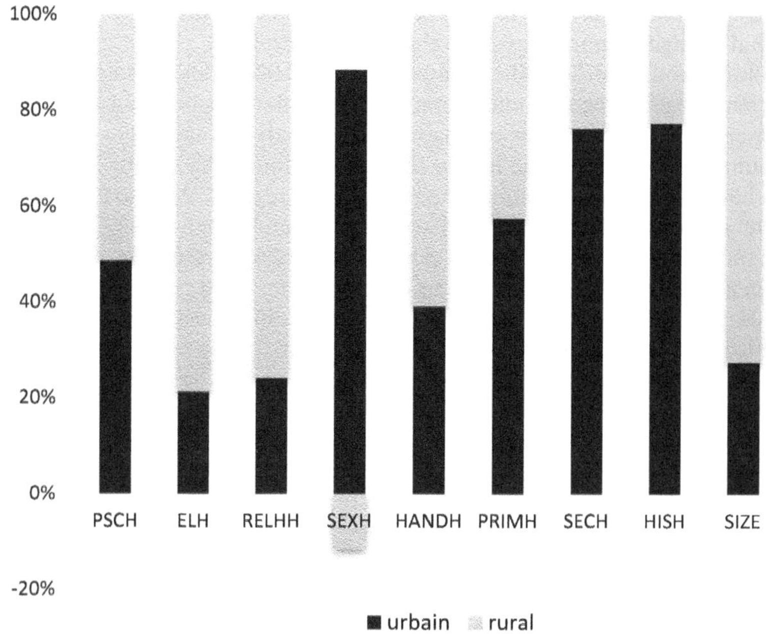

Fig. 3. Decomposition of IOP in Access to Employment for Young People by Localization. *Source*: Authors, data from the Fourth Cameroon Household Survey (FCHS4, 2014).

in the immobility of their children in the labour market between the two generations (Hellier, 2016; Solom, 2017).

Indeed, several studies have focused on the developing countries triptych to show that the intergenerational transmission of PSC, or the correlation and decomposition of inequalities in human capital of the head of household's PSC, explains labour market status.

The breakdown of the D_index by place of residence confirms the general trend observed at regional level. Indeed, the PSCH remains the most decisive circumstance in the distribution of employment opportunities among young people, with a higher contribution in rural areas (44%) than in urban areas (41.14%). It is also followed by the circumstance of having at most a primary education. In particular, the circumstance related to the level of education of the head of the household is more decisive in urban areas (32.81%) than in rural areas (24.45%), regardless of the level of education of the latter. However, this contribution decreases as the level of education increases. On the other hand, socio-demographic factors (household size, religion and disability of the head of the household) are more decisive for young people's access to employment in rural areas than in urban areas. In order to check the robustness of results from the magnitude of IOP computed, the bootstrapping analysis through 250 and 500 replications is used, and the findings from Fig. 3 and in Tables A2–A3 show the marginal changes, comparatively to the baseline results.

Tables 6 and 7 present the results from OB decomposition approach. The coefficients (e.g. in the columns) represent the difference between the values of the observed IOP (the values on the main diagonal) and the value derived from the counterfactual (the value of the IOP in a region if the labour force had the same characteristics as the labour force in another region). We also found a gap in the level of opportunity inequality between rural and urban areas.

On the main diagonal of Table 6, 6.84% and 8.82% represent the proportion of homogeneity in urban and rural areas due to the observed circumstances. On the other diagonal, we can estimate the proportion of differences due to the composition effect. The second value in the first column (6.726%) represents 98% of the initial value (6.84%), which tells us that in urban areas, the differences in access to opportunities in urban areas are mainly due to differences in circumstances and outcomes, and are only slightly explained by differences in the structure of circumstances. This conclusion also holds for the rural labour market.

If we take Douala, for example, as the study or reference region, the first column provides information on the size of the gap in IOPs, determined by assigning to the coefficients of the regression for the Douala region, the characteristics of each of the other regions. Finally, it appears that the values obtained in the other regions are very close to those of Douala; this shows that the differences in access to employment between Douala and each of the other regions are due more to the composition effect than to the structural effect.

This result gives a general idea of the results of the Oxaca-Blinder (OB) decomposition. Thus, the interregional gap in access to job opportunities is essentially (or in some cases entirely) related to the heterogeneity in the distribution of circumstances between regions. In some cases, however, it turns out that the contribution of the effort factors 25% to the IOP of access to employment between two regions (North-Douala; Yaounde-Far North, etc.) plays a non-negligible role.

Finally, our results point to the crucial role of geographical proximity in the interregional distribution of circumstances. Indeed, the MORAN spatial autocorrelation test (I) is valid for the coverage rate ($I = 0.58$) and the HOI ($I = 0.55$), but invalid for the D index ($I = 0.21$). In other words, access to opportunity and employment coverage in one region are influenced by those observed in neighbouring regions, whereas inequality in the distribution of available jobs in one region does not depend on that observed in neighbouring regions. This link may be related to, among other things, high geographical labour mobility,

Table 6. Oaxaca-Blinder Decomposition of IOP Between Rural and Urban Localization.

Localization	Urban	Rural
Urban	6,846	8,581
Rural	6,726	8,824

Source: Authors, data from the Fourth Cameroon Household Survey (CHS4, 2014).

Table 7. Oaxaca-Blinder Decomposition of IOP by Worker Location.

Distribution	DLA	YDE	ADW	CEN	EAS	FAN	LITT	NORTH	NOES	WEST	SOU	SOW
DLA	0.06453	0.06926	0.07339	0.06457	0.06591	0.07224	**0.07985**	0.0719	0.07267	0.07314	0.0708	0.06645
YDE	0.06305	0.06787	0.07116	0.06273	0.06464	0.06816	0.07763	0.0693	0.07162	0.0711	0.0690	0.0650
ADW	0.05602	0.06454	0.07980	0.06292	0.07142	0.09202	0.06509	0.0952	0.0706	0.08716	0.0695	0.06619
CEN	0.06250	0.06907	0.07978	0.06275	0.07260	0.09025	0.07149	0.0909	0.07085	0.08716	0.06955	0.06619
EAS	0.05746	0.06450	0.07489	0.05862	0.06819	0.08788	0.06556	0.0871	0.0664	0.08419	0.06411	0.06209
FAN	0.05019	0.05834	0.07474	0.05833	0.06378	0.09755	0.04820	0.0995	0.05933	0.09018	0.0568	0.06524
LITT	0.06694	0.07421	0.08029	0.06854	0.07490	0.09218	0.07971	0.0932	0.07710	0.0937	0.07289	0.07129
NORTH	0.04738	0.05501	0.07061	0.05390	0.06204	0.09057	0.04751	0.0909	0.05711	0.08087	0.05548	0.05835
NOES	0.06663	**0.07538**	0.08879	**0.07083**	**0.07951**	**0.09827**	0.06945	**0.1015**	**0.07830**	**0.09816**	**0.07319**	**0.07493**
WEST	0.06294	0.06928	0.07807	0.06324	0.07182	0.09342	0.07302	0.0948	0.06968	0.08909	0.06833	0.06788
SOUTH	0.06237	0.06891	0.07656	0.06138	0.07007	0.09073	0.07224	0.0869	0.07046	0.08307	0.0669	0.06449
SUW	**0.06484**	0.07180	0.07994	0.06569	0.07250	0.08606	0.07425	0.088	0.07439	0.08817	0.0700	0.06800

Source: Authors, data from the Fourth Cameroon Household Survey (CHS4, 2014).
They correspond to the highest value of IOP for each area under the study.

as discussed in Meka'a (2015) in his analysis of the impact of migration and internal remittances from migrants on the labour market. Overall, the difference in coverage and access to employment opportunities for young people between two regions is partly explained by geographical externalities. If we take Douala as the study or reference region, for example, the first column gives us information on the size of the gap in IOPs, determined by assigning to the coefficients of the regression for the Douala region.

It appears that young people aged 10–25 have an employment coverage rate of 28% and an employment access rate (EAR) of 19%. In addition, we found that around 30% of the share of available jobs should be allocated to the non-employed on an equal opportunities basis to ensure equal access to these opportunities at the national level. Although this is a relatively high proportion, there are large disparities between areas of residence. We found that the East and North regions are the most egalitarian in Cameroon in terms of the distribution of jobs to young people, with a dissimilarity index of 27% each, while the North West region is the most unequal, with a dissimilarity index of 34%, followed by the West and Littoral regions. It was also found that the distribution of jobs is more heterogeneous in rural areas (30%) than in urban areas (28%), and this pattern is similar when looking at the coverage rate and the access rate to job opportunities. In order to determine the marginal contribution of the circumstance to the IOP, we proceeded, on the one hand, as follows to the decomposition by the Shapley method. With a contribution of between 23% and 50%, the socio-professional.

5. DISCUSSIONS

Analyzing the determinants of the IOP among the young in the Cameroonian labour market, and by using the HOI and Shapley/Oaxaca decomposition methods, findings show that: The category of the head of household is the main factor influencing young people's access to employment; this is the case in all areas of residence (regional, urban, rural), with the exception of the eastern and coastal regions, where the main factor is the religion of the head of household. Moreover, these factors, to which the educational level of the head of household must be added, are the most decisive for the future of young workers in rural and urban areas. In Cameroon, Bindop (2019) identifies family background as a decisive factor that 'conditions the positioning of their descendants on the labour market'. He also shows that the level of education is a determining factor in this process (Hellier, 2016). Furthermore, the Blinder-Oaxaca decomposition method suggests that there is a significant gap in the opportunity index between regions and between rural and urban areas, and that this gap is explained by differences in circumstances (composition effect) rather than by the coefficients of these circumstances (structure effect). Our results confirm those of Fambon et al. (2018). Similarly, Mkinley and Draft (2001) found that, in contrast to urban areas, rural unemployment rises more slowly than the employment rate; and that this is essentially the consequence of the massive shift of the labour force from low productivity rural areas to high productivity urban centres. This argument is based on the neoclassical theory of migration and its impact on development as presented by Lewis (1957), Haris and Todaro (1970). Moreover, the exploratory analysis of the data suggests the existence of a spatial autocorrelation, in particular between employment coverage rates on the one hand and interregional access rates to employment on the other. This result is partly in line with Raj-Chetty et al. (2015), who justify the role of neighbourhoods in job access, and with Islam (2015), who argues for the impact of geographical factors on the future outcomes of an individual on the labour market.

Although Becker (1964), Arrow (1972) and Phelps (1972) have justified the presence of inequalities in the labour market, other important factors have been identified. In the present study, the socio-professional category of the parents and the possession of a primary school diploma were found to be more decisive for the access of their child aged between 10 and 25 years in each region of Cameroon. In indeed, Bindop (2019) explains in his study that ethnic origin and social norms are circumstantial factors that explain inter-relational mobility in the Cameroonian labour market. The author also points out that socio-professional category affects the position of their descendants in the labour market directly, or indirectly through educational attainment. Our findings broadly confirm Abras et al. (2013), who in their study of European and Asian labour markets showed that inequalities in access to paid employment are largely determined by opportunity factors. According to Talla et al. (2017) and Diffouo (2009), the persistence of inequalities between children and their place of residence is indicative of inequalities in employment opportunities in adulthood, which requires remedial economic policies.

6. CONCLUSION AND POLICY IMPLICATIONS

While several studies have already examined IOP in the Cameroonian labour market, our contribution to this debate is threefold. First, by limiting our population to those aged between 10 and 25, who represent the working population most affected by unemployment. Second, we have focused on the role of the location (region, urban, rural) in order to highlight heterogeneity at a more disaggregated level, which is necessary for the orientation of targeted public employment policies. Thirdly and finally, the methodology used is that of the HOI, using a decomposition technique that goes beyond the Shapley method and seeks to examine which of the compositional and structural effects is decisive in explaining differences in the magnitude of HOI across residential settings. Using data from the NSI (2014) on 5,486 individuals from the Fourth Cameroonian Household Survey, findings show first that overall, the average rate of HOI, coverage rate, Dissimilarity and IOP index are almost 20%, 28%, 30% and 29.9%, respectively, implying that the inequality on the labour market are still relatively higher as well as the inaccessibility rate to employment. However, rather than an investigation at the national level, it is arising the important spatial disparities in Cameroonian's labour marker among the young workers. Indeed, two main subgroups emerges: IOPs are highest in littoral, West and rural regions and, while they are lowest in North West, East and urban ones. Moving to D-index, a similar trend is occurred.

Meaning that, the distribution of employment in the first subgroup region is more heterogeneous, whereas this more homogeneous in the second subgroup. Additionally, Regions with the higher opportunities are North and East; contrary to North West and Centre where that are lowest. These findings further prevail that the former subgroup region is more covered in terms of accessibility to job by young people, while the latter subgroup reveal a most difficulty to getting job in the regions including. regions are on the other hand are the. According to Shapley-Shorrock decomposition method, the evidence arises that, except for littoral, managerial position is the most relevant circumstance factor to explain the IOP in each region. It appears that the main circumstances contributing to the D-index are socio-professional category, primary education and religious obedience of the household head which explain from 51% to 79% the overall IOP. While on the other hand, the Blinder-Oaxaca decomposition shows that 80% of the gap in D-Index is explained by disparities in circumstances, rather than individual efforts. Finally, our conclusions argue in favour of effective decentralization, for a more inclusive employment policy that takes into account local labour market features. Indeed, the various policy reforms undertaken by the Cameroonian government in the aftermath of the independent elections already alluded to interregional social and economic disparities. Therefore, these include the policy of regional balance, which has been ineffective because it has led to the exacerbation and stagnation of inequalities rather than their reduction. Finally, this result helps the Cameroonian government direct its policies towards employment and the reduction of inequalities, which is a key objective in its national strategy document (NDS30) and a priority for achieving sustainable development by 2030, according to the United Nations.

NOTES

1. On the one hand, Africa is likely to be the world's largest provider of labour via emigration of workers. On the other hand, wages in the manufacturing sector could increase. Finally, a high concentration of workers in urban areas could stimulate innovation (World Bank, 2014).
2. The former support that the fight against inequality requires the maximisation of the utility function of each individual. There is equality if the marginal utilities are the same for all individuals.
3. Administratively, Cameroon has 10 regions: Centre, Littoral, West, East, South, North-West, South-West, Adamaoua, North and Extreme North, Douala and Yaoundé. However, the dismemberment of the INS makes the city of Douala (the economic capital) and that of Yaounde (the political capital) regions in their own right.
4. Shapiro Francia (1972) test has the advantage as it not limited to the sample size.

REFERENCES

Aaronson, D. (1998). Using sibling data to estimate the impact of neighborhoods on children's educational outcomes. *Journal of Human Resources*, 915–946.

Abras, A., Hoyos, A., Narayan, A., & Tiwari, S. (2013). Inequality of opportunities in the labor market: Evidence from life in transition surveys in Europe and Central Asia. *IZA Journal of Labor & Development*, *2*, 1–22.

Ahmed, H. M. M., Osman, E. A. M., & Mahran, H. A. (2020). Inequality of opportunity in the labor market: Evidence from Sudan. *Journal of Social Science Studies*, *7*(2), 38–56.

Aiyar, S., & Ebeke, C. (2020). Inequality of opportunity, inequality of income and economic growth. *World Development*, *136*, 105115.

Alesina, A., & Rodrik, D. (1994). Distributive politics and economic growth. *The Quarterly Journal of Economics*, *109*(2), 465–490.

Anis, S., & Mekki, H. (2021). Level of Fairness and justice in labor market: Evidence from Tunisia Post-Revolution. *Journal of the Knowledge Economy*, *12*(3), 1187–1214.

Anyanwu, J. C. (2014). Does intra-African trade reduce youth unemployment in Africa? *African Development Review*, *26*(2), 286–309.

Arneson, R. J. (1989). Equality and equal opportunity for welfare. *Philosophical Studies*, *56*(1), 77–93.

Arrow, K. J. (1972). Models of job discrimination. *Racial Discrimination in Economic Life*, *83*.

Assaad, R., Hendy, R., & Salehi-Isfahani, D. (2019). Inequality of opportunity in educational attainment in the Middle East and North Africa: Evidence from household surveys. *International Journal of Educational Development*, *71*, 102070.

Becker, G. S. (1964). *Human capital New York*. Columbia University for the National Bureau of Economic Research.

Blinder, A. S. (1973). Wage discrimination: Reduced form and structural estimates. *Journal of Human Resources*, 436–455.

Bourguignon, F., Ferreira, F. H., & Menéndez, M. (2013). Inequality of opportunity in Brazil: A Corrigendum. *Review of Income and Wealth*, *59*(3), 551–555.

Brunori, P., Palmisano, F., & Peragine, V. (2019). Inequality of opportunity in sub-Saharan Africa. *Applied Economics*, *51*(60), 6428–6458.

Cohen, G. A. (1989). On the currency of egalitarian justice. *Ethics*, *99*(4), 906–944.

Contreras Guajardo, D., Larrañaga Jiménez, O., Puentes Encina, E., & Rau Binder, T. (2009). The Evolution of Opportunities for Children in Chile 1990-2006.

De Barros, R., Ferreira, F. H. G., Molinas, V., Jose, R., & Saavedra, C. J. (2009). *Measuring inequality of opportunities in Latin America and the Caribbean*. World Bank; Palgrave Macmillan.

Diffouo, G. Y. (2009). Le principe de légale d'accès aux emplois et la fonction publique à l'épreuve de la tribalité positive au Cameroun. *juridis périodique, n°9*, 88–99.

Dimova, R., & Stephan, K. (2020). Inequality of opportunity and (unequal) opportunities in the youth labour market: How is the Arab world different? *International Labour Review*, *159*(2), 217–242.

Durlauf, S. N. (1996). A theory of persistent income inequality. *Journal of Economic Growth*, *1*, 75–93.

Dworkin, R. (2018). What is equality? Part 2: Equality of resources. *Philosophy and Public Affairs*, *10*(4), 143–205.

El-Saadani, S., & Metwally, S. (2019). Inequality of opportunity linked to disability in school enrollment among youth: Evidence from Egypt. *International Journal of Educational Development*, *67*, 73–84.

Fambon, S., Sekou Siewe, A., Ngoho Tchakoute, R., Kouakep, S. O., Ndjafa, K. S., & Cheboun, D. (2018). *Diagnostic et determinant des depenses de consommation des ménages au Cameroun dans les années 1990, 2000 et 2010* (p. 37). Agence Francaise du Development.

Ferreira, F. H., Gignoux, J., & Aran, M. (2011). Measuring inequality of opportunity with imperfect data: The case of Turkey. *The Journal of Economic Inequality*, *9*, 651–680.

Filmer, D., & Fox, L. (2014). *Youth employment in sub-Saharan Africa*. World Bank Publications.

Fleurbaey, M. (1994). On fair compensation. *Theory and Decision*, *36*, 277–307.

Fotso Koyeu, F. P., Ningaye, P., & Talla Fokam, D. N. D. (2019). How does inequality of opportunities affect the distribution of economic wellbeing in Cameroon.

Harris, R. J., & Todaro, P. M. (1970). Migration, unemployment and development: A two-sector analysis. *The American Economic Review*, *60*, 126–142.

Harsanyi, C. J. (1955). Cardinal welfare, individual ethics, and interpersonal comparison of utility. *Journal of Political Economy*, *63*(4), 309–321.

Hellier, J. (2016). *Education, intergenerational mobility and social stractification: Theory, LEM discussion paper*. Lille Economie Management.

Hussain, M. A., & Awad, A. (2022). Inactive youth in Sub-Saharan Africa: Does inequality of opportunity matter? *Economies*, *10*(1), 27.

Institut National de la Statistique. (2014). Résultat de la Quatrième Enquête Camerounaise après des Ménages (ECAM 4). *République du Cameroun.*

Islam, T. T. (2013). Childhood neighborhood conditions and the persistence of adult income. *Regional Science and Urban Economics*, *43*(4), 684–693.

Krafft, C., & Alawode, H. (2018). Inequality of opportunity in higher education in the Middle East and North Africa. *International Journal of Educational Development*, *62*, 234–244.

Krafft, C., & Assaad, R. (2016). Inequality of opportunity in the labor market for higher education graduates in Egypt and Jordan. In *The Middle East economies in times of transition* (pp. 159–185). Palgrave Macmillan UK.

Kuznets, S. (1955). Economic growth and income inequality. *The American Economic Review*, *45*(1), 1–28.

Le Gallo, J. (2002). Econometrie spatiale : L'autocorrélation spatiale dans les modèles de regression lineaire. *Economie & Précision*, *155*, 139–157.

Lewis, W. A. (1954). Economic development with unlimited supplies of labor. *Manchester School Economics Social Studies*, *22*(2), 139–191.

Mbenga Bindop 1, K. M. (2019). Les inégalités d'accès au marché du travail au Cameroun: le rôle de l'école. *Revue d'économie du développement*, *27*(2), 45–86.

Meka'a, C. B. (2015). Transferts de fonds des migrants et dépenses des ménages: application au cas du Cameroun. *Région et Développement*, *41*, 201–230.

Mkinley, T., & Draft, F. (2001). Employment generation and poverty reduction in Sudan. *World*, *38*, 18–15.

Motiran, S. (2018). Inequality of opportunity in India: Concept, measurement and empirics. *Indian Journal of Human Development*, *12*(2), 1–12.

Myrdal, G. (1965). *The political element in the development of economic theory*. Harvard University Press.

Naidu, S., & Yuchtman, N. (2013). Coercive contract enforcement: law and the labor market in nineteenth century industrial Britain. *American Economic Review*, *103*(1), 107–144.

Njikam G.B., Tchoffo R.M., & Mwaffo V.F. (2005). Caractéristiques et déterminants de l'emploi des jeunes au Cameroun. Cahier de la stratégie de l'emploi, département de la stratégie en matière de l'unité des politiques de l'emploi, OIT, Genève.

Oaxaca, R. (1973). Male-female wage differentials in urban labor markets. *International Economic Review*, 693–709.

Pasquier-Doumer, L. (2010). *Inequality of opportunity on the urban labour market in West Africa*. Working Paper No. DT/2010-09, Paris: Universite Paris Dauphine.

Phelps, E. S. (1972). The statistical theory of racism and sexism. *The American Economic Review*, *62*(4), 659–661.

Raj Chetty, Hendren, N., & Katz, F. L. (2015). The effects of exposure to better neighbourhoods on children: New evidence from the moving to opportunity experiment. *American Economic Review*, *106*(4), 855–902.

Ramos, X., & Van de Gaer, D. (2012). Empirical approaches to inequality of opportunity: Principles, measures, and evidence. *Journal of Economic Surveys*, *30*(5), 855–883.

Rawls, J. (1971). *A theory of justice*. Harvard Univ.

Roemer, J. E. (1996). *Theories of distributive justice*. Harvard University Press.

Roemer, J. (2002). Equality of opportunity: A progress report, social choice and welfare. *Social Choice and Welfare*, *19*(1), 455–471.

Roemer, J. E., & Trannoy, A. (2016). Equality of opportunity: Theory and measurement. *Journal of Economic Literature*, *54*(4), 1288–1332.

Sen, A. (1980). *Equality of What? The Tanner Lecture on Human Values*, 197-220. Cambridge University Press.

Shapley, L. S. (1953). A value for n-person games. In H. W. Kuhn & A. W. Tucker (Eds.), *Contributions to the theory of games* (Vol. 2). Princeton University Press.

Shorrocks, A. (2013). Decomposition procedures for distributional analysis: A unified framework based on the Shapley value. *The Journal of Economic Inequality*, *11*(1), 99–126.

Solon (2017). *What do we known so far about multigenerational mobility?* Institute of labor market, discussion paper, n°10623.

Stiglitz, J. (1982). Self-selection and pareto efficient taxation. *Journal of Public Economics*, *17*(2), 213–240.

Talla, F. D. N. D. (2017). *Inégalité d'opportunité sur le marché du travail, emploi et mobilité professionnelle au Cameroun*. Thèse de Doctorat, Université de Dschang.

Talla, F. D., Ningaye, P., & Chameni, N. C. (2017). Inégalité d'opportunités sur le marché d'emploi en Afrique subsaharienne: une application au contexte camerounais. *Les cahiers du CEDIMES*, *11*(2).

Thieme, T. (2010). Youth, waste and work in Mathare: Whose business and whose politics? *Environment and Urbanization*, *22*(2), 333–352.

Thorbecke, E. (2013). The interrelationship linking growth, inequality and poverty in sub-Saharan Africa. *Journal of African Economies*, *22*(1), 15–48.

Van De Gaer D (1993) *Equality of opportunity and investment in human capital*. [Ph.D. Thesis, Katholieke Universiteit Leuven, Leuven, Belgium].

Van de Gaer, D., Vandenbossche, J., & Figuero, L. J. (2013). *Children's Health opportunities and project evaluation: Mexico's opportunidas program*. Open Knowledge Repository.

World Bank. (2006). *Inequality and development* (p. 340). WB report, n°32204.

World Bank. (2009). *Measuring inequality of opportunities in Latin America and the Caribbean*, Washington, DC, 1(1), n°46827.

APPENDIX

Table A1. Determinants of Young Access in Cameroonian Labour Market: Probit Regression.

Variables	NAT	DLA	YDE	ADW	CEN	EAS	FAN	LIT	NOR	NOW	WEST	SOU	SOW
PSCH	−1.698***	−1.133***	−1.421***	−1.663***	−1.902***	−1.482***	−2.069***	−2.114***	−2.250***	−1.694***	−2.213***	−1.251***	−1.563***
	(0.0615)	(0.202)	(0.215)	(0.216)	(0.238)	(0.216)	(0.177)	(0.338)	(0.185)	(0.233)	(0.239)	(0.285)	(0.231)
ELH	−0.902***	−0.194	−0.294	−1.596***	−0.641	−0.246	−1.049***		−1.184***	−0.293	−2.026*	−0.332	−1.873**
	(0.108)	(1.050)	(0.652)	(0.379)	(0.503)	(0.367)	(0.225)		(0.251)	(0.309)	(1.037)	(0.644)	(0.742)
RELHH	−0.470**	−0.340	−0.0104		0.0809	1.261	−0.875**	−0.621	−1.610**	1.343	−0.0465		−1.691
	(0.197)	(0.562)	(0.639)		(0.887)	(0.906)	(0.404)	(1.071)	(0.778)	(0.975)	(0.471)		(1.090)
SEXH	−0.944***	−0.665***	−0.980***	−0.825***	−0.886***	−0.506***	−1.354***	−1.414***	−1.123***	−1.030***	−0.930***	−0.918***	−1.023***
	(0.0390)	(0.128)	(0.135)	(0.164)	(0.145)	(0.142)	(0.115)	(0.182)	(0.113)	(0.149)	(0.129)	(0.173)	(0.154)
HANDH	−0.878***	−0.772**	−0.852**	−0.603	−0.210	−0.296	−2.878***	−1.539***	−0.665**	−0.751	−0.318	−1.108***	−0.729
	(0.116)	(0.304)	(0.366)	(0.569)	(0.336)	(0.363)	(0.754)	(0.556)	(0.337)	(0.674)	(0.347)	(0.417)	(0.536)
PRIMH	−1.434***	−1.569***	−1.771***	−1.154***	−1.154***	−1.083***	−0.969***	−2.018***	−1.014***	−1.820***	−1.315***	−1.519***	−1.292***
	(0.0634)	(0.199)	(0.205)	(0.237)	(0.231)	(0.222)	(0.204)	(0.307)	(0.229)	(0.246)	(0.234)	(0.274)	(0.221)
SECH	−1.535***	−2.178***	−1.813***	−2.839***	−1.030***	−0.931**	−0.522	−1.925***	−0.377	−0.935**	−1.615***	−1.564***	−1.570***
	(0.109)	(0.297)	(0.270)	(1.031)	(0.356)	(0.419)	(0.499)	(0.568)	(0.433)	(0.383)	(0.441)	(0.439)	(0.367)
HISH	−1.443***	−1.455***	−1.460***	0.476	−0.792					−1.104		−1.093	−1.973*
	(0.219)	(0.407)	(0.375)	(1.148)	(0.739)					(0.827)		(1.096)	(1.054)
SIZE	−0.196***	−0.425***	−0.491***	−0.309***	−0.421***	−0.195*	−0.256***	−0.158	−0.196***	−0.346***	−0.398***	−0.129	−0.310***
	(0.0288)	(0.0968)	(0.0991)	(0.105)	(0.115)	(0.108)	(0.0822)	(0.161)	(0.0755)	(0.123)	(0.114)	(0.128)	(0.117)
AREA	0.404***			0.444***	−0.272**	0.0939	0.949***	−0.290*	0.787***	−0.145	0.423***	−0.0897	−0.107
	(0.0371)			(0.159)	(0.137)	(0.149)	(0.123)	(0.171)	(0.121)	(0.143)	(0.127)	(0.169)	(0.143)
C	1.001***	1.153***	1.844***	0.916**	1.978***	0.773**	1.195***	2.548***	1.035***	2.048***	1.373***	1.331***	1.834***
	(0.0946)	(0.256)	(0.270)	(0.390)	(0.394)	(0.388)	(0.292)	(0.478)	(0.284)	(0.369)	(0.369)	(0.431)	(0.399)
Obs	19,021	1,864	1,697	1,183	1,478	1,205	2,389	1,043	2,405	1,506	1,764	1,001	1,337

Source: Authors *** $p<0.01$, ** $p<0.05$, * $p<0.1$.

Table A2. Robustness Decomposition: Bootstrap Analysis.

	500 Replications											
Variable	DLA	YDE	ADW	CEN	EAS	FAN	LIT	NOR	NOW	WEST	SOU	SOW
IOP	**0.292263**	**0.295214**	**0.288820**	**0.287114**	**0.225148**	**0.294748**	**0.388988**	**0.267718**	**0.344765**	**0.321431**	**0.300020**	**0.290944**
PSCH	40.83%	34.08%	34.56%	48.77%	48.04%	40.61%	38.54%	44.48%	40.97%	45.11%	32.49%	41.65%
RELHH	9.59%	0.85%	1.19%	6.09%	6.32%	19.13%	−6.74%	17.73%	13.65%	5.53%	4.12%	7.53%
SEXH	1.46%	0.91%	0.44%	0.02%	0.20%	5.03%	2.06%	2.28%	0.04%	2.49%	−0.65%	1.23%
HAND	−0.04%	0.26%	5.60%	2.71%	1.07%	2.82%	3.60%	3.02%	1.88%	1.65%	2.75%	2.42%
ELH	3.10%	5.23%	3.26%	1.32%	1.28%	3.47%	4.49%	1.85%	0.84%	1.56%	9.85%	1.11%
PRIMH	27.27%	28.79%	32.01%	27.90%	32.60%	13.85%	31.00%	15.55%	33.16%	28.25%	31.81%	29.38%
SECH	6.93%	24.37%	15.96%	5.94%	4.55%	1.21%	6.34%	1.41%	3.53%	6.26%	8.52%	8.09%
HISH	1.37%	3.52%	4.44%	0.50%	−0.23%	−0.01%	−0.20%	−0.22%	0.84%	−0.45%	1.63%	2.35%
SIZE	4.01%	2.00%	2.54%	1.66%	2.57%	3.73%	4.97%	4.81%	1.52%	3.21%	6.13%	3.59%
AREA	3.76%	0.00%	0.00%	4.90%	1.08%	9.28%	3.42%	8.46%	2.96%	5.56%	1.17%	2.65%
TOTAL	100.00%	100.00%	100.00%	100.00%	100.00%	100.00%	100.00%	100.00%	100.00%	100.00%	100.00%	100.00%
	250 Replications											
PSCH	40.83%	34.08%	34.56%	45.28%	48.04%	40.61%	38.54%	44.48%	40.97%	45.11%	32.49%	41.65%
RELHH	9.59%	0.85%	1.19%	18.35%	6.32%	19.13%	−6.74%	17.73%	13.65%	5.53%	4.12%	7.53%
SEXH	1.46%	0.91%	0.44%	−0.05%	0.20%	5.03%	2.06%	2.28%	0.04%	2.49%	−0.65%	1.23%
HAND	−0.04%	0.26%	5.60%	3.57%	1.07%	2.82%	3.60%	3.02%	1.88%	1.65%	2.75%	2.42%
ELH	3.10%	5.23%	3.26%	1.87%	1.28%	3.47%	4.49%	1.85%	0.84%	1.56%	9.85%	1.11%
PRIMH	27.27%	28.79%	32.01%	21.43%	32.60%	13.85%	31.00%	15.55%	33.16%	28.25%	31.81%	29.38%
SECH	6.93%	24.37%	15.96%	5.89%	4.55%	1.21%	6.34%	1.41%	3.53%	6.26%	8.52%	8.09%
HISH	1.37%	3.52%	4.44%	0.39%	−0.23%	−0.01%	−0.20%	−0.22%	0.84%	−0.45%	1.63%	2.35%
SIZE	4.01%	2.00%	2.54%	1.75%	2.57%	3.73%	4.97%	4.81%	1.52%	3.21%	6.13%	3.59%
AREA	3.76%	0.00%	0.00%	1.13%	1.08%	9.28%	3.42%	8.46%	2.96%	5.56%	1.17%	2.65%
TOTAL	100.00%	100.00%	100.00%	100.00%	100.00%	100.00%	100.00%	100.00%	100.00%	100.00%	100.00%	100.00%

Source: Authors.

Table A3. Robustness Check for IOP.

Resampling	250 Bootstrap	500 Bootstrap
National	28,72	
DLA	29,52	0.292263
YDE	28,88	0.295214
ADW	28,97	0,28882
CEN	28,65	0.290802
EAS	21,94	0.225148
FAN	29,21	0.294748
LIT	34,02	0.388988
NO	26,6	0.267718
NOW	34,21	0.344765
WES	31,87	0.321431
SOU	29,34	0.300020
SOW	29,09	0.290944

CHAPTER 4

THE EFFECT OF COLLECTIVE BARGAINING AGREEMENTS ON EMPLOYEES' WELFARE AT THE FIRM LEVEL: EVIDENCE FROM SPAIN

Fernando Pinto[a] and Raquel Sebastian[b]

[a]*Universidad Rey Juan Carlos de Madrid (Spain), EQUALITAS, Madrid, Spain*
[b]*Universidad Complutense de Madrid (Spain), ICAE and EQUALITAS, Madrid, Spain*

ABSTRACT

This study examines the effects of firm-level collective bargaining agreements (CBAs) on workers' welfare within Spanish firms, focusing on the trade-off between wage inequality and mean wage levels within firms. Results indicate that while firm-level CBAs contribute to increased intra-firm wage inequality, they also significantly enhance intra-firm average wage levels, with these positive effects being consistently observed across firm types and employee skill levels. Most notably, the increase in mean wages tends to offset the adverse effects associated with wage disparities, thereby leading to an overall improvement in workers' welfare within firms. These findings provide crucial policy implications, advocating for tailored approaches in supporting effective collective bargaining practices that can foster equitable wage growth and enhance workers' welfare, particularly in smaller firms and those employing low-skilled workers. Our results underscore the importance of firm-level negotiations in

Opportunity, Mobility and Inequality
Research on Economic Inequality, Volume 31, 91–119

ISSN: 1049-2585/doi:10.1108/S1049-258520250000031005

shaping equitable and prosperous labour market outcomes in contemporary economic settings.

Keywords Collective bargaining agreements; wage inequality; welfare; individual characteristics; firms; occupation skills

1. INTRODUCTION

The architecture of a nation's collective bargaining model holds significant implications for economic policy, given its capacity to define wage structures and employment conditions. This model is instrumental in shaping labour outcomes, as it directly impacts labour demand and the rate of unemployment. Consequently, the collective bargaining framework, with a specific emphasis on its wage-setting protocols, constitutes a critical mechanism in the modulation of labour market dynamics.

Much of the existing research has studied the effect of Collective Bargaining Agreements (CBAs) on employment (unemployment) and wages. In an exhaustive survey of existing research, Aidt and Tzannatos (2008) found that extensive bargaining coverage tends to correlate with elevated levels of inflation and unemployment. Gnocchi et al. (2015) using a dataset for 19 OECD countries over the span of four decades, established that wage bargaining mechanisms characterized by flexibility enhance the adaptability of real wages to fluctuations in labour productivity and unemployment rates, thus mitigating the impacts of economic cycles. More recently, the OECD (2019) reported that systems featuring organized decentralization exhibit superior outcomes in terms of employment performance and productivity when compared to alternative frameworks.

In the examination of wage dynamics, consensus among scholars suggests that employees under firm-level agreements typically receive higher remuneration compared to those governed by sectoral agreements (Dahl et al., 2013). Two primary rationales underpin this observation: first, decentralization is posited to more effectively incentives individual performance, enhancing wage outcomes (Lucifora & Origo, 2015). Thus, the propensity for firm-level negotiations to yield superior wages is attributed to the mechanisms of efficiency wages (Cahuc et al., 2014). Second, the negotiations between trade unions and employers tend not to fully consider the macroeconomic consequences of their agreements. That is, the actors involved in these negotiations often focus on achieving immediate benefits for their respective parties, such as wage increases or cost reductions, without fully internalizing the potential long-term impacts on the overall economy, such as increased inflation, higher unemployment, and potential loss of international competitiveness (Calmfors, 1993). The existence of a positive wage premium associated with firm-level collective agreements has been confirmed for many countries: Italy (Dell'Aringa & Lucifora, 1994), Belgium (Rycx, 2003), Denmark (Plasman et al., 2007), France (Leclair & Petit, 2004), Greece (Daouli et al., 2013), Portugal (Cardoso & Portugal, 2005), Spain (Card & de la Rica, 2006), Sweden (Granqvist & Regner, 2008) and for Europe (Dell'Aringa & Pagani, 2007).

The works of Bertola et al. (2012), Galuscak et al. (2012), along with Druant et al. (2012) demonstrate that wage flexibility is greater in decentralized bargaining frameworks as opposed to more centralized structures. Additionally, Boeri (2014) underscored the ineffectiveness of two-tier bargaining systems, pointing out their inability to combine the adaptability inherent in decentralized arrangements with the organizational advantages of centralized systems.

Recently, following the financial crisis of 2008, researchers have sought to understand whether collective bargaining agreements impact wage inequality. According to studies by the OECD (2018 and 2019), a consensus has emerged that countries with more decentralized systems (company agreements) exhibit higher wage inequality, while those with more centralized systems (sector-level agreements) show lower wage inequality.

The exploration into the role of collective bargaining in mitigating wage inequality has taken a new turn with the contributions of Boeri et al. (2024). This study incorporates productivity into the analysis and concludes that wage dispersion is lower in Italy (a centralized country) compared to Germany (a decentralized country). However, since wages in Italy do not adjust according to productivity, this leads to significant inefficiency costs for Italy in terms of employment and wages. In more detail, the study demonstrates that the German wage-setting framework, characterized by voluntary employer engagement, sectoral bargaining at the regional level, and the widespread adoption of opening clauses, facilitates wage flexibility in alignment with regional productivity variations. This mechanism contributes to sustaining elevated employment levels across the country, notably in regions of lower productivity such as East Germany. Conversely, the Italian model, which enforces uniform wage thresholds nationwide with minimal opportunities for local wage negotiation, effectively decouples wages from regional productivity metrics. This disconnection results in diminished employment prospects in areas of lower productivity, notably in Southern Italy.

In the context of Spain, the empirical insights into wage differentials and premiums associated with different types of agreements are limited. Card and de la Rica (2006) and Plasman et al. (2007) identified a favourable wage premium for agreements negotiated at the firm level compared to those at the sectoral level. Concerning wage dispersion, the findings of Card and de la Rica (2006), Dell'Aringa and Pagani (2007), Canal and Rodríguez (2016), and more recently, Ramos et al. (2022), converge on the notion that firm-level agreements marginally elevate wage inequality.

To the best of our knowledge, this is the first article to examine the impact of firm-level CBAs on workers' welfare at the firm level. We focus on Spain for two reasons. First, the Great Recession led to the flexibilization of collective bargaining agreements to boost economic growth and reduce unemployment. Second, Spain's economy is predominantly made up of small and medium-sized enterprises, so it is an ideal country for our study about the effects of CBAs. For this task, we will use the 2018 Structure of Earnings Survey of Spain (*Encuestra de Estructura Salarial*, ESS, in Spanish) which is the most recent year available in Eurostat.

This study advances the field in two significant ways: Firstly, it pioneers the measurement of wage inequality at the company level. As far as we know, it is a dimension previously unexplored in existing literature which has predominantly focused on individual-level wage disparities. The rationale behind this novel approach is underscored by some key findings: there is a demonstrable positive correlation between salary and company size (Idson & Oi, 1999). This significant firm-size wage premium observed in larger enterprises is attributable to sectoral affiliation, enhanced productivity, and workforce stability (Lallemand et al., 2005). Also, there is a positive link between overall wage inequality at the national level and the expansion of the country's largest firms (Mueller et al., 2017).

Secondly, this research sheds light on the intricate balance between equity (as measured by wage inequality) and efficiency (reflected in the average salary) from a company-centric perspective, showing the complex relationship between employees' welfare and organizational performance metrics.

Our study begins by examining the effect of collective bargaining agreements on wage inequality at the company level. It has been repeatedly observed that countries with collective bargaining agreements at the company level have higher levels of inequality. However, it is important to estimate the size of this effect in a broader framework, a one where welfare -not just inequality- is considered. Among all inequality indices, we use the Gini index at the company level since it adheres to the basic principles of the literature on inequality: progressive transfers, principle of symmetry, scale invariance, and population replication (see for example, Lambert, 2002). Furthermore, the Gini index will allow us to calculate workers' welfare within firms as in Sen (1974) and it is the most widely used inequality index in the literature.

The previous examination would remain partial without addressing the impact of CBAs at the company level on the average wage within firms. Thus, a high level of wage inequality within a firm does not inherently signify diminished welfare. It is conceivable for both intra-firm wage inequality and average intra-firm wages to be on an upward trajectory simultaneously.

To elucidate this issue, we apply an abbreviated Social Welfare Function (SWF) (Sen, 1974). This function assumes that the marginal utility of society is inversely related to its position in the income distribution. In other words, individuals with lower incomes gain more utility from an additional unit of income compared to those with higher incomes. Consequently, redistributing income from wealthier individuals to poorer ones can enhance overall social welfare, as the additional utility gained by poorer individuals outweighs the utility lost by wealthier individuals (Chakravarty, 2009). This implies that transferring income from the highest-income groups to the lowest-income groups generally increases societal welfare, provided that the mean wage remains constant. From this perspective, Sen's vision of the SWF applied to wages at the firm level considers not only the average wage within the firm but also the Gini coefficient of wage distribution within the company. In this manner, we connect the two effects: intra-firm wage inequality and intra-firm mean wage. The abbreviated SWF solves the trade-off between mean wage (efficiency) and wage inequality (equity).

The main findings of this work are the following two. First, our research indicates that CBAs at the company level significantly affect wage structures, resulting in both increased wage inequality and average wages within firms. Importantly, the impact of these agreements is not consistent across all firms; rather, it varies depending on firm size and the skill level of the workforce. High-skilled firms experience the most pronounced benefits in terms of wage increases, indicating a direct correlation between workforce skill intensity and the effectiveness of collective bargaining mechanisms.

Second, our analysis extends to the broader implications of these wage dynamics on workers' welfare within firms, where the positive effects on average wages generally outweigh the potential drawbacks associated with increased wage dispersion. This balance suggests that, under certain conditions, collective bargaining can serve as a mechanism to improve workers' welfare within firms, despite the challenges posed by wage inequality.

The structure of this chapter is organized as follows: after this introduction, in Section 2, we provide an overview of collective bargaining agreements in Spain. In Section 3, we outline our dataset and the empirical methodology employed. Section 4 presents the effects of firm-level collective agreement on intra-firm wage inequality, intra-firm mean wage, and intra-firm welfare. Finally, Section 5 concludes.

2. INSTITUTIONAL FRAMEWORK: COLLECTIVE BARGAINING AGREEMENTS IN SPAIN

Under the Franco dictatorship, Spain's labour market was highly centralized and regulated. Collective bargaining was in place, governed by existing labour laws (*Ordenanzas Laborales*). While legal trade unions and employers' organizations engaged in contract negotiations, the state played a direct role in dictating the results of these negotiations (Milner & Metcalf, 1994).

Following the end of the dictatorship in 1975, Spain transitioned back to a democratic system, initiating a series of regulatory measures for the labour market. A landmark development in this process was the enactment of the Workers' Statute (*Estatuto de los trabajadores*) in 1980, which was designed to structure the wage system, with a particular focus on collective bargaining agreements. This initial version of the Workers' Statute confronted challenges such as low union membership and the under-representation of unions, issues attributed to the nascent state of democracy.[1] Additionally, the economic landscape of Spain during this period, which persists to some extent today, was characterized by a predominance of small and medium-sized enterprises.

At the risk of oversimplification, the Spanish system of collective agreements outlined in the Workers' Statute, although subject to various modifications, was applied in Spain until 2012. It can be summarized as follows: firstly, unions have the authority to negotiate collective agreements if they achieve a minimum of 10% at the national level and 15% at the regional level in union elections, irrespective of their membership size. The second characteristic is the automatic extension of agreements. This implies that once a collective agreement is approved, it applies to all firms and employees in the sector/region, regardless of their affiliation with the signing social partners. Thirdly, collective agreements remain in effect until a new agreement is reached, irrespective of the expiration date, a concept known as ultra-activity. Lastly, negotiations occur between employer associations and unions at national, regional, provincial, or sectoral levels, with provincial negotiations being the most common. There is also the option to sign agreements at the company level. In this case, negotiations take place between the board of directors and the work council (or worker representatives in companies with fewer than 50 employees). Additionally, a company-level agreement cannot be less favourable than a sectoral agreement.

The legal constraints described above, along with the small size of Spanish companies, explain the limited impact of decentralized negotiations and the low percentage of workers covered by company-level negotiations. In practice, company agreements are negotiated at the initiative of the firm workers' committee in large enterprises with a high union presence, resulting in higher wages than sectoral agreements. Using data for Spain, we have calculated that most employees, 85% in 2006, are covered by collective agreements at higher than firm level (sectoral, provincial, regional or national), with 14% of employees affected by firm-level collective agreements. Fig. 1 illustrates the distribution of collective bargaining agreements by type over the years. It is evident from the figure that sectoral, provincial, regional, or national agreements have consistently covered

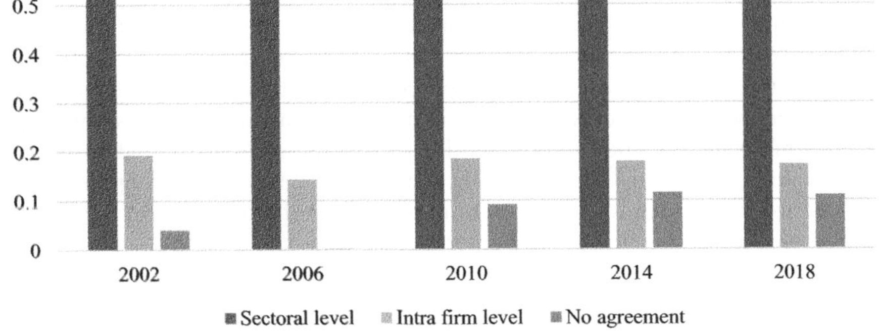

Fig. 1. Collective Bargaining Agreements by Type. *Source*: authors' calculation from EES (2002, 2006, 2010, 2014 and 2018). *Notes*: The 'no agreement' category is only available from 2010 onwards. For the years 2002 and 2006, this category is equivalent to 'no information'.

the majority of employees. Although the proportion of employees covered by firm-level agreements has shown a slight increase from approximately 10% in 2002 to about 16% in 2018, higher-level agreements still dominate, covering around 75-80% of employees throughout the period. The introduction of the 'no agreement' category in 2010, which remains relatively small, further highlights the extensive coverage of collective agreements in Spain. This data underscores the challenges faced by decentralized negotiations in smaller firms and the significant role of higher-level agreements in shaping wage structures and outcomes.

The collapse of Lehman Brothers, followed by the global recession that commenced in 2008, had profound economic repercussions in Spain by 2010. This period witnessed a significant escalation in unemployment rates, culminating at 26.94% in the final quarter of 2012. In response to these challenges, it became imperative to implement strategies aimed at stimulating employment, enhancing wage flexibility, and facilitating the rapid adjustment of salaries and employment conditions. Such measures were essential for ensuring the alignment of the labour market with the prevailing economic cycle.

In response to the deteriorating labour market and adverse macroeconomic conditions, Spain enacted a labour reform in July 2012.[2] This legislative overhaul targeted collective bargaining and wage structures, focusing on three key areas:

i) Decentralization of collective bargaining: the reform prioritized company-level agreements over sectorial-level accords to enhance negotiation flexibility. This was achieved by abolishing the 'ultra-activity' clause, which previously allowed the indefinite extension of collective bargaining agreements when new ones could not be negotiated, and by promoting 'open clauses' in sector-level agreements. 'Open clauses' allow companies to deviate from sector-level agreements under specific conditions, providing greater flexibility in adapting working conditions to the economic realities of individual firms. These clauses can include provisions for adjusting wages, working hours, and other employment terms in response to economic crises or specific company needs, thereby aiming to preserve jobs and ensure economic viability during challenging periods (Brändle & Heinbach, 2013).
ii) Reduction in severance pay: the reform simplified severance pays regulations by eliminating the 'express dismissal' provision, which previously allowed employers to immediately dismiss employees by paying the severance compensation upfront, thereby avoiding the prolonged legal process and additional costs associated with pending salaries during legal disputes. The reform standardized compensation at 33 days' pay per year of service (previously 45 days), capped at 24 months, for unfair dismissals. It also simplified the criteria for economic dismissals, making it easier for companies to reduce their workforce based on economic grounds.
iii) Increased internal flexibility: the legislation allowed firms greater flexibility in modifying employment conditions previously governed by sectoral agreements, including adjustments to wages, working hours, and schedules. This measure was designed to equip companies with the essential tools to adapt more quickly to changing economic circumstances.

The last labour reform in Spain has had several significant effects. First, it has promoted the decentralization of wage bargaining through firm-level agreements that had a priority over sectoral agreements and opt-out clauses (Bentolila et al., 2012; Doménech et al., 2018). Second, the reform has increased the likelihood of transitioning from unemployment to permanent employment, raising the monthly transition rates from 1.7% to 2.6% on average during the first six months of unemployment. It has also reduced the probability of dismissal for workers on temporary contracts by approximately 11%, enabling companies to use internal flexibility measures instead of dismissal (García-Pérez & Domènech, 2019). In addition, it has influenced wage differentials and increased wage inequality (Ramos et al., 2022).

The existing body of research on the impact of labour reforms on wage dispersion, employment, and wage inequality is limited. Empirical analyses indicate that wage adjustments post-reform have not been uniformly experienced across the workforce: specifically, low-wage earners (López-Mourelo & Malo, 2015) and individuals on new contracts (Fernández-Kranz, 2015) have been disproportionately affected. Additionally, Canal and Rodríguez (2016) have found that wage dispersion was more pronounced among workers engaged in company-level bargaining compared to those under multi-employer bargaining agreements. From a macroeconomic viewpoint, the reforms are associated with increased wage flexibility, leading to a broader moderation in wage growth (Izquierdo et al., 2013; Izquierdo & Puente, 2015).

3. DATA AND EMPIRICAL STRATEGY

3.1. Database and Variables

Our analysis utilizes microdata from the 2018 Structure of Earnings Survey of Spain (*Encuesta de Estructura Salarial*, ESS, in Spanish), the most recent dataset published by Eurostat. To our knowledge, this is the first study to employ data from this year.[3] The sampling process follows a two-stage methodology. First, firms are selected through random sampling from the records available in the Social Security General Register of Payments. Then, within each of these randomly chosen firms, workers are also selected via a random sampling method. This extensive dataset offers insights into the dynamics affecting wage structures within Spanish firms, incorporating a broad spectrum of variables at both the individual and firm levels.

At the individual level, we consider characteristics such as gender, age, nationality, and education, stratified into basic, medium, and high levels. We also include tenure with the firm and supervisory positions. Regarding contract type, we include whether it is indefinite or temporary, and full-time or part-time. Occupational roles are classified into white-collar or blue-collar, and low-skilled or high-skilled positions.

From a firm perspective, our analysis includes economic activity (industry, occupation, or service sector), ownership (private or public), and market scope (local, regional, national, or international). Furthermore, we explore the effect of firm size, characterizing three types: small (2–49 employees), medium (50–199 employees) and large (more than 200 employees).[4]

For the empirical analysis, we divide the sample based on two key dimensions: the skill level of the workforce and the size of the firm. Firms are categorized into low-skilled, middle-skilled, and high-skilled based on the predominant skill level of their employees, allowing us to capture the differential impacts of firm-level CBAs across various skill compositions. Additionally, segmenting firms by size (small, medium and large) enables us to analyze how firm size influences wage dynamics, inequality, and overall welfare.

Using this microdata, this study seeks to elucidate to what extent company-level CBAs influence, first, intra-firm wage inequality, second, the average wage dispersion of firms, and as a result the welfare of the employees at the firm level.

Before moving into the empirical strategy, we first explain the intra-firm Gini index distribution.[5] Different from the Gini index at the individual level, in this case, we calculate wage inequality inside each company. We exclude firms with only one employee since there is no inequality for these firms. The formula that we use is the following:

$$G(w_k) = \frac{1}{2n_k^2\mu_k} \sum_{i=1}^{n_k} \sum_{j=1}^{n_k} p_{ki}\, p_{kj} \left| w_{ki} - w_{kj} \right|, \tag{1}$$

where w_k represents the wage distribution of firm k, w_{ki} is the salary of individual i in firm k, μk is the mean wage of firm k, and p_{ki} and p_{kj} are the relative weights associated with the observations w_{ki} and w_{kj}, respectively. As said in the Introduction, we use this inequality index for two reasons. First, the Gini coefficient is the most popular inequality index, widely used in the empirical literature. Second, using this inequality index together with the average wage within firms will allow us to apply the abbreviated Social Welfare Function (SWF) proposed in Sen (1974) (see later in this section).

Fig. 2 illustrates the distribution of the intra-firm Gini index, revealing a wide range of inequality levels and highlighting a heterogeneous landscape of wage dispersion. The spread of the Gini index values suggests that while some firms maintain relatively equitable wage structures (with a Gini index close to 0), others exhibit pronounced disparities (with a Gini index bigger than 0.4). This diversity underscores the complexity of wage distribution dynamics, influenced by factors such as industry, company policies, and labour market conditions. For the distribution of the intra-firm Gini index by company size see Appendix 1, Figs. A1, A2, and A3.

Another variable that will be fundamental to our analysis is social welfare.[6] Once the incidence of CBAs at the firm level on wage inequality and wage averages within firms is studied, we will need to jointly analyze both variables to measure the impact on workers' welfare.

Tracing its roots back to Bergson (1938), an abbreviated social welfare function has predominantly been applied to assess the repercussions of various phenomena (such as economic growth, business cycles, and tax-benefit systems) on an economy, especially in the context of balancing efficiency and equity (Mukhopadhaya, 2003). SWF can be succinctly represented as $W = W(S, I)$, where W signifies the overall social welfare, S embodies the total income of society reflecting economic efficiency, and I denotes the degree of inequality within

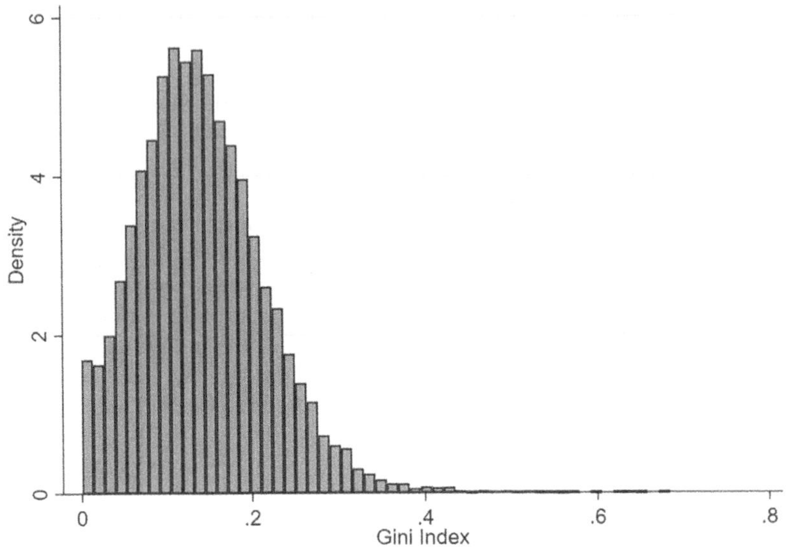

Fig. 2. Distribution of the Intra-Firm Gini Index. *Source:* authors' calculation from EES (2018).

the society. Fundamentally, it is expected that $\partial W/\partial S > 0$ and $\partial W/\partial \theta < 0$, indicating that social welfare should increase with society's total income and decrease with rising inequality. Furthermore, the SWF is typically presumed to be concave, illustrating a societal preference for equity, which, as Mukhopadhaya (2003) elucidates, manifests when redistributing income from wealthier to poorer individuals enhances social welfare. Additionally, adherence to the Pareto Principle is essential, stipulating that any increase in an individual's income, with all others' incomes held constant, should lead to an uplift in welfare levels.

Under an axiomatic approach, after assuming that the marginal utility of income is decreasing, Sen (1974) proposes a SWF that after being adapted to own framework is as follows:

$$W_f = \mu_f \left[1 - G\left(w_k\right)\right], \tag{2}$$

where μ_f is the average wage for each company, and $G(w_k)$ is the intra-firm Gini coefficient.[7] It is easy to see the following trade-off between efficiency and equality.

3.2. Empirical Strategies

Our final goal is to calculate the effect that CBAs at the firm level have on workers' welfare at the firm level. By using an abbreviated SWF, we analyze the impact of CBAs on the dilemma between equity (inequality) and efficiency (mean wages) within firms. Thus, from the literature it seems that CBAs at high levels increase inequality but also mean wages. Therefore, it is important to consider both to estimate worker's welfare in the aggregate. This could justify decentralizing CBAs since they increase mean wages as much as to more than compensate the raise in wage dispersion. After all, both variables (equity and efficiency) are sides of the same coin. For this task, we consider three related models.

First, we investigate whether the presence of a CBAs at the firm level (rather than at the national level) influences wage inequality within the firm while controlling for various other factors that could impact wage dispersion. In particular, we estimate the following regression:

$$Intrafirm\ G_f = \beta_0 + \beta_1 CBA_f + \beta_2 X_i + \beta_3 Z_f + \in_{if}, \tag{3}$$

where the dependent variable is conceptualized as a measure of wage inequality (Gini) within the firm *f*. CBA_f represents a variable indicating the presence and intensity of firm-level collective bargaining agreements for the firm *f*: it takes value 0 if the agreement is at the national, regional, or local level, and value 1 if the CBAs is at the firm level. The model incorporates two categories of control variables: firstly, firm-level characteristics, symbolized as Z_f (for each firm *f*), which include the sector of activity, size of the firm, market of the firm and ownership status (public versus private). Secondly, individual-level attributes, denoted by X_i (for each individual *i*), including the following: gender, age, educational attainment, nationality, length of service, contract type (permanent versus temporary and full-time versus part-time), supervisory roles, and occupational classification (independent variables are defined in Appendix 2).

The second model tries to measure whether collective agreements at the firm level influence the mean wage at the firm level. To do so, we change the dependent variable. Thus, we estimate the following equation:

$$Wage\ average_f = \beta_0 + + \beta_1 CBA_f + \beta_2 X_i + \beta_3 Z_f + v_{if}, \tag{4}$$

where the dependent variable represents the average wage at the firm level, while the independent variables are the same as those considered in Equation (3).

Finally, we replicate the same estimation for measure social welfare at the firm level:

$$W_f = \beta_0 + + \beta_1 CBA_f + \beta_2 X_i + \beta_3 Z_f + u_{if}, \tag{5}$$

where the dependent variable is now the welfare within a firm, whereas the independent variables align with those specified in Equation (3).

4. MAIN RESULTS

4.1. The Effects of Firm-Level Collective Agreements on Intra-Firm Wage Inequality

Table 1 presents the results of the impact of firm-level collective bargaining agreements on intra-firm wage inequality. Column (1) shows the simple effect of firm-level CBAs without additional controls. Column (2) includes individual characteristics such as gender, age, nationality, and educational attainment. Column (3) adds firm-level characteristics, including the sector of activity, market type, and firm size. Finally, column (4) incorporates all the controls. Table 1 shows a positive and statistically significant impact of firm-level CBAs on intra-firm wage inequality. This relationship remains robust across different econometric specifications, underscoring the substantive influence of firm-level negotiations on wage inequality within firms. The magnitude of this effect might appear modest; however, a closer inspection reveals its significance. Specifically, a coefficient of 0.003 in the specification (4) translates to a 4% increase in the standard deviation of the Gini coefficient, indicating a non-negligible effect on wage inequality.

Examining the effects of other variables, we observe noteworthy patterns. Individual characteristics such as sex, age, nationality, and educational attainment exhibit significant associations with wage inequality, as do various firm characteristics, including sector of activity, market type, and firm size. For instance, higher educational levels are correlated with greater wage dispersion, which might reflect

Table 1. The Effect of Firm-Level Collective Bargaining on Intra-Firm Wage Inequality.

	(1)	(2)	(3)	(4)
Company-level CBAs	0.011***	0.018***	0.002***	0.003***
	(0.000)	(0.000)	(0.000)	(0.001)
Individual characteristics				
Sex		0.003***		0.001**
		(0.000)		(0.000)
Age		−0.001***		0.000
		(0.000)		(0.000)
Nationality		−0.005**		−0.003**
		(0.001)		(0.001)
Education: Basic		0.007***		0.004***
		(0.001)		(0.000)
Education: Medium		0.021***		0.016***
		(0.001)		(0.001)
Education: High		0.034***		0.024***
		(0.001)		(0.001)
Tenure		0.001***		0.000***
		(0.000)		(0.000)
Contract		−0.001		−0.000
		(0.000)		(0.000)
Part-time		−0.009***		−0.005***
		(0.000)		(0.000)
Occ: low-skilled white-collar		−0.024***		−0.022***
		(0.000)		(0.000)
Occ: high-skilled blue-collar		−0.033***		−0.025***
		(0.001)		(0.001)
Occ: low-skilled blue-collar		−0.023***		−0.025***
		(0.001)		(0.001)
Supervisor		0.008***		
		(0.001)		

Table 1. (*Continued*)

	(1)	(2)	(3)	(4)
Firm characteristics				
Activity: Construction			−0.014***	−0.012***
			(0.001)	(0.001)
Activity: Service			0.007***	0.002***
			(0.000)	(0.000)
Property			0.010***	0.009***
			(0.000)	(0.000)
Type of market: National			0.024***	0.020***
			0.000	(0.000)
Type of market: EU			0.023***	0.019***
			0.001	(0.001)
Type of market: World			0.038***	0.026***
			0.001	(0.001)
Type of firm size: 50–200			0.037***	0.035***
			0.000	(0.000)
Type of firm size: >200			0.048***	0.045***
			0.000	(0.000)
R^2	0.004	0.120	0.163	0.222
Observations (firms)	19,439	19,439	19,439	19,439

Source: Authors' calculation from EES (2018). The dependent variable is wage inequality at the firm level.
Notes: Results obtained from the estimation of model (3). ***, ** and * indicate that the coefficients are statistically significant at 1%, 5% and 10%, respectively. The reference categories for each variable can be seen in Table B1 of Appendix 2.

the premium on skills and education within the labour market (Budría & Moro-Egido, 2008). The sector of activity and the market in which the firm operates play a role in determining wage inequality within firms. Companies engaged in international markets, especially those operating globally, tend to exhibit higher wage inequality at the firm level, possibly due to the diverse skill requirements and competitive pressures in these environments (Klein et al., 2013). Additionally, factors such as age, nationality, and experience significantly influence within company wage inequality. Younger workers often face higher unemployment rates and lower wages compared to older workers due to their limited work experience and higher likelihood of precarious employment conditions (Reinecke & Grimshaw, 2015; Sebastian, 2018). Similarly, nationality can impact wage structures, with migrant workers frequently experiencing lower wage returns on their labour market experience compared to native workers (Brunow & Jost, 2022; Sebastian & Ulceluse, 2019). Moreover, the type of market also matters; firms in markets with high levels of employment protection tend to exhibit greater wage inequality between temporary and permanent workers (Fauser & Gebel, 2023).

From now on, we focus on the effects of collective bargaining at the company level, although the results of the rest of explicative variables are available to the reader upon request.

Our investigation extends to the dynamics of wage inequality within firms, segmented by the prevailing skill levels of their workforce. In operationalizing this analysis, firms are categorized based on the predominant skill level of their employees: high-skilled firms (where at least 80% of workers are high-skilled workers), low-skilled firms (where at least 20% of workers are deemed low-skilled) and middle-skilled firms (encompassing the remaining firms, effectively capturing an intermediate skill level for the majority, about 60%, of the workforce). We adopt this strategy to understand how different skill levels within firms' impact wage distribution patterns, ensuring our analysis reflects the realities of workforce composition.

In the context of low-skilled firms, our analysis indicates a more significant increase in wage inequality associated with firm-level CBAs, underscoring the variability of bargaining outcomes across different firm types (see Table 2). This variance can be attributed to the divergent operational and labour dynamics prevalent within these firm categories. Middle-skilled firms, conversely, occupy an intermediate position, exhibiting a varied impact of firm-level CBAs on wage dispersion, reflective of the heterogeneity within this group.

The regression coefficients provide a statistically robust basis for these observations, with firm-level CBAs showing a positive and significant effect on wage

Table 2. Effects of Firm-Level CBAs on Intra-Firm Wage Inequality by the Type of Firm.

	(1)	(2)	(3)	(4)
Low-skilled firm				
Company-level CBAs	0.034*** (0.001)	0.027*** (0.001)	0.008*** (0.001)	0.006*** 0.001
Individual characteristics		√		√
Firm characteristics			√	√
R^2	0.039	0.083	0.224	0.224
Observations (firms)	5,891	5,891	5,891	5,891
Middle-skilled firm				
Company-level CBAs	0.018*** (0.001)	0.013*** (0.001)	−0.002** (0.001)	0.004*** (0.000)
Individual characteristics		√		√
Firm characteristics			√	√
R^2	0.009	0.070	0.157	0.241
Observations (firms)	7,249	7,249	7,249	7,249
High-skilled firm				
Company-level CBAs	0.019*** (0.001)	0.013*** (0.001)	0.004*** (0.001)	0.003*** (0. 001)
Individual characteristics		√		√
Firm characteristics			√	√
R^2	0.008	0.086	0.191	0.212
Observations (firms)	6,299	6,299	6,299	6,299

Source: authors' calculation from EES (2018).
Notes: Results obtained from the estimation of model (3) by the type of firm incorporating the controls detailed in Table 1. ***, **, and * indicate that the coefficients are statistically significant at 1%, 5% and 10%, respectively. The sign indicates if the model takes individual characteristics (column 2), firm characteristics (column 3), or both characteristics (column 4). The reference categories for each variable can be seen in Table B1 of Appendix B.

inequality within low and high-skilled firms, albeit to differing extents. The effects remain consistent upon controlling for individual characteristics and firm-specific factors, thereby affirming the substantive influence of firm-level bargaining processes on the internal wage structure.

The data reveal that high-skilled firms (or firms that are more technologically advanced) experience a less pronounced increase in intra-firm wage inequality resulting from firm-level CBAs (refer to column 4). (Canal & Rodríguez, 2004). This outcome suggests a more equitable distribution of bargaining power within high-skilled firms mitigates the potential adverse effects of firm-level bargaining on wage inequality.

This segmented analysis highlights the complexity of collective bargaining's impact on wage inequality, showing how the skill composition of a firm's workforce can influence the outcomes of such negotiations. Our finding calls for a deeper exploration into the mechanisms through which firm-level bargaining shapes wage distributions, particularly in the context of skill-based disparities.

Next, we divided the sample by firm size. Thus, we created three groups: small-sized firms (2 to 49 employees), medium-sized firms (50 to 200 employees), and large firms (over 200 employees). The results are shown in Table 3. We find that intra-firm wage inequality intensifies as firm size decreases. In particular, the regression analysis in Table 3 indicates a statistically significant increase in wage inequality within smaller firms (employing between 2 and 49 workers) associated with the implementation of firm-level CBAs. In contrast, larger firms (with more than 200 employees) exhibit a negligible or even negative relationship between firm-level CBAs and wage inequality. This disparity raises questions about the underlying mechanisms that might contribute to these differences, including the potential role of skill level distributions and bargaining power dynamics within firms of varying sizes.

Our analysis suggests a nuanced interplay between firm size and wage inequality, where smaller firms might inherently struggle more with wage dispersion issues than their larger counterparts. One plausible explanation could involve the correlation between firm size and the skill level of the workforce; larger firms might not only possess a broader distribution of skills but also more resources and structures in place to manage wage negotiations more effectively, thus mitigating the extent of wage inequality.

The observed trend holds relevance for the Spanish labour market, characterized by a substantial presence of small to medium-sized enterprises (SMEs). In Spain, the percentage of SMEs is extremely high. According to data from the Ministry of Industry, as of January 1, 2023, 99.8% of companies in Spain are SMEs, which amounts to 3,202,717 out of a total of 3,207,580 companies. This line may help understand why social actors such as trade unions are cautious about pushing for negotiations at the firm level. Our results highlight the importance for policymakers and stakeholders in the Spanish labour market to adopt customized strategies in overseeing collective bargaining procedures, especially in assisting smaller businesses in handling wage negotiations and promoting fairness in the labour market.

Table 3. Effects of Firm-Level CBAs on Intra-Firm Wage Inequality by Firm Size.

	(1)	(2)	(3)	(4)
Small-sized firms (2–49)				
Company-level CBAs	0.026***	0.016***	0.017***	0.013***
	(0.002)	(0.002)	(0.002)	(0.002)
Individual characteristics		√		√
Firm characteristics			√	√
R^2	0.008	0.127	0.074	0.165
Observations (firms)	11,844	11,844	11,844	11,844
Medium-sized firms (50–200)				
Company-level CBAs	−0.000	−0.000	0.000	0.001
	(0.000)	(0.001)	(0.001)	(0.001)
Individual characteristics		√		√
Firm characteristics			√	√
	0.000	0.063	0.023	0.083
Observations (firms)	3,970	3,970	3,970	3,970
Large-sized firms (>200)				
Company-level CBAs	−0.004***	−0.003***	−0.002***	−0.000
	(0.000)	(0.000)	(0.000)	(0.000)
Individual characteristics		√		√
Firm characteristics			√	√
R^2	0.001	0.045	0.007	0.055
Observations (firms)	3,625	3,625	3,625	3,625

Source: Authors' calculation from EES (2018).
Notes: Results obtained from the estimation of model (3) by firm size incorporating the controls detailed in Table 1. ***, ** and * indicate that the coefficients are statistically significant at 1%, 5% and 10%, respectively. The sign indicates if the model takes individual characteristics (column 2), firm characteristics (column 3), or both characteristics (column 4). The reference categories for each variable can be seen in Table B1 of Appendix B.

4.2. The Effects of Firm-Level Collective Agreements on Intra-Firm Mean Wages

In the previous section, we showed a rise in wage inequality within firms. However, it may happen that while wage inequality within the company is increasing, wages are also increasing for all workers. That is why so far, we have measured the effects of collective bargaining on wage inequality within firms, and now we focus on assessing its impact on average wages within companies. Collective bargaining can improve effort encouraging employees to work harder, increase their productivity, and therefore, their wages, but at the price of increase wage dispersion within the firm.

Table 4 presents the effects of firm-level collective bargaining on the intra-firm mean wages. It shows a positive and statistically significant impact of firm-level CBAs on the average wage of employees within firms. Quantitatively, an observed coefficient of 1.141 represents a 16.57% of the variation (see column 4).[8] This share highlights the effect of firm-level bargaining on elevating average wage levels within firms.

The implication of this finding is important because it suggest that firm-level collective bargaining not only serves as a mechanism for wage negotiation but also plays a pivotal role in enhancing the overall wage structure within firms. For policymakers and labour market stakeholders, these insights offer a compelling rationale for fostering and facilitating effective bargaining processes at the firm level, aimed at achieving equitable and sustainable wage growth.

Now, we study how firm-level CBAs affect the average wage of workers within firms, categorized by the main skill level of their employees. Table 5 indicates that CBAs at the firm level have a substantial positive impact on the intra-firm mean wage, regardless the type of skilled firm. More precisely, we observed that firm-level collective bargaining raises average wage levels within companies, particularly in those with high-skilled employees.

This observation suggests a direct correlation between the skill intensity of a firm and the efficacy of collective bargaining in enhancing wage outcomes. High-skilled firms, typically characterized by a workforce with higher productivity levels, seem to leverage collective bargaining mechanisms more effectively, translating into more substantial wage gains for their employees.

This phenomenon highlights a linkage between firm-level bargaining and productivity: the capacity for collective bargaining to yield positive wage adjustments is arguably contingent upon the productive capital of the workforce. Although our dataset does not include direct measures of productivity, the inferred relationship from wage outcomes suggests a compelling association between productivity levels and the potency of collective bargaining impacts.

Table 4. The Effect of Firm-Level CBAs on Intra-Firm Mean Wage.

	(1)	(2)	(3)	(4)
Company-level CBAs	3.121*** (0.053)	2.081*** (0.058)	1.1154*** (0.053)	1.141*** (0.000)
Individual characteristics		√		√
Firm characteristics			√	√
R^2	0.045	0.295	0.164	0.342
Observations (firms)	19,439	19,439	19,439	19,439

Source: Authors' calculation from EES (2018).

Notes: Results obtained from the estimation of model (4) incorporating the controls detailed in Table 1. ***, ** and * indicate that the coefficients are statistically significant at 1%, 5% and 10%, respectively. The sign indicates if the model takes individual characteristics (column 2), firm characteristics (column 3), or both characteristics (column 4). The reference categories for each variable can be seen in Table B1 of Appendix B.

Table 5. The Effect of Firm-Level CBAs on Intra-Firm Mean Wage by Type of Firm.

	(1)	(2)	(3)	(4)
Low-skilled firm				
Company-level CBAs	2.271*** (0.056)	1.752*** (0.053)	1.047*** (0.045)	0.869*** (0.045)
Individual characteristics		√		√
Firm characteristics			√	√
R^2	0.085	0.181	0.210	0.264
Observations (firms)	5,891	5,891	5,891	5,891
Middle-skilled firm				
Company-level CBAs	3.036*** (0.070)	2.128*** (0.067)	1.106*** (0.069)	1.257*** (0.067)
Individual characteristics		√		√
Firm characteristics			√	√
R^2	0.054	0.197	0.205	0.328
Observations (firms)	7,249	7,249	7,249	7,249
High-skilled firm				
Company-level CBAs	4.485*** (0.148)	3.081*** (0.142)	2.991*** (0.141)	2.381*** (0.135)
Individual characteristics		√		√
Firm characteristics			√	√
R^2	0.051	0.230	0.198	0.288
Observations (firms)	6,299	6,299	6,299	6,299

Source: authors' calculation from EES (2018).
Notes: Results obtained from the estimation of model (4) by type of firm incorporating the controls detailed in Table 1. ***, ** and * indicate that the coefficients are statistically significant at 1%, 5% and 10%, respectively. The sign indicates if the model takes individual characteristics (column 2), firm characteristics (column 3), or both characteristics (column 4). The reference categories for each variable can be seen in Table B1 of Appendix B.

Our investigation further investigates how firm-level CBAs influence mean wages within companies by firm size (Table 6). The results indicate that the benefits of firm-level CBAs on mean wages are positive, significant, and robust across all firm sizes, underscoring the widespread efficacy of such bargaining in enhancing wage levels. Interestingly, the magnitude of these benefits is not uniform but exhibits a U-shaped pattern across the spectrum of firm sizes. Thus, smaller firms (employing between 2 and 49 workers) and larger firms (with more than 200 employees) experience greater improvements in mean wages through firm-level CBAs compared to medium-sized firms (employing between 50 and 200 workers).

Table 6. The Effect of Firm-Level CBAs on Intra-Firm Wage Means by Firm Size.

	(1)	(2)	(3)	(4)
Small-sized firms (2–49)				
Company-level CBAs	2.552*** (0.156)	1.655*** (0.134)	1.665*** (0.153)	1.232*** (0.135)
Individual characteristics		√		√
Firm characteristics			√	√
R^2	0.016	0.219	0.079	0.246
Observations (firms)	11,844	11,844	11,844	11,844
Medium-sized firms (49–200)				
Company-level CBAs	1.249*** (0.097)	0.757*** (0.087)	0.653*** (0.109)	0.663*** (0.092)
Individual characteristics		√		√
Firm characteristics			√	√
R^2	0.009	0.270	0.0549	0.2923
Observations (firms)	3,970	3,970	3,970	3,970
Large-sized firms (>200)				
Company-level CBAs	1.895*** (0.062)	1.477*** (0.055)	1.131*** (0.059)	1.248*** (0.055)
Individual characteristics		√		√
Firm characteristics			√	√
R^2	0.020	0.305	0.121	0.332
Observations (firms)	3,625	3,625	3,625	3,625

Source: Authors' calculation from EES (2018).
Notes: Results obtained from the estimation of model (4) by size firm incorporating the controls detailed in Table 1. ***, ** and * indicate that the coefficients are statistically significant at 1%, 5% and 10%, respectively. The sign indicates if the model takes individual characteristics (column 2), firm characteristics (column 3), or both characteristics (column 4). The reference categories for each variable can be seen in Table B1 of Appendix B.

This pattern suggests a significant relationship between firm size and the effectiveness of collective bargaining in shaping wage structures. For smaller and larger firms, the negotiation processes appear to yield more substantial wage increments, a dynamic that might be influenced by various factors including bargaining power, organizational structures, and the strategic priorities of the negotiating parties.

The observed U-shaped pattern challenges notions of a trade-off between efficiency and equity in the context of firm-level bargaining. For firms with more than 49 workers, the data indicate that collective bargaining positively affects mean wages without adversely impacting wage inequality to a significant extent.

This finding implies that firm-level negotiations can concurrently support wage growth and maintain equitable wage distributions, especially in larger organizational settings.

4.3. The Effects of Firm-Level Collective Agreement on Intra-Firm Workers' Welfare

Having observed the effect of collective bargaining on inequality and average wages at the company level, we analyze whether workers at the firm level experience an increase in their well-being because of such negotiation. On one hand, we have seen that inequality within companies increases, which will reduce workers' well-being (Section 4.1). On the other hand, we have shown that collective bargaining at the company level improves average wages within the company, which will increase workers' well-being (Section 4.2). Therefore, it is not clear what will happen to workers' well-being as there exists a clear trade-off between efficiency (average salary) and equity (inequality) for workers at the company level. In what follows we try to answer this question: does the enhancement in mean wages, facilitated by collective bargaining, outweigh the potential adverse impacts of increased wage inequality on workers' welfare within companies?

Table 7 presents the impact of firm-level CBAs on intra-firm workers' welfare. It demonstrates that CBAs at the firm level have a positive and statistically significant effect on the welfare of workers within companies. Thus, the enhancement in efficiency, indicated by higher mean wages, considerably outweighs the negative effects linked with increased wage inequality. Consequently, workers' welfare within companies improves because of CBAs at the firm level. This finding aligns

Table 7. The Effect of Firm-Level Collective Bargaining on Intra-Firm Workers' Welfare.

	(1)	(2)	(3)	(4)
Company-level CBAs	2.434*** (0.042)	1.616*** (0.039)	0.982*** (0.042)	0.952 *** (0.038)
Individual characteristics		√		√
Firm characteristics			√	√
R^2	0.045	0.292	0.153	0.331
Observations (firms)	19,439	19,439	19,439	19,439

Source: authors' calculation from EES (2018).
Notes: Results obtained from the estimation of model (5) incorporating the controls detailed in Table 1. ***, ** and * indicate that the coefficients are statistically significant at 1%, 5% and 10%, respectively. The sign indicates if the model takes individual characteristics (column 2), firm characteristics (column 3), or both characteristics (column 4). The reference categories for each variable can be seen in Table B1 of Appendix B.

with the hypothesis that collective bargaining mechanisms, which typically aim to negotiate better wages, indirectly contribute to improving the overall welfare of the workforce by elevating wage levels.

We move into understanding the impact of firm-level CBAs on the welfare of workers across by type of skilled firm. Table 8 confirms that all types of skilled firms experience improved welfare due to collective bargaining, with high-skilled firms experiencing particularly significant improvements. This outcome likely reflects the higher bargaining power and the potential for greater wage gains within these firms.

Table 8. The Effect of Firm-Level CBAs on Intra-Firm Workers' Welfare by Type of Firm.

	(1)	(2)	(3)	(4)
Low-skilled firm				
Company-level CBAs	1.716***	1.319***	0.849***	0.704***
	(0.046)	(0.043)	(0.038)	(0.037)
Individual characteristics		√		√
Firm characteristics			√	√
R^2	0.075	0.169	0.200	0.253
Observations (firms)	5,891	5,891	5,891	5,891
Middle-skilled firm				
Company-level CBAs	2.458***	1.734***	1,028***	1.007***
	(0.054)	(0.050)	(0.053)	(0.054)
Individual characteristics		√		√
Firm characteristics			√	√
R^2	0.064	0.214	0.204	0.316
Observations (firms)	7,249	7,249	7,249	7,249
High-skilled firm				
Company-level CBAs	3.539***	2.373***	2.417***	1.882***
	(0.118)	(0.113)	(0.114)	(0.109)
Individual characteristics		√		√
Firm characteristics			√	√
R^2	0.051	0.232	0.175	0273
Observations (firms)	6,299	6,299	6,299	6,299

Source: authors' calculation from EES (2018).
Notes: Results obtained from the estimation of model (5) by type of firm incorporating the controls detailed in Table 1. ***, ** and * indicate that the coefficients are statistically significant at 1%, 5% and 10%, respectively. The sign indicates if the model takes individual characteristics (column 2), firm characteristics (column 3), or both characteristics (column 4). The reference categories for each variable can be seen in Table B1 of Appendix B.

In the final stage of the analysis, we estimate whether the impact of firm-level CBAs varies across different firm sizes concerning workers' welfare. The results in Table 9 reveal a positive and statistically significant impact of collective bargaining on workers' welfare within firms, irrespective of the size of the company.

Furthermore, our findings indicate a non-monotonic, U-shaped relationship between firm size and the welfare benefits for workers derived from firm-level collective bargaining agreements: the greatest benefits in workers' welfare from collective bargaining are obtained in the smallest (2–49 workers) and largest firms (>200 workers). Interestingly, in smaller firms, these benefits accrue despite an increase in wage disparity (result obtain in Section 4.1), suggesting that the positive impact on average wages significantly contributes to overall welfare improvements.

Table 9. The Effect of Firm-Level CBAs on Intra-Firm Workers' Welfare by Firm Size.

	(1)	(2)	(3)	(4)
Small-sized firms (2-49)				
Company-level CBAs	1.941*** (0.123)	1.260*** (0.106)	1.241*** (0.118)	0.906*** (0.104)
Individual characteristics		√		√
Firm characteristics			√	√
R^2	0.016	0.209	0.068	0.230
Observations (firms)	11,844	11,844	11,844	11,844
Medium-sized firms (49-200)				
Company-level CBAs	1.140*** (0.079)	0.718*** (0.070)	0.586*** (0.090)	0.573*** (0.076)
Individual characteristics		√		√
Firm characteristics			√	√
R^2	0.013	0.292	0.061	0.312
Observations (firms)	3,970	3,970	3,970	3,970
Large-sized firms (>200)				
Company-level CBAs	1.687*** (0.050)	1.304*** (0.044)	0.998*** (0.048)	1.058*** (0.045)
Individual characteristics		√		√
Firm characteristics			√	√
R^2	0.025	0.309	0.139	0.341
Observations (firms)	3,625	3,625	3,625	3,625

Source: authors' calculation from EES (2018).

Notes: Results obtained from the estimation of model (5) by size firm incorporating the controls detailed in Table 1. ***, ** and * indicate that the coefficients are statistically significant at 1%, 5% and 10%, respectively. The sign indicates if the model takes individual characteristics (column 2), firm characteristics (column 3), or both characteristics (column 4). The reference categories for each variable can be seen in Table B1 of Appendix B.

5. CONCLUSIONS

This article studies the impacts of firm-level collective bargaining agreements on workers' welfare within the Spanish labour market; that is, the trade-off between wage inequality within companies (equity) and mean wages at the firm level (efficiency). Moreover, the analysis provides a detailed examination of how these agreements influence wage inequality, mean wage levels, and overall worker well-being across various firm sizes and different levels of employee skill.

Our findings show a detailed interaction between wage inequality and mean wages within companies under firm-level CBAs. While these agreements lead to an increase in wage disparities within firms, they also significantly boost average wage levels at the company level. This trend is consistently observed across all skill levels of employees, from low-skilled to high-skilled, and across various firm sizes. Despite the negative implications of increased wage inequality within firms, the overall effect of firm-level CBAs is beneficial, as they elevate welfare levels within companies. More precisely, the positive impact on mean wages at the company level generally offsets the adverse effect of increased wage disparity within firms, leading to an improvement in workers' welfare at the firm level. This improvement is particularly important in companies with high-skilled workers, where the impact of CBAs on raising wages is most significant. On the other hand, the advantages of CBAs are influenced by firm size, highlighting the importance of considering the specific context of the firm, including its workforce composition and industrial sector, in shaping the outcomes of collective bargaining.

From a policy perspective, these insights emphasize the need to foster and facilitate effective collective bargaining practices that enhance both wage equality and workers' welfare. Policymakers and labour market analysts should consider the skill composition of the labour force when formulating labour relations policies and designing collective bargaining frameworks. The positive wage effects observed across different firm types advocates for a supportive policy environment that encourages firm-level bargaining to foster wage growth. The sectoral differences in the impact of CBAs on mean wages point to the necessity for tailored approaches in labour policy and collective bargaining practices, ensuring that the benefits of negotiations are equitably distributed across the workforce, regardless of the skill intensity of their employment sectors. These insights underscore the vital role of skill and productivity considerations in shaping the outcomes of collective bargaining processes.

The findings advocate for a nuanced application of CBAs as a mechanism for economic and social improvement, emphasizing their potential to foster equitable and prosperous labour market outcomes. Thus, this study offers practical guidance for policymakers, labour unions, and employers on leveraging collective bargaining for the benefit of workers and the broader economy.

NOTES

1. See Bentolila and Jimeno (2002) for a description of the evolution of the legislation on collective bargaining in Spain since the eighties until the end of the nineties.

2. Visser (2016) provides a detailed examination of modifications to collective bargaining agreements within OECD nations provoked by the Great Recession.

3. The EES, administered by the National Statistics Institute of Spain (*Instituto Nacional de Estadística*, INE, in Spanish), guarantees the data's reliability and representativeness. The survey employs a stratified random sampling design, ensuring a representative cross-section of the Spanish labour market.

4. See Appendix B, Table 1 for more details on the variables. The correlation matrix from this dataset shows no problems with multicollinearity, ensuring the reliability of our analysis and is available to the reader upon request.

5. Among all the possible inequality indices in the literature on inequality we adopt the Gini coefficient as it fulfils the basic principles found in the literature: progressive transfer, symmetry, scale invariance and replication of the population.

6. Refer to Sebastian (2022) for an analysis of the labour market, income per capita, and welfare in Europe.

7. Rodríguez & Salas, 2014b) showed that for a set of income (wage) distributions that are symmetric under the same transformation, the result of applying the SWF proposed by Sen (1974) agrees with the majority voting result.

8. The standard deviation of the intra-firm mean wage is 6.885.

ACKNOWLEDGEMENTS

We are grateful for the editor and referee's comments and suggestions that helped to improve the paper. All errors remain our own. The authors acknowledge funding Fundación La Caixa (Sebastian), 'Atracción de talent' from Comunidad de Madrid under project 2022-T1/SOC-23949 (Sebastian), and from the Ministerio de Ciencia e Innovación under project PID2022-137352NB-C43 (Sebastian).

REFERENCES

Aidt, T. S., & Tzannatos, Z. (2008). Trade unions, collective bargaining and macroeconomic performance: A review. *Industrial Relations Journal*, *39*(4), 258–295.

Bentolila, S., Dolado, J. J., & Jimeno, J. F. (2012). The new labour market reform in Spain: Objectives, instruments, and shortcomings. *CESifo DICE Report*, *10*(2), 3–7.

Bentolila, S., & Jimeno, J. F. (2002). *La reforma de la negociación colectiva en España*. (No. 2002-03). Fedea.

Bergson, A. (1938). A Reformulation of Certain Aspects of Welfare Economics. *Quarterly Journal of Economics*, *52*(2), 310–334.

Bertola, G., Dabusinskas, A., Hoeberichts, M., Izquierdo, M., Kwapil, C., Montornés, J., & Radoswki, D. (2012). Price, wage and employment response to shocks: Evidence from the WDN survey. *Labour Economics*, *19*(5), 783–791.

Brändle, T., & Heinbach, W. D. (2013). Opening clauses in collective bargaining agreements: More flexibility to save jobs? *Review of Economics*, *64*(2), 159–192.

Boeri, T. (2014). *Two-tier bargaining*. IZA Discussion Paper. N8358.

Boeri, T., Ichino, A., Moretti, E., & Posch, J. (2024). Wage equalization and regional misallocation: Evidence from Italian and German Provinces. *Journal of the European Economic Association*, *19*(6), 3249–3292.

Brunow, S., & Jost, O. (2022). Wages of skilled migrant and native employees in Germany: New light on an old issue. *International Migration Review*, *56*(2), 410–432.

Budría, S., & Moro-Egido, A. I. (2008). Education, educational mismatch, and wage inequality: Evidence for Spain. *Economics of Education Review*, *27*(3), 332–341.

Cahuc, P., Carcillo, S., & Zylberberg, A. (2014). *Labor economics* (2nd ed., Chapter 7). MIT Press.

Canal, J. F., & Rodríguez, C. (2004). Collective bargaining and within-firm wage dispersion in Spain. *British Journal of Industrial Relations*, *42*, 481–506.

Card, D., & de la Rica, S. (2006). Firm-level contracting and the structure of wages., *Industrial and Labor Relations Review*, *59*(4), 573–593.

Cardoso, A. R., & Portugal, P. (2005). Contractual wages and the wage cushion under different bargaining settings. *Journal of Labor Economics*, *23*(4), 875–902.

Chakravarty, S. (2009). Equity and efficiency as components of a social welfare function. *International Journal of Economic Theory*, *5*, 181–199.

Calmfors, L. (1993). Centralisation des négociations de salaires et performances macroéconomiques – une analyse. *Revue Économique de l'OCDE*, *21*, 172–206.

Canal, J. F., & Rodríguez, C. (2016). Collective bargaining, wage dispersion and the economic cycle: Spanish evidence. *The Economic and Labour Relations Review*, *27*(4), 471–489.

Dahl, C., le Maire, D., & Munch, J. (2013). Wage dispersion and decentralisation of wage bargaining. *Journal of Labor Economics*, *31*(3), 501–533.

Daouli, J. Demoussis, M. Giannakapoulos, N., & Laliotis, I. (2013). Firm-level collective bargaining and wages in Greece: A quantile decomposition analysis. *British Journal of Industrial Relations*, *51*(1), 80–103.

Dell'Aringa, C., & Lucifora, C. (1994). Collective bargaining and relative earnings in Italy. *European Journal of Political Economy*, *10*(4), 727–747.

Dell'Aringa, C., & Pagani, L. (2007). Collective bargaining and wage dispersion in Europe. *British Journal of Industrial Relations*, *45*(1), 29–54.

Doménech, R., García, J.R., & Ulloa, C. (2018) The effects of wage flexibility on activity and employment in Spain., *Journal of Policy Modelling*, *40*(6), 1200–1220.

Druant, M., Fabiani, S., Kezdi, G., Lamo, A., Martins, F., & Sabbatini, R. (2012). Firms' price and wage adjustment in Europe: Survey evidence on nominal stickiness. *Labour Economics*, *19*(5), 772–782.

Fauser, S., & Gebel, M. (2023). Labor market dualism and the heterogeneous wage gap for temporary employment: A multilevel study across 30 countries. *Socio-Economic Review*, *21*(4), 2069–2091.

Fernández-Kranz, D. (2015). Ingresos salariales en España durante la crisis económica: ¿ha sido efectiva la reforma de 2012? *Cuadernos de Información Económica*, *246*(May/June).

Galuscak, K., Keeney, M., Nicolitsats, D., Smets, F., Strzelecki, P., & Vodopivec, M. (2012). The determination of wages of newly hired employees: Survey evidence on internal versus external factors. *Labour Economics*, *19*, 809–812.

García-Pérez, J. I., & Domènech, J. M. (2019). The impact of the 2012 Spanish labour market reform on unemployment inflows and outflows: A regression discontinuity analysis using duration models. *Hacienda Publica Espanola*, (231), 157–200.

Granqvist, L., & Regner, H. (2008). Decentralized wage formation in Sweden. *British Journal of Industrial Relations*, *46*(3), 500–520.

Gnocchi, S., Lagerborg, A., & Pappa, E. (2015). Do labor market institutions matter for business cycles? *Journal of Economic Dynamics and Control*, *51*, 299–317.

Idson, T. L., & Oi, W. Y. (1999). Workers are more productive in large firms. *American Economic Review*, *89*(2), 104–108.

Izquierdo, M., & Puente, S. (2015). *La respuesta de los salarios ante cambios en la situación cíclica: una estimación a partir de la Muestra Continua de Vidas Laborales (MCVL)*. Boletín Económico, (June). Banco de España.

Izquierdo, M., Lacuesta, A., & Puente, S. (2013). *La reforma laboral de 2012: Un primer análisis de algunos de sus efectos*. Boletín Económico, (September). Banco de España.

Klein, M. W., Moser, C., & Urban, D. M. (2013). Exporting, skills and wage inequality. *Labour Economics*, *25*, 76–85.

Lallemand, T., Plasman, R., & Rycx, F. (2005). Why do large firms pay higher wages? Evidence from matched worker-firm data. *International Journal of Manpower*, *26*(7/8), 705–723.

Lambert, P. (2002). *The distribution and redistribution of income* (3rd ed.). Manchester University Press.

Leclair, M., & Petit, P. (2004). Présence syndicale dans les établissements: Quel effet sur les salaires masculins et féminins? Économie *et Statistique*, *371*, 23–47.

López-Mourelo, E., & Malo, M. A. (2015). El mercado de trabajo en España: El contexto europeo, los dos viejos desafíos y un nuevo problema. *Ekonomiaz*, *87*, 32–59.

Lucifora, C., & Origo, F. (2015). Performance-related pay and firm productivity: Evidence from a reform in the structure of collective bargaining. *Industrial and Labor Relations Review*, *68*, 1–27.

Milner, S., & Metcalf, D. (1994). *Spanish Pay setting institutions and performance outcomes*. Banco de España Documento de Trabajo No. 9420. Madrid: Banco de España.

Mueller, H. M., & Ouimet, P. O., & Simintzi, E. (2017). Wage inequality and firm growth. *The American Economic Review*, *107*(5), 379–83.

Mukhopadhaya, P. (2003). A generalized social welfare function and its disaggregation by components of income: The method and applications. In J. Bishop & Y. Amiel (Eds.), *Inequality, welfare and poverty: Theory and measurement* (Research on Economic Inequality, *9*, pp. 245–264). Emerald Publishing Limited.

OECD. (2018). *OECD employment outlook 2018*. OECD.

OECD. (2019). *Negotiating our way up*. OECD.

Plasman, R., Rusinek, M., & Rycx, F. (2007). Wages and the bargaining regime under multi-level bargaining: Belgium, Denmark and Spain. *European Journal of Industrial Relations*, *13*(2), 161–180.

Ramos, R., Sanromá, E., & Simón, H. (2022). Collective bargaining levels, employment and wage inequality in Spain. *Journal of Policy Modelling*, *44*, 375–395.

Reinecke, G., & Grimshaw, D. (2015). Labour market inequality between youth and adults: a special case? In *Labour markets, institutions and inequality*. Edward Elgar and ILO.

Rodríguez, J. G., & Salas, R. (2014a). The Gini coefficient: Majority voting and social welfare. *Journal of Economic Theory*, *152*, 214–223.

Rodríguez, J. G., & Salas, R. (2014b). Majority voting and Gini-based social welfare: testing the hypothesis of symmetry. *Applied Economic Letters*, *22*(8), 658–663.

Rycx, F. (2003). Industry wage differentials and the bargaining regime in a corporatist country. *International Journal of Manpower*, *24*(4), 347–366.

Sebastian, R. (2018). Explaining job polarisation in Spain from a task perspective. *SERIEs*, *9*(2), 215–248.

Sebastian, R., & Ulceluse, M. (2019). The effect of immigration on natives' task specialisation: The case of Germany. *International Journal of Manpower*, *40*(5), 939–957.

Sebastian, R. (2022). The labour market, income per capita and welfare in Europe: An overview of the last two decades. *Ekonomiaz*, *101*, 158–183.

Sen, A. K. (1974). Informational bases of alternative welfare approaches: Aggregation of income distribution. *Journal of Public Economics*, *3*(4), 387–403.

Visser, J. (2016). What happened to collective bargaining during the great recession? *IZA Journal of Labor Policy*, *5*(9), 1–35.

APPENDIX 1

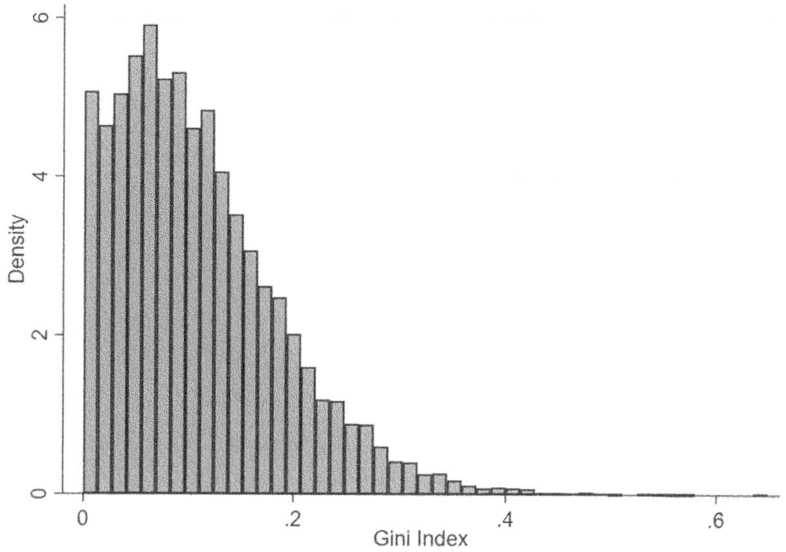

Fig. A1. Distribution of the Gini Index by Companies Between 2 and 49 Workers. *Source:* Authors' calculation from EES (2018).

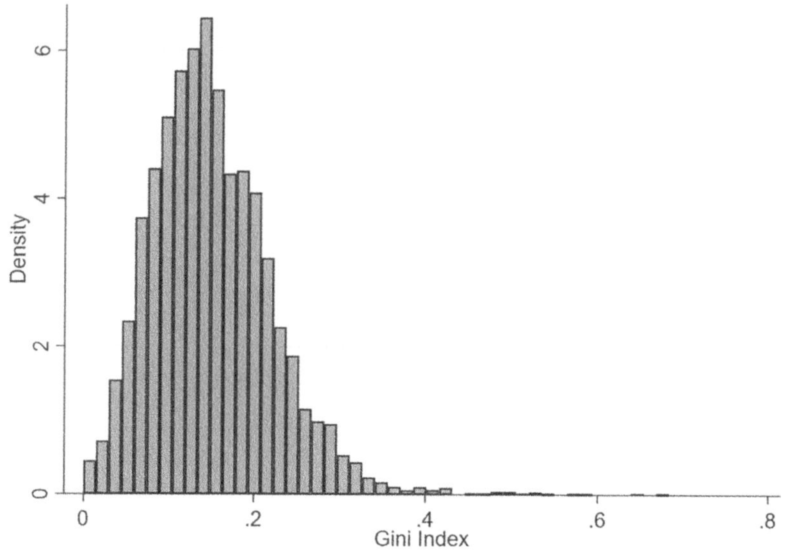

Fig. A2. Distribution of the Gini Index by Companies Between 50 and 200 Workers. *Source:* Authors' calculation from EES (2018).

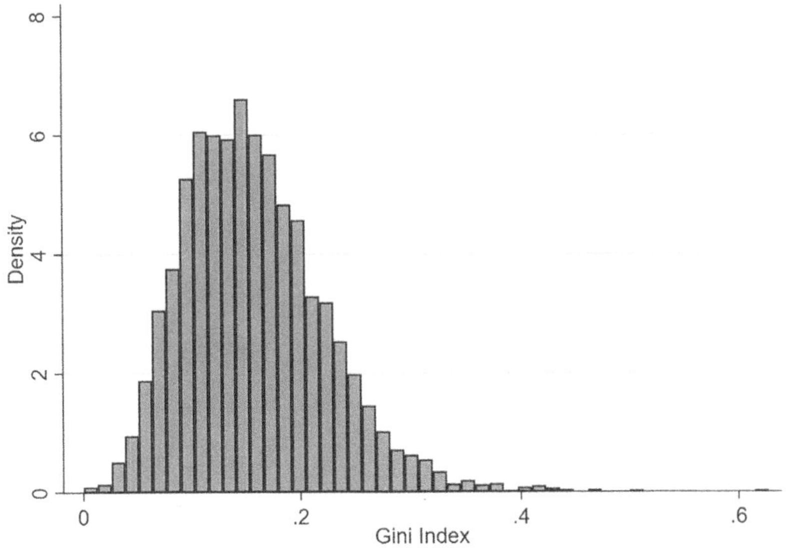

Fig. A3. Distribution of the Gini Index by Companies with More Than 200 Workers. *Source:* Authors' calculation from EES (2018).

APPENDIX 2

Table B1. Variable Definitions.

Dependent variable	
Intra-firm Gini index	Gini index calculated using the salaries of the company's employees. Gini index is a measure of distribution inequality, commonly used to compare income or wealth inequality within a population. A Gini index of 0 represents perfect equality, where everyone has the same income, while a Gini index of 1 represents perfect inequality.
Intra-firm mean wage	Calculated as the average wage paid to employees within a single firm. This statistic provides insight into the general level of compensation offered by the company to its workforce.
Intra-firm welfare	The balance between efficiency, represented by the average salary, and equity, which refers to the inequality among wages within a firm. This definition emphasizes that intra-firm welfare is influenced by how these two factors interact and impact the overall well-being of employees.
Independent variable	
Collective Bargaining Agreements (CBAs)	CBAs binary variable taking the value 0 for firm-level and work centre level agreement, and 1 for national, subnational and sectoral agreement.
Individual characteristics	
Sex	Sex binary variable taking value 0 for men and 1 for women.
Age	Variable that represents the number of years since an individual's birth.
Nationality	Nationality binary variable taking value 0 for Spanish, and 1 for Foreign.
Education	Education categorical variable taking value 1 for elementary education (taken as a reference in the models), 2 for basic education, 3 for high education.
Tenure	Variable that measures the duration of an employee's experience in months at a company. It quantifies the length of time an individual has been employed by the same employer, indicating their stability and potentially their seniority within the organization.
Contract	Contract binary variable taking value 0 for indefinite, and 1 for temporary.
Part-time	Part-time binary variable taking value 0 for full-time, and 1 for part-time.
Occupation	Occupation categorical variable taking value 1 for high-skill white-collar, 2 for low-skill white-collar, 3 high-skill blue-collar, and 4 for low-skill blue-collar (taken as a reference in the models).
Supervisor	A binary variable indicating whether an employee has a supervisor. It is coded as 1 if the employee has a supervisor and 0 if the employee does not have a supervisor.
Firm Characteristics	
Activity	Activity categorical variable taking value 1 for industry (taken as a reference in the models), 2 for construction, and 3 for services.
Property	Property binary variable taking value 0 for private and 1 for public.
Type of market	Type of market categorical variable taking value 1 local or regional market (taken as a reference in the models), 2 for national market, 3 for international market.
Type of size firm	Type of market categorical variable taking value 1 for 'between 2 and 49 workers' (taken as a reference in the models), 2 'between 50 and 199 workers', and 3 'for more than 200 workers'.

Source: Authors' elaboration.

CHAPTER 5

CHOOSING A JOB: WHO INFLUENCES YOU THE MOST, PARENTS OR FRIENDS?

Pablo De la Vega Suárez[a], Juan Prieto-Rodriguez[b] and Juan Gabriel Rodríguez[c]

[a]*Next Education, Madrid, Spain*
[b]*Universidad de Oviedo, Oviedo, Spain*
[c]*Universidad Complutense de Madrid, Madrid, Spain*

ABSTRACT

This chapter examines the relative influence of parents (vertical channel) and friends (horizontal channel) when deciding between employment in the public or private sector. Using a novel database and applying network analysis, the influence of peers is first measured. Next, the peer effect is compared with the impact of parental background on individual preferences. For the private sector, findings indicate that the influence (marginal effect) of friends is greater than that of parents. The opposite is observed for the public sector. However, in the case of public sector employment, the overall effect of the horizontal channel may surpass the vertical channel, as individuals typically have two parents but may have many friends. Additionally, it is found that both parents and friends exert a greater influence on women than on men.

Keywords: Social network; intergenerational transmission; private sector job; public sector job; gender; peer's effect

Opportunity, Mobility and Inequality
Research on Economic Inequality, Volume 31, 121–152

Published under exclusive licence by Emerald Publishing Limited
ISSN: 1049-2585/doi:10.1108/S1049-258520250000031006

1. INTRODUCTION

The occupational choice of an individual is a fundamental decision that affects her entire life. Another important decision is the choice between working for the public or for the private sector, especially for people living in countries where public examination is a necessary step to work in the public sector. Despite this importance, the dynamics choosing to seek a public or private sector job are, however, largely unknown. Thus, the literature on this issue is scarce and has mainly focused on the motivational bases of public service (Perry et al., 2010). Perry (1997) studied the socialization context on the formation of the Public Service Motivation, however, among other things, we still do not know who exerts a higher influence on the individual's propensity to work in the public or private sector, parents or friends. In this chapter, we analyze whether the self-declared willingness to work in the public or private sectors is linked to a larger extent to the family (vertical channel) or to the peers (horizontal channel).

From the inequality-of-opportunity literature, we know that the main channels through which parents can affect the income earning capacity of their children are: wealth; provision of social connections which are relevant in the labour market; formation of skills in children, through family culture and investment; genetic transmission; and instillation of preferences and aspirations (Dardanoni et al., 2006). Given these factors and the restrictions imposed by data availability, this literature has widely used the level of parental education or occupational status as a proxy for the first three factors (Ferreira et al., 2011; Marrero & Rodríguez, 2012; Rodríguez, 2008; Roemer et al., 2003), and the ethnic group or race as a direct measure of the fourth factor (Marrero & Rodríguez, 2011). However, little has been done about the last one (Alesina & Giuliano, 2010). For example, we know that low risk aversion encourages the choice for entrepreneurship (Cramer et al., 2002), but we do not know how this trait is transmitted vertically.

In addition to the traditional influential factor, the family, the social network of friends is also important in determining individuals' preferences and aspirations. Recent developments in the technology of interpersonal communications (cell phones and applications like WhatsApp, Facebook, Instagram, etc.) and new lifestyles (provoked by single-parent families and families where both parents work out of the house) have changed the share of time that children expend with their parents. As a result, peers (horizontal channel) could be more influential now. In fact, it has been found that social networks can reduce intergenerational persistence (Bervoets & Zenou, 2017). The peer effect (and social network) have been used to better understand the level of productivity at work (Mas & Moretti, 2009), alcohol use (Balsa et al., 2018), and, fundamentally, educational performance(Brunello et al., 2010; Calvó-Armengol et al., 2009), finding in general that there is a positive effect of peers on the individual. However, as far as we are aware, the influence of the social network on occupational choice has not yet been explored.

To fill this gap, we study the simultaneous influence that parents and friends have on the willingness to work in the public and private sectors.

Bisin and Verdier (2001) were the first to develop a model where the transmission of cultural traits could be vertical (from the parents) and horizontal (from the social network). Following this chapter, researchers tried later to model this phenomenon by including continuous traits (Cheung & Wu, 2018) and the social network structure (Buechel et al., 2014).[1] Unfortunately, a similar analysis has not been developed for the occupational choice. Existing studies on this topic have only focused on vertical transmission. For instance, Aina and Nicoletti (2018) have analyzed the intergenerational transmission of liberal professions and Fairlie and Robb (2007) have studied the intergenerational transmission of small business ownership.

In our attempt to study simultaneously both parents' and friends' influence, we first create a new database elaborated from a survey formed by 24 questions asking for individual socio-economic characteristics, parental background and participants' social networks. For parental background, we use the education level and occupation of both the father and the mother. Later, based on an open-ended survey methodology and techniques from the social networks' analysis, we calculate two potential network effects. First, the *pure peer effect* based on a matrix of influences that collects the direct and indirect influences between peers (nodes of the network). Second, the *network-structure effect*, i.e. the effect due to the way peers are distributed in the network. At last, we estimate a model to measure which channel of transmission (parents or friends) has a major impact on individual's occupational choice.

By comparing the relative marginal effect of both channels, friends seem to be more important than parents for choosing the private sector. On the contrary, for the public sector, the intergenerational mechanism of transmission shows a larger impact, i.e. the effect exerted by parents is larger than the one exerted by friends. Nonetheless, the horizontal channel has the potential to counterbalance the vertical channel effect if a sufficiently large number of friends have a different opinion than the parents.

In addition, we analyze if there are differences between men and women in the transmission of preferences about the working sector. The literature has found that the opinion of parents about the woman's role in society affects daughters' decisions about work (Farré & Vella, 2013; Fernandez et al., 2004). However, it is not clear yet if this influence is larger than the one from peers. To highlight this, we estimate our model separately for men and women. We observe that women are more influenced by parents and friends than men. In particular, daughters are influenced by their mothers working in the public sector in a positive and significant way, while sons are not influenced by any of their parents. With respect to the horizontal channel, peers affect women at a higher degree.

The chapter is structured as follows. In the next section, we explain the network methodology that is used to measure the peer effect. In Section 3, we comment on the construction of our database and the main variables employed in the analysis. Section 4 presents the model. In Section 5, we show the main findings for the whole sample and by gender. Finally, Section 6 provides some concluding remarks.

2. MEASURING THE PEER EFFECT: THE ROLE OF THE SOCIAL NETWORK

2.1. Background

Traditionally, the study of economics has orbited around the concept of the 'economic agent,' either the individual or the firm. However, as important as the economic agents themselves, is the relationship among them. Here is where the analysis of networks becomes important, because there is always a web where the economic agent takes position and creates links with others from who she is influenced and to whom she affects.

Network analysis is a multidisciplinary field that has been applied in nearly all branches of knowledge. In economics, it has been recently used in several fields, such as game theory (Slikker & Nouweland, 2001), altruism (Leider et al., 2009), accessibility (Fu et al., 2016), and the market of art (Yogev & Grund, 2012). In labour economics, the selection problem (Greenwalds, 1986; Weiss, 1981) leads companies to use informal channels to hire people (Shapiro & Stiglitz, 1984). In this respect, Granovetter (1995) points out that 69% of workers in his sample had gotten their jobs through a friend. Moreover, there are models that analyze the positive effect of social networks on employment status (Calvó-Armengol, 2004; Glitz, 2017) and wages (Arrow & Borzekowski, 2004; Calvó-Armengol & Jackson, 2004; Fontaine, 2008; Montgomery, 1991). From an empirical perspective, there is a wide literature about the effect of social networks on employment and wages (Gee et al., 2017; Goel & Lang, 2019; Kramarz & Skans, 2014; Saygin et al., 2019). Results show that the impact of the network size on employment status is positive, although the effect of the network on wages is controversial.[2]

One promising element of the network analysis is the measurement of the *peer effect*, i.e. the influence that people receive from their equals. This influence, the horizontal transmission channel, is actually a composite measure of two elements, the *pure-peer effect* and the *network effect*, where the latter refers to the structure of the network and how the information circulates through it. Because there is no hierarchy in friends' networks, the structure of the network can be a useful tool for measuring the overall peer effect. As Halliday and Kwak (2012) have highlighted, the use of social networks methodologies avoids the traditional underestimation of the total peer effect.

2.2. Methodology

Let us begin with the *pure peer effect*. First, we need to measure the influence of peers on individual i. The literature on social networks offers some measures that do this, being the one proposed by Bonacich (1987) the most complete of all since it allows the use of different weights to measure the indirect effect of the network.[3] Following this proposal, we calculate the matrix of perceived relationships between individuals (nodes) i and j. Unfortunately, individuals do not usually perceive their relationships in the same way, so we are forced to calculate instead the symmetrized matrix of the network, A, by imposing that the relationship between individuals i and j is equal to the maximum perceived value between them. This influence matrix represents, however, only the direct relationship between nodes i and j. In addition, we should consider the indirect paths that join any pair of nodes (for example, through a common friend).

Because each cell ij in a squared matrix represents the interaction between nodes i and j in a path of size two, Bonacich (1987) proposes the estimation of the following relationship matrix:

$$\boldsymbol{c} = (\boldsymbol{I} - \beta \boldsymbol{A})^{-1} - \boldsymbol{I}, \tag{1}$$

where $\boldsymbol{I}$ is the identity matrix and β is a parameter. The appealing property of this expression is that when the absolute value of β is lower than the largest eigenvalue of $\boldsymbol{A}$, the influence matrix in (1), $\boldsymbol{c}$, converges to the following infinite sum:

$$\boldsymbol{c} = \sum_{k=1}^{\infty} \beta^{k-1} \boldsymbol{A}^k = \left(\boldsymbol{A} + \beta \boldsymbol{A}^2 + \beta^2 \boldsymbol{A}^3 + \ldots\right) \tag{2}$$

Each cell ij of the matrix $\boldsymbol{c}$ captures the total influence (the direct plus the indirect effects) of node i on node j. To guarantee that the convergence condition for equation (2) is fulfilled, we follow the literature (Bonacich, 1987; Borgatti et al., 2002) and consider that the indirect paths are weighted by $\beta = 0.995$/largest eigenvalue of $\boldsymbol{A}$.

Once we have calculated the influence matrix $\boldsymbol{c}$, we construct two dummy variables which capture the individual willingness to work in the public and the private sectors. The size of the influence matrix $\boldsymbol{c}$ is $N \times N$ (where N is the number of individuals) and the two dummy variables are $N \times 1$ vectors. Consequently, the result of multiplying the influence matrix by each of the two vectors gives a new vector of size $N \times 1$ where each element measures the total influence over individual i of all the members of the network who want to work in the public sector (*Public_peers*) or the private sector (*Private_peers*).

We are aware of the endogeneity problem that this approach might have. We are assuming that the effect is always from the peers to the individual, when in fact, the individual is also influencing the peers. This can be a problem because observations are not statistically independent (if they were, the network analysis would make no sense!). However, the literature has shown that the reflection problem stated in Manski (1993) when estimating the peers' effect can be solved with network data (Bramoullé et al., 2009; Calvó-Armengol et al., 2009). Following Bramoullé et al. (2009), the identification of social effects is guaranteed when $\boldsymbol{I}$, $\boldsymbol{A}$ and $\boldsymbol{A}^2$ are linearly independent, and this condition is fulfilled when there are no individuals isolated in the network, which is the case in our dataset.

An additional related problem is the simultaneity of the mutual influence. To check that the observed influence of peers is not due to the simultaneity of the mutual influence, we reformulate the peer effect variable. Instead of multiplying the influence matrix $\boldsymbol{c}$ by the declared willingness to work in each sector, we multiply it by the observed job sector of the parents of each peer. The problem of simultaneity is possible between peers, but it is impossible that parents' decision about their type of occupation is influenced by peers. As stated in Appendix 2, the results of this analysis are consistent with the main results of the chapter.

Another issue that may be affecting our results is a selection bias in our dataset. Given that we use a sample of students, it exists the possibility that prior conditions might have affected the degree selection and, therefore, our results. In order to control for this issue, we have made a robustness check. Basically, we analyzed if parents' characteristics are conditioning individual degree selection and if that is affecting their willingness to work for a certain sector. These robustness check results are consisting with the ones presented in the main document, which indicates that our model is not affected by a selection bias. These results and a further explanation are presented in Appendix 3.

To measure the network effect, we use the variable *Hierarchy*, that measures how constrained is the network for individual *i*, i.e. how costly is for node *i* to get the information that circulates through the network. To calculate this variable, we use the following two equations (Burt, 2004):

$$C_{ij} = \left(p_{ij} + \sum\nolimits_q p_{iq} p_{qj}\right)^2 \quad (3)$$

$$c_i = \sum\nolimits_j c_{ij} \quad (4)$$

where p_{ij} is the strength of the relationship between individuals *i* and *j*. The strength is measured by the time spent between individuals *i* and *j*. If individual *i* wants to be efficient in terms of networking, she will share time with people that have no friends in common ($p_{qj} = 0$). In this manner, she will have more opportunities to make new friends because her network is loose. On the contrary, if the individual spends her time with people who are already friends with each other, her network will be constrained and the value of *Hierarchy* will be higher.

As a reminder, it is important to note that the pure peer effect variables (*Public peers* and *Private peers*) and the network-structure variable (*Hierarchy*) come from the same network matrix but capture different aspects of it. If an individual has three friends who are only friends between them and neither of them has declared a preferred sector, she will not receive any influence from her peers. However, her *Hierarchy* value will be high because her network structure is quite restricted.

3. A NEW DATABASE

When studying network effects, one of the worst problems that scholars typically have to face is the lack of network data. To solve this problem, they usually create a new database, and this is also our case. To this end, we created a survey formed by 24 questions about individual socioeconomic characteristics, parental background and participants' social networks.[4] The data collection was done face-to-face. We personally went from class to class asking students in the final year of their degree to answer the questions of the survey. We had a total of 904 respondents from 22 classes, one class per degree, and 2 universities (Universidad de Oviedo and Universidad Complutense de Madrid, both in Spain). Both universities are public founded, but one is located in a small city (Oviedo) where the private job opportunities are scarce, whilst the Universidad Complutense is the largest university in Spain, located at the biggest city. In this manner, we aimed to collect information from different backgrounds.

We decided to survey just students in the final year of their degree for two reasons. First, the social networks of these students are expected to be more developed. Second, these students will enter into the labor market soon and should have a clear idea regarding the kind of job they would like to have.

The social network was created by using an open-ended survey methodology. This method asks each student to declare a maximum of 5 people from their class with whom they had the best relationship, without giving to them any list of classmates. We decided to limit the number of declared friends to 5 to force the students to declare their 'real' friends. Later, when calculating the symmetrized matrix, very popular individuals were assigned more than 5 friends, given the fact that more people than 5 cite them as their friends. The final network is formed by 904 nodes (students) and 3,936 links among them. In addition, the students were asked to assess the strength of their link with peers in four different ways: the number of times per week spent with a friend physically outside the university; the number of times per week spent with a friend through online social networks (Facebook, Instagram, WhatsApp, etc.); if they had gone to the same high school; and if their parents know each other. The strength of the link was ranged from 1 (weak relationship) to 7 (strong relationship).

We collected data about individual characteristics like age, gender, average marks, type of school (private or public), work experience, and degree (science, health, social science, engineering); parental background (the education and occupation of the mother and father); and job sector preferences (public or private sector). The descriptive statistics and a full explanation of these variables is given in the following section.

In addition to the usual descriptive statistics of the variables used in the model, we include some descriptive information about the network (see Table 1). *Density* measures the number of links in the network divided by the total number of possible ones. *Components* is the number of groups of people interconnected, while the *Component Ratio* is the number of components divided by the number of nodes minus 1. The number of components is not large, which indicates that even inside of some classrooms there are disconnected groups of people. *Fragmentation* measures the proportion of pairs that are unreachable, and *Connectedness* is defined

Table 1. The Structure of the Network.

Density	0.005
Components	67
Component Ratio	0.073
Fragmentation	0.954
Connectedness	0.046
Closure	0.546
Average Distance	4.525
SD Distance	2.508
Diameter	16
Average Degree	4.137
H Index	9

as 1 minus the fragmentation value. According to these two variables the network is highly disconnected. This result was expected because our network is formed by groups of people in different degrees without direct connection between them.

There is a transitive triple when if we have three nodes, A, B and C, where A is linked to B and B is linked to C, it is expected that A is linked to C (Granovetter, 1973). On the other hand, a path of size two is formed by two nodes that are connected through an intermediate one. Then, *Closure* is defined as the ratio between the number of transitive triples and the number of paths of size two. This variable measures the proportion of individuals whose friends are also friends among them in comparison with the proportion of individuals whose friends do not know each other. It proxies the capacity of information to reach other areas of the network. In our case, the relative high value of this variable shows a large transitivity of information within small groups. The *Average distance* is the average size of paths in the network and *SD Distance* is its standard deviation. *Diameter* is the maximum size of paths in the network. These measures give us another vision of the network, even if groups are disconnected, individuals inside them are interconnected. The *Average Degree* defines the average number of friends declared by students, which was limited to 5 in the survey. Finally, The *H Index* is the maximum value of H such that a given individual is friend of H individuals that have each been cited as a friend at least H times.[5]

We represent our network in Fig. 1, where each point is an individual linked to her self-declared friends by lines and each shape represents a different class

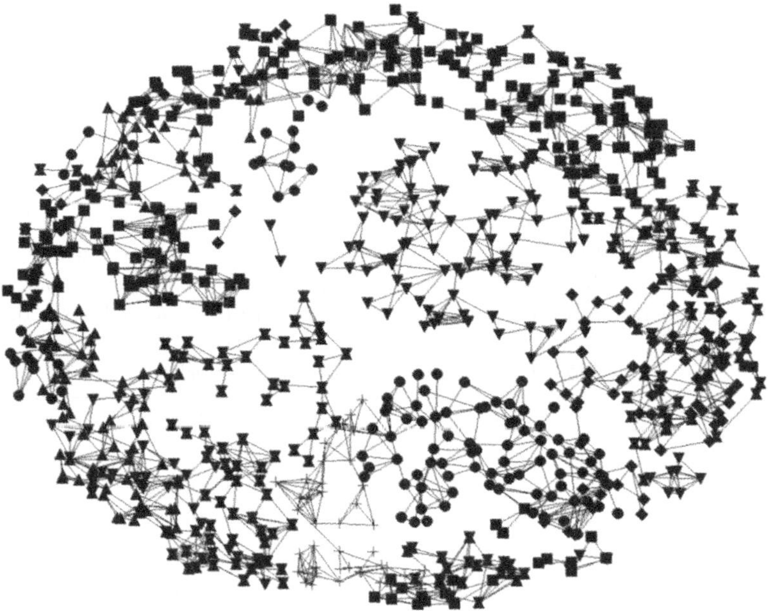

Fig. 1. The Structure of the Network. *Notes*: Each shape represents a different degree. Distances in the graph do not reflect the closeness of individuals in reality.

(degree). The visualization of the network shows some of its properties. First, the disconnection between clusters: each degree is an independent component so there are no links between nodes belonging to different degrees. Second, the effect of a given position in the cluster depends on the structure of the network since some degrees have a more centralized structure (i.e. the triangles in the middle-left) than others (i.e. the circles in the middle-right).

4. EMPIRICAL MODEL

To understand the factors that influence the individual choice between a private and a public sector job we estimate the following probit for each sector:

$$\Pr(LaborSector) = f(Network, Parents, Personal, Degree).$$

For the *Public Sector*, we use the self-declared decisions of working for the public sector as a civil servant. For the *Private Sector*, we use the self-declared decisions of working for the private sector either as employee or entrepreneur. Students were not forced to answer this question,[6] so we find individuals whose response is zero for both variables. As a result, our findings will be no symmetric for both types of jobs because the decisions to work for the public and private sectors do not cover the whole space of probability.[7]

The explanatory variables in our model are grouped as follows:

- *Network*: this group of variables reflects the network's characteristics of each individual and will control for the horizontal transmission channel. Here, we include three variables: *Public_peers, Private_peers* and *Hierarchy*. The first two variables measure the peer effect, with *Public_peers* being the variable that considers the friends' choice to be a public servant, and *Private_peers* being the variable that accounts for the peer influence to work in the private sector. The variable of *Hierarchy* reflects the individual's network structure by measuring her constrain, i.e. how easily a person can go outside her network and meet new people. The precise formulation of these variables is given in the section Network Methodology.
- *Parents*: This set of variables control for the vertical transmission channel. We include the job sector (public or private) and schooling years of parents. Parents' job sector is intended to control for the information that parents transmit to their children, encouraging or discouraging them to work in the same sector. This variable (*Parents_public/private*) is a dummy that takes value one when at least one parent works in the considered sector. *Years of Education* accounts for parental human capital. The prefix, F or M, accounts for the father or the mother. This variable is calculated from the level of studies achieved by the parents of the individual.
- *Personal*: This group represents the set of individual characteristics. Here we include *gender*, *Average_mark* (the average grade from 0 to 10 achieved in the university) and *Squared Average mark*. In addition, we include a dummy

Table 2. Variables of the Questionnaire.

	Mean	Sd	Min	Max
Public Sector	0.421	0.494	0	1
Private Sector	0.377	0.485	0	1
Public Peers	1.451	1.336	0	6.041
Private Peers	1.191	1.152	0	5.037
Hierarchy	0.219	0.275	0	1
Parents Public	0.342	0.475	0	1
Parents Private	0.633	0.482	0	1
F_Years of Education	12.59	4.432	0	20
M_Years of Education	13.22	3.951	0	20
Age	22.72	3.469	20	58
Gender	0.407	0.492	0	1
Average mark	6.732	1.454	0	9.800
Squared average mark	47.35	14.52	0	96.04
Non public school	0.313	0.464	0	1
Work experience	0.489	0.502	0	2
Science	0.175	0.380	0	1
Health	0.238	0.426	0	1
Social science	0.378	0.485	0	1
Engineering	0.0664	0.249	0	1
Madrid	0.0973	0.297	0	1

variable for work experience (*Work_exp*) which takes value 1 if the individual has worked previously, and *non_public* which is a dummy variable that takes value 1 if the individual has attended a non-public school.[8]

- *Degree*: This group of variables represents the characteristics of the individual's degree. We include four dummy variables to control for the unobserved specific attributes of each field: *Eng* (Engineering), *Science*, Social (Social Science) and *Health* (Health Sciences). In addition, we include a dummy variable, *Madrid*, to control for the students who belong to Universidad Complutense de Madrid.

Table 2 depicts the descriptive statistics of some of the variables collected in the data.

5. RESULTS

Table 3 provides the findings for the two probit models. First, there is a positive and significant effect of *Public peers* and *Hierarchy* on the decision to work for the public sector. For the private sector, only *Private peers* is positive and significant. Thus, the horizontal transmission channel is relevant for both sectors, although there are no significant cross effects between sectors. Despite our expectations, a negative peer effect on the self-declared willingness to work in the public sector from friends willing to work in the private sector, and vice versa, was not found.

Moreover, the structure of the network does not affect both decisions equally because a more hierarchical individual's network only increases the willingness to be a public servant. In a typical public sector job, network skills are not important for outcomes, but they are relevant to climb the career ladder in the private sector (Shipilov et al., 2007). Therefore, the positive effect of *hierarchy* for the public

Table 3. Probit Results for the Public and Private Sectors.

Variables	Public Sector	Private Sector
Peers_public	0.297***	−0.036
	(0.038)	(0.039)
Peers_private	−0.0042	0.192***
	(0.043)	(0.043)
Hierarchy	0.593***	0.243
	(0.178)	(0.177)
Parents_public	0.348***	−0.151
	(0.110)	(0.112)
Parents_private	−0.073	0.087
	(0.102)	(0.104)
M_Years of Education	−0.012	−0.017
	(0.014)	(0.014)
F_Years of Education	−0.012	0.003
	(0.012)	(0.012)
Average Mark	−0.334***	0.251***
	(0.087)	(0.084)
Average Mark_sq	0.043***	−0.033***
	(0.009)	(0.008)
Gender	−0.001	0.195**
	(0.094)	(0.094)
Non_public school	−0.060	0.515***
	(0.100)	(0.099)
Work experience	−0.215**	0.072
	(0.091)	(0.092)
Engineering	−1.236***	0.273
	(0.255)	(0.190)
Science	−0.242*	0.059
	(0.131)	(0.131)
Social	−0.193*	−0.446***
	(0.107)	(0.110)
Madrid	−0.417***	0.763***
	(0.160)	(0.159)
Constant	0.039	−0.769**
	(0.345)	(0.365)
Wald chi2	155.74***	153.42***
Log-pseudolikelihood	−524.258	−515.924
AIC	1083.056	1065.849
BIC	1164.753	1147.546

Notes: Standard error in parentheses: ***$p < 0.01$, **$p < 0.05$, *$p < 0.1$.

sector means that people who are worse in networking have a higher probability of willing to be a civil servant.

Parents public and *Parents private* represent the transmission of traits from parents to children. We find that there is a positive and significant effect of parents on children's declared preferences for future jobs only for the public sector. The lack of any effect from parental education is surprising. It seems that parental human capital does not influence the child's inclination in favor of either the public or the private sector.[9]

For the set of individual characteristics, we find another important difference among both sectors. In both cases, there is a non-linear effect, although the relationship is concave for the private sector while it is convex for the public one. This result implies that the best students tend to prefer the public sector to the private one. The best students seem to care more about the higher average earning of the public sector than the potential higher salaries existing in the private sector, i.e. better students have a higher risk aversion. This result is consistent with the previous literature where studies have shown that there is a positive relationship between risk aversion and the decision to work for the public sector (Bellante & Link, 1981; Pfeifer, 2010). Also, this literature has found that the motivation for working in the public sector is more related with non-monetary factors like work-life balance (Buelens & Van den Broeck, 2007; Rashid & Rashid, 2012).

The positive and significant effect of *non_public school* for the private sector shows that students receiving private and concerted education exhibit a higher probability of willing to work for the private sector. The *work exp* variable has a negative effect for the public sector which indicates that having job experience decreases the probability of willing to work for the public sector, most probably because this early work experience took place in the private sector. *Gender* shows a positive effect for the private sector, i.e. men display a higher probability of working in the private sector.

The results for the student's degree are as expected. Thus, compared with health, other fields exhibit a lower probability of willing to work for the public sector.[10] The negative coefficient of *Social* for the private and public sectors may be explained by the fact that students in Social Sciences have large opportunities to work in both sectors so preferences are highly dispersed. Unsurprisingly, the result for *Madrid* is negative for the public sector and positive for the private one. Madrid is the capital of Spain, while Asturias is a small region where the opportunities to work in the private sector are significantly fewer.

5.1. Marginal Effects: Parents Versus Friends

The results introduced in the previous section indicate the direction of the effects, but the main motivation of this chapter is to disentangle which channel of transmission have a major impact on the individual's declared choice. While there is no conflict between the two channels for the private sector since only peers' preferences are significant, both channels are positive and significant for the public sector. Which is the most important transmission channel? To assess this issue, we first analyze the relative marginal effect of the variables representing the horizontal and vertical transmission channels. Following Cameron and Trivedi (2005), the ratio between the two marginal effects (*Mg*) is:

$$\frac{Mg_i}{Mg_j} = \frac{\beta_i}{\beta_j}, \tag{5}$$

where β_i and β_j are the estimated coefficients. In our case, the relative marginal effect of the vertical channel (coefficient of *Parents public*) over the horizontal channel (coefficient of Peers *public*) is 1.17. At first glance, the vertical channel appears to dominate the horizontal channel.

For robustness, we carry out three additional exercises. First, we calculate the marginal effect of each channel at different points of the *Peers_public* distribution (from those individuals with no friends willing to work in the public sector to those individuals with all friends willing to work in the public sector). Fig. 2 represent the marginal effects for *Peers_public* and *Parents_public* as the peer effect increases. The vertical channel shows a larger impact than the horizontal one for the entire distribution of the peer effect variable, being the difference between both channels almost the same across the whole distribution. Thus, having a parent working for the public sector increases the probability of willing to be a civil servant more than having a friend who wants to be a civil servant.

Second, we calculate the marginal effects of the variable *Peers_public* conditional on having a parent who is civil servant (Fig. 3). For people with low peer

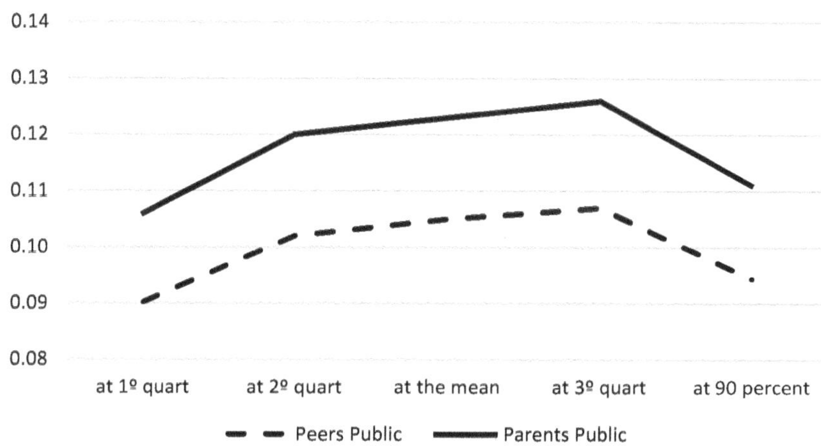

Fig. 2. Marginal Peer's and Parents' Effects.

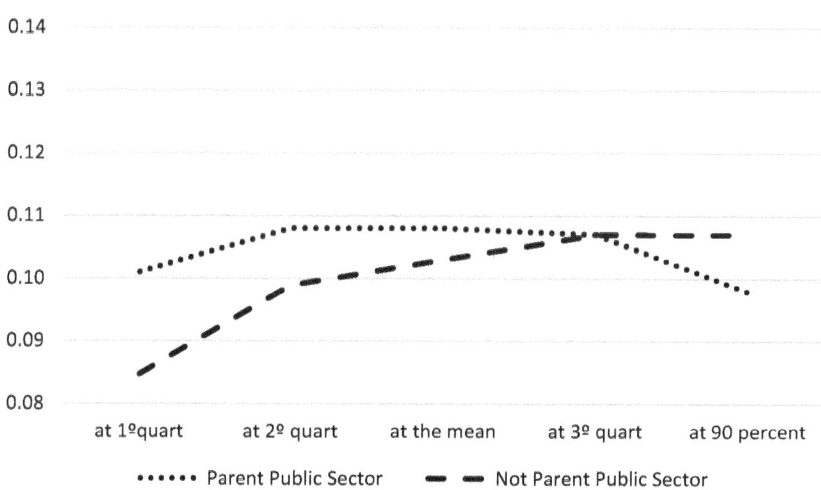

Fig. 3. Peers Public Marginal Effects Conditional on the Parental Job.

influence (first quartiles of the distribution), having a parent working in the public sector reinforces the effect of the horizontal channel. At the other tail of the peer distribution (those who have many friends who want to be a civil servant), having a parent working in the public sector diminish the effect of the horizontal channel. It seems that individuals reduce their preference for an option when almost everybody around (friends and parents) point to the same direction.

Thus far, we have observed that the vertical channel has a larger effect than the horizontal one. However, individuals have only two parents, while they can have many friends. Consequently, we have not fully answered yet the question, who influences you more? For this task, we assess the effect of increasing the peer influence. First, we multiply the influence matrix by a vector of dummies that takes value 1 when the individual did not have a clear idea about the sector she wants to work because she did not answer this question for the survey (*peers_doubt*).[11] Thus, this new variable will account for the social influence from individuals who did not know which sector they prefer. Then, this variable is used to estimate the new peer effect if some undecided friends (50%, 75% and 90%) change their mind and show a clear will to work in a given sector. So, we are putting together the influence from *public_peers* (already included in the model) and the influence from *peers_doubt*. In Table 4, we present the variation of the marginal peer effect for an individual who was receiving the mean influence from the *Peers_public* or *Peers_private* and is now also receiving the influence of the *peers_doubt* (for three different proportions).

So, this result can be read as: when half of your peers, who did not decide a sector, choose to work for the public sector the marginal effect of the horizontal channel is increased by 0.8. When the share of peers who 'change their mind' increase to 90% of them, this marginal effect gets to more than 0.3, which is higher than the marginal effect from the vertical channel.

Despite that the vertical channel has a larger marginal effect than the horizontal channel, the latter has the potential to be more important than the former because the change in the decision of an average undecided friend has a significant positive effect on the horizontal channel. People usually have more than two friends, therefore, even if the influence of the closest friend is smaller than the one of parents, the total influence from friends can still be greater than parents'.

Table 4. Marginal Peer Effects When Undecided Friends Change Their Opinion.

	From doubt to willing to work at the Public Sector	From doubt to willing to work at the Private Sector
at mean	0.105***	0.071***
	(0.016)	(0.014)
at mean + 50% of peers in doubt	+0.080***	+0.049***
	(0.019)	(0.017)
at mean + 75% of peers in doubt	+0.108***	+0.066***
	(0.021)	(0.0195)
at mean + 90% of peers in doubt	+0.214***	+0.135***
	(0.030)	(0.033)

Notes: Standard error in parentheses: ***$p < 0.01$, **$p < 0.05$, *$p < 0.1$.

6. TRANSMISSION CHANNELS BY GENDER

Now, we test if there are gender differences in the transmission of traits. For this task, we replicate our estimations for men and women (see Table 5). First, similarly to the general model, we do not find any pattern in the vertical transmission of preferences for the private sector. However, the vertical transmission of

Table 5. Results by Gender.

	Public Sector		Private Sector	
	Women	Men	Women	Men
Peers_public	0.339***	0.261***	−0.013	−0.078
	(0.048)	(0.064)	(0.05)	(0.063)
Peers_private	0.024	−0.012	0.202***	0.170**
	(0.056)	(0.069)	(0.057)	(0.067)
Hierarchy	0.673***	0.642**	0.527	−0.259
	(0.235)	(0.286)	(0.236)	(0.281)
Mother_public	0.448**	0.202	−0.241	−0.067
	(0.179)	(0.210)	(0.187)	(0.206)
Father_public	−0.048	0.295	0.150	−0.006
	(0.192)	(0.227)	(0.197)	(0.223)
Mother_private	−0.041	0.013	0.074	−0.022
	(0.138)	(0.174)	(0.141)	(0.167)
Father_private	−0.016	−0.281	−0.001	0.221
	(0.144)	(0.176)	(0.147)	(0.174)
Average mark	−0.473***	−0.144	0.391***	0.065
	(0.121)	(0.145)	(0.119)	(0.138)
Average mark_sq	0.052***	0.028*	−0.041***	−0.017
	(0.012)	(0.014)	(0.01)	(0.014)
M_Years of Education	−0.02	−0.004	−0.028	−0.005
	(0.019)	(0.022)	(0.02)	(0.022)
F_Years of Education	0.015	−0.046**	−0.002	0.003
	(0.017)	(0.019)	(0.017)	(0.019)
Non_public school	−0.165	0.089	0.531***	0.521***
	(0.134)	(0.159)	(0.133)	(0.155)
Work experience	−0.112	−0.392***	−0.01	0.172
	(0.118)	(0.149)	(0.123)	(0.145)
Engineering	−1.299***	−1.133***	0.278	0.181
	(0.418)	(0.342)	(0.315)	(0.253)
Science	−0.539***	0.165	0.213	−0.196
	(0.180)	(0.203)	(0.179)	(0.2)
Social	−0.379***	0.135	−0.272*	−0.704***
	(0.139)	(0.177)	(0.143)	(0.178)
Madrid	−0.387*	−0.534**	0.903***	0.707***
	(0.226)	(0.238)	(0.23)	(0.231)
Constant	0.256	−0.229	−1.254**	0.005
	(0.458)	(0.578)	(0.539)	(0.553)
N	535	368	535	368
Wald chi2	100.13	78.41***	90.74***	65.92***
Log-pseudolikelihood	−306.399	−204.097	−289.154	−217.466
AIC	648.799	444.195	614.308	470.932
BIC	725.880	514.540	691.389	541.277

Note: Standard error in parentheses: ***$p < 0.01$, **$p < 0.05$, *$p < 0.1$.

Table 6. Marginal Peers' Effect.

	Public Sector		Private Sector	
	Women	Men	Women	Men
Peers_public	0.110***	0.081***	−0.004	−0.026
	(0.014)	(0.019)	(0.015)	(0.021)
Peers_private	0.007	−0.003	0.061***	0.057***
	(0.018)	(0.022)	(0.017)	(0.022)

Notes: Standard error in parentheses: ***$p < 0.01$, **$p < 0.05$, *$p < 0.1$.

preferences for the public sector that we obtained in the general model is associated only to the influence that daughters receive from their mothers. Here, the effect of gender on the vertical channel is important because sons are not significantly influenced by none of their parents while daughters experience a big influence from their mothers to work in the public sector. This result is consistent with previous literature that shows that the effect on the intergenerational transmission of cultural traits is greater from mother to daughter (Alan et al., 2017).

Despite that the influence of parents' occupation is not important for men, there is a negative effect of father's education on sons' preferences for the public sector, i.e. men with a highly educated father exhibit a lower probability of willing to work for the public sector. Regarding the preferences to work in the public sector, there is an intergenerational transmission via the vertical channel that operates differently for sons than for daughters, women are only affected by their mothers and men only by their fathers.

Second, peer effects are confirmed for both men and women, although they are bigger for the latter in both sectors (see also the marginal effects in Table 6). Because the horizontal channel is more important for women, and also the vertical one (see above), it can be said that women are more influenced than men.

With respect to the network structure variable (*hierarchy*), both men and women exhibit a positive effect on their declared preferences for working in the public sector. Again, students with a less efficient network prefer to work for the public sector where networking abilities are less needed.

Finally, it is worth recalling that for the general model we found that the best students prefer to work for the public sector. By gender, this relationship exists for women, but it is not significant for men. This result may be caused by a strategy of the best educated women to limit wage discrimination and promotion issues (the glass ceiling problem).

7. CONCLUDING REMARKS

In this chapter, we study the transmission mechanisms of preferences that influence the individual's willingness to work in the public and private sectors. In particular, our main goal is to determine who has a larger influence on the formation of preferences for a given job sector, your parents or your friends.

For the public sector only the determinants of the Public Service Motivation (PSM) have been studied. However, the transmission of these traits and its effect on the selection of the job sector were unknown. This chapter shed some light on the importance of the parent's sector and the peers interest on the willingness to work for the public sector.

Previous literature on inequality of opportunity has stated that parental education and occupation are important individual circumstances for the determination of individual's preferences (Ferreira & Gignoux, 2011; Marrero & Rodríguez, 2012; Roemer et al., 2003). In the same manner, the literature on social networks has found that peers exert a significant influence on individual's choices (Balsa et al., 2018; Calvó-Armengol et al., 2009; Mas & Moretti, 2009). To the best of our knowledge, this is the first analysis that compares both the vertical and horizontal channels simultaneously.

For this task, we construct an original database from a survey of students at their last-year in college. Our first result shows that there is a positive horizontal transmission effect for both sectors, i.e. the more friends willing to work in a particular sector, the higher the probability of a person to will the same. For the vertical channel, our results are significant only for the public sector. In this respect, it is interesting to bear in mind that rates of unemployment in Spain were above 20% during the Great Recession. This fact may have induced parents to discourage their children to work for the private sector, even if their pre-crisis preferences were in favor of the private sector. If this is true, being occupied in the private sector will not be a good predictor for preferring the private sector. Regarding the public sector, both channels are significant, although the estimated marginal effects seem to give prevalence to the vertical channel. However, because people usually have more than two friends (but only two parents), the cumulative marginal effect of a group of friends may, however, overcome parental influence.

Also, our results show that the best students prefer to work for the public sector. Despite that the highest salaries are found in the private sector; it seems that good students prefer the public sector because it has a higher average wage and lower risk. The last factor is likely the most important since the effect of marks is significant only for women, the gender with the highest risk aversion (Borghans et al., 2009). In addition, we find that women are significantly more influenced than men for both channels.

The literature on inequality of opportunity has typically considered parental transmission as one of the most fundamental channels through which initial conditions (circumstances) affect individual earnings. Our results show that the transmission of preferences from peers can be even more important. In this case, future research should investigate whether peers help to equalize individual opportunities or not.

NOTES

1. See Bisin & Verdier (2011) for a revision of the literature on this topic.
2. Some studies, focused on Europe, find that wages tend to be lower for jobs attained through a friend or a relative (Kramarz & Skans, 2014; Pistaferri, 1999). This is explained

by the fact that small firms in Europe, which usually pay lower salaries than big companies, have a higher probability of hiring through informal channels like friends or relatives.

3. This method is a generalization of the Eigenvector Centrality proposed by Bonacich (1972). A complete discussion of the advantages of the used measure can be found in Bonacich (2007).

4. See Appendix 1 for a complete presentation of the questionnaire.

5. This metric is used, as many others network measures, by Google Scholar to rank authors and publications.

6. There is 721 respondents of this question out of the 904 participants on the survey.

7. In order to test that there is not a problem of auto selection on the non-respondents we have calculated a model using the respondents only. Results are in line with the one presented in the main document and can be found on Appendix 4.

8. There are two types of non-public schools in Spain, the regular full private school and the concerted school which is fully supported with public funds but privately managed.

9. We also considered the quadratic form, but the result did not change.

10. A large share of students in the field of health end up working for the National Health System (Seguridad Social) in Spain.

11. Remind that this is the same exercise that we did to create the *public* and *private peers* variables. However, here we are using those individuals who did not answer the question in the survey.

REFERENCES

Aina, C., & Nicoletti, C. (2018). The intergenerational transmission of liberal professions. *Labour Economics*, *51*, 108–120.

Alan, S., Baydar, N., Boneva, T., Crossley, T. F., & Ertac, S. (2017). Transmission of risk preferences from mothers to daughters. *Journal of Economic Behavior & Organization*, *134*, 60–77.

Alesina, A., & Giuliano, P. (2010). The power of the family. *Journal of Economic Growth*, *15*, 93–125.

Arrow, K. J., & Borzekowski, R. (2004). Limited Network Connections and the Distribution of Wages. *SSRN Electronic Journal*.

Balsa, A., Gandelman, N., & Roldán, F. (2018). Peer and parental influence in academic performance and alcohol use. *Labour Economics*, *55*, 41–55.

Bellante, D., & Link, A. N. (1981). Are public sector workers more risk averse than private sector workers? *Industrial and Labor Relation Review*, *34*(3), 408–413.

Bervoets, S., & Zenou, Y. (2017). Intergenerational correlation and social interactions in education. *European Economic Review*, *92*, 13–30.

Bisin, A. & Verdier, T. (2011). The economics of cultural transmission and socialization. in J. Benhabib, A. Bisin & M. O. Jackson (Eds.), *Handbook of social economics* (Vol. 1, pp. 339–416). Amsterdam, The Netherlands: North-Holland.

Bonacich, P. (1972). Factoring and weighting approaches to status scores and clique identification. *The Journal of Mathematical Sociology*, *2*(1), 113–120.

Bonacich, P. (1987). Power and centrality: A family of measures. *American Journal of Sociology*, *92*(5), 1170–1182.

Bonacich, P. (2007). Some unique properties of eigenvector centrality. *Social Networks*, *29*(4), 555–564.

Borgatti, S. P., Everett, M. G., & Freeman, L. C. (2002). *Ucinet 6 for Windows: Software of social network analysis*. Analytics Technologies.

Bramoullé, Y., Djebbari, H., & Fortin, B. (2009). Identification of peer effects through social networks. *Journal of Econometrics*, *150*(1402), 41–55. https://doi.org/10.1016/j.jeconom.2008.12.021

Brunello, G., De Paola, M., & Scoppa, V. (2010). Peer effects in higher education: Does the field of study matter? *Economic Inquiry*, *48*(3), 621–634. https://doi.org/10.1111/j.1465-7295.2009.00235.x

Buechel, B., Hellmann, T., & Pichler, M. M. (2014). The dynamics of continuous cultural traits in social networks. *Journal of Economic Theory*, *154*, 274–309.

Buelens, M., & Van den Broeck, H. (2007). An analysis of differences in work motivation between public and private sector organizations. *Public Administration Review*, *67*(1), 65–74.

Burt, R. S. (2004). Structural holes and good ideas. *American Journal of Sociology*, *110*(2), 349–399.
Calvó-Armengol, A. (2004). Job contact networks. *Journal of Economic Theory*, *115*(1), 191–206.
Calvó-Armengol, A., & Jackson, M. O. (2004). Social networks and resulting patterns and dynamics of employment and wages. *American Economic Review*, *94*(3), 426–454.
Calvó-Armengol, A., Patacchini, E., & Zenou, Y. (2009). Peer effects and social networks in education. *Review of Economic Studies*, *76*(4), 1239–1267.
Cameron, A. C., & Trivedi, P. K. (2005). *Microeconometrics methods and applications*. Cambridge University Press.
Cheung, M.-W., & Wu, J. (2018). On the probabilistic transmission of continuous cultural traits. *Journal of Economic Theory*, *174*, 300–323.
Cramer, J., Hartog, J., Jonker, N., & Van Praag, C. (2002). Low risk aversion encourages the choice for entrepreneurship: An empirical test of a truism. *Journal of Economic Behavior & Organization*, *48*(1), 29–36.
Dardanoni, V., Fields, G. S., Roemer, J. E., & Puerta, M. L. S. (2006). How demanding should equality of opportunity be, and how much have we achieved? In S. Morgan, D. Grusky & G. S. Fields (Eds.), *Mobility and inequality : Frontiers of research from sociology and economics* (p. 463).
Fairlie, R. W., & Robb, A. (2007). Families, human capital, and small business: Evidence from the characteristics of business owners survey. *ILR Review*, *60*(2), 225–245.
Farré, L., & Vella, F. (2013). The intergenerational transmission of gender role attitudes and its implications for female labour force participation. *Economica*, *80*(318), 219–247.
Fernandez, R., Fogli, A., & Olivetti, C. (2004). Mothers and sons: Preference formation and female labor force dynamics. *The Quarterly Journal of Economics*, *119*(4), 1249–1299.
Ferreira, F. H. G., Gignoux, J., & Aran, M. (2011). Measuring inequality of opportunity with imperfect data: The case of Turkey. *The Journal of Economic Inequality*, *9*(4), 651–680.
Fontaine, F. (2008). Why are similar workers paid differently? The role of social networks. *Journal of Economic Dynamics and Control*, *32*(12), 3960–3977.
Fu, G., Wilkinson, S., & Dawson, R. J. (2016). A spatial network model for civil infrastructure system development. *Computer-Aided Civil and Infrastructure Engineering*.
Gee, L. K., Jones, J., & Burke, M. (2017). Social networks and labor markets: How strong ties relate to job finding on Facebook's social network. *Journal of Labor Economics*, *35*(2), 485–518.
Glitz, A. (2017). Coworker networks in the labour market. *Labour Economics*, *44*, 218–230.
Goel, D., & Lang, K. (2019). Social ties and the job search of recent immigrants. *ILR Review*, *72*(2), 355–381.
Granovetter, M. S. (1973). The strength of weak ties. *American Journal of Sociology*, *78*(6), 1360–1380.
Granovetter, M. S. (1995). *Getting a job: A study of contacts and careers*. University of Chicago Press.
Greenwalds, B. C. (1986). Adverse selection in the labour market. *Review of Economic Studies*, *53*(3), 325–347.
Halliday, T. J., & Kwak, S. (2012). What is a peer? The role of network definitions in estimation of endogenous peer effects. *Applied Economics*, *44*(3), 289–302.
Kramarz, F., & Skans, O. N. (2014). When strong ties are strong: Networks and youth labour market entry. *Review of Economic Studies*, *81*(3), 1164–1200.
Leider, S., Möbius, M. M., Rosenblat, T., & Do, Q.-A. (2009). Directed altruism and enforced reciprocity in social networks. *The Quarterly Journal of Economics*, *124*(4), 1815–1851.
Manski, C. F. (1993). Identification of endogenous social effects: The reflection problem. *The Review of Economic Studies*, *60*(3), 531.
Marrero, G. A., & Rodríguez, J. G. (2011). Inequality of opportunity in the United States: Trends and decomposition. In *Inequality of opportunity: Theory and measurement* (pp. 217–246).
Marrero, G. A., & Rodríguez, J. G. (2012). Inequality of opportunity in Europe. *Review of Income and Wealth*, *58*(4), 597–621.
Mas, A., & Moretti, E. (2009). Peers at work. *American Economic Review*, *99*(1), 112–145.
Montgomery, J. D. (1991). Social networks and labor-market outcomes: Toward an economic analysis. *American Economic Review*, *81*(5), 1408–1418.
Perry, J. L. (1997). Antecedents of public service motivation. *Journal of Public Administration Research and Theory*, *7*(2), 181–197.

Perry, J. L., Hondeghem, A., & Wise, L. R. (2010). Revisiting the motivational bases of public service: Twenty years of research and an agenda for the future. *Public Administration Review*, *70*(5), 681–690.

Pfeifer, C. (2010). Risk aversion and sorting into public sector employment. *German Economic Review*, *12*(1), 85–99.

Pistaferri, L. (1999). Informal networks in the Italian labor market. *Giornale Degli Economisti e Annali Di Economia*, 355–375.

Rashid, S., & Rashid, U. (2012). Work motivation differences between public and private sector. *American International Journal of Social Science*, *1*(2), 24–33.

Rodríguez, J. G. (2008). Partial equality-of-opportunity orderings. *Social Choice and Welfare*, *31*(3), 435–456.

Saygin, P. O., Weber, A., & Weynandt, M. A. (2019). Coworkers, networks, and job-search outcomes among displaced workers. *ILR Review*.

Shapiro, C., & Stiglitz, J. E. (1984). Equilibrium unemployment as a worker discipline device. *The American Economic Review*, *74*(3), 433–444.

Shipilov, A., Labianca, G., Kalnysh, V., & Kalnysh, Y. (2007). Career-related network building behaviors, range social capital, and career outcomes. *Academy of Management Proceedings*, *2007*(1), 1–6.

Slikker, M., & Nouweland, A. (2001). *Social and economic networks in cooperative game theory*. Springer US.

Weiss, A. (1981). Self-selection in the labor market. *The American Economic Review*, *71*(3), 275–284.

Yogev, T., & Grund, T. (2012). Network dynamics and market structure: The case of art fairs. *Sociological Focus*, *45*(1), 24–40.

APPENDIX 1. THE QUESTIONNAIRE

This is a translated copy of the questionnaire used in the survey to collect our database. It must bear in mind that some questions do not have a straightforward translation to the English language. For instance, the term 'orla', the usual picture that all recent graduates take at the end of their studies, is translated as 'graduate photograph'; 'colegio concertado', a private school supported with public funds, is translated as 'charter school'; 'PAU' is an exam that all students need to pass in order to get into a Spanish university.

Date: ____________

Faculty: __________ **Degree:** ___________

1. PERSONAL DATA

1.1 Name and surname:

1.2 Year of birth:

1.3 Gender (Mark with an X):

Male		Female	

1.4 Have you ever participated in the 'graduate photograph'? (Mark with an X)

Yes	
No	

1.5 Number of years in the faculty (including the current one): _______

1.6 Nationality: ___________________

1.7 Current city of residence: _______________________

1.8 Family's city of residence: ___________________

1.9 Sexual orientation (Mark with an X):

Heterosexual	
Homosexual	
Bisexual	
Others	

2.1 Attained level of studies of your parents (Mark with an X):

	Father	Mother
No studies		
Primary school		
Vocational studies		
High School		
University		
Master or PhD		

If they have university studies, please indicate which one:
Mother: ____________________
Father: ____________________

2.2 Parents' occupation (Mark with an X):

	Father	Mother
Civil Servant		
Entrepreneur with LESS than 5 workers		
Entrepreneur with MORE than 5 workers		
Employee in a company with LESS than 5 workers		
Employee in a company with MORE than 5 workers		
Unemployed for LESS than a year		
Unemployed for MORE than a year		
Retired		
Housekeeper		
Student		
Others:____________________		

2.3 Average mark on the degree (out of 10): _____
2.4 Mark obtained to enter to the university (PAU + High school): ______
2.5 Do you have any need-based grant? (Example: Ministry of Education and Culture) (Mark with an X)

Yes	
No	

2.6 To which type of school did you go? (If you have gone to more than one school, please, indicate in which you have been more years) (Mark with an X)

Public school	
Charter School	
Private school	

2.7 With respect to the near future, in which segment of the labor market would you like to work? (Mark with an X)

Public sector (Civil servant)	
Private sector as an employee	
Private sector as an entrepreneur	

2.8 Are you currently working or have you ever worked? (Mark with an X)

No	

Go to question **3.1**

Yes	

→ Regarding the most recent job:

When?

I am currently working	
I have worked until less than a month	
I have worked for over a year	

How much time did you work?

3 months or less	
Between 3 and 6 months	
Between 6 months and a year	
More than a year	

2.9 Only if your answer in 2.8 was 'yes': Is the job related with the degree you are studying? (Mark with an X)

No	

Yes	

→ **Were you doing your university practices?**

Yes	
No	

2.10 If the job was not university practices, how did you get the job? (Mark with an X)

Through a friend	
Through an employment office	
Through an app (i.e. LinkedIn)	

3.1 Cite a maximum of 5 people in this class with whom you have the best relationship and are also completing the questionnaire. Write down their names and surname (you can use a social media like Facebook or ask them directly if you do not know their surname). In a scale of 1 to 4 indicate the cell that corresponds with the time you spend with that person.

Note: Freq. Physical communication indicates the number of times that you physically speak out of the university. Freq. social network communication indicates the number of times that you speak through social media (Whatsapp, Facebook, Skype) out of the university.

Name and surname	Freq. Physical communication				Freq. Social network communication			
	1	2	3	4	1	2	3	4
A								
B								
C								
D								
E								

1: If you speak once or less in an average week.
2: If you speak two times in an average week.
3: If you speak two or three times in an average week.
4: If you speak almost every day in an average week.

3.2 Indicate if you went to the same school as the people you have indicated in question 3.1 and if your parents know each other.

	Have you gone to the same school?		Do your parents know each other?	
	Yes	**No**	**Si**	**No**
A				
B				
C				
D				
E				

Thank you very much for your participation in this survey. To finish, we would like to ask you about your personal e-mail, not the one of your university. This request is to ask you in the future about your labor situation to analyze the patterns of integration in the labor market.

E-mail:

APPENDIX 2. A PARENTAL PEER VARIABLE

We have reformulated the peer's effect variable by multiplying the influence matrix not by the self-declared willingness to work in a given sector but for the actual job sector of the parents. Thus, the issue of simultaneity is avoided because parents' decision about the type of occupation cannot be influenced by peers. Results are presented in Table A2.1.

Table A2.1. Results for the Parents' Peer Variable.

Variables	Public Sector	Private Sector
Public parents peers	0,029***	−0,044***
	(0,014)	(0,021)
Private parents peers	−0,009***	0,011***
	(0,003)	(0,004)
Hierarchy	0,228	0,1
	(0,163)	(0,162)
Parents public	0,349***	−0,139
	(0,107)	(0,11)
Parents private	−0,072	0,096
	(0,099)	(0,102)
Avg mark	−0,347***	0,240***
	(0,087)	(0,089)
Avg mark2	0,043***	−0,031***
	(0,008)	(0,008)
M_Years of Education	−0,012	−0,016
	(0,013)	(0,014)
F_Years of Education	−0,014	0,004
	(0,011)	(0,012)
Gender	−0,056	0,211***
	(0,091)	(0,093)
Nonpublic school	0,026	0,502***
	(0,097)	(0,098)
Work exp	−0,245***	0,081
	(0,0895)	(0,091)
Madrid	−0,489***	0,787***
	(0,161)	(0,158)
Science	−0,28***	0,044
	(0,13)	(0,132)
Eng	−1,254***	0,3
	(0,242)	(0,188)
Social	−0,191**	−0,515***
	(0,105)	(0,11)
Constant	0,633**	−0,519
	(0,327)	(0,348)
Wald-Chi2	159.82***	147.47***
Log-pseudolikelihood	−519.7782	−510.724
AIC	1173.03	1083.83
BIC	1182.476	1164.368

Notes: Standard error in parentheses: ***$p < 0.01$, **$p < 0.05$, *$p < 0.1$.

First, similarly to the original model, we find parents that do not answer the question about the public/private sector in the survey which guarantees that both probit estimations are different. Second, the results for the variables not related to the network are consistent with previous findings (see main text). Third, the coefficients of the new peer's effect variables show a reinforcement of the desire of working in a given sector. Thus, individuals who receive a greater influence from peers whose parents work in the public (private) sector display a higher probability of willing to work for the public (private) sector. Nonetheless, there is a negative effect from the peers with parents working in a sector that is different from the one declared as preferred by the individual. Finally, Hierarchy is now not significant.

APPENDIX 3. SELECTION BIAS ROBUSTNESS CHECK

As said in the main text, we have tried two different empirical approaches to control for a possible selection bias. The first approach is a two-stages model being the first stage an estimation of thc field chosen by the students using as explanatory variables those of the full model plus the field chosen by parents with a college degree. *Science, Health, Social, Eng* (that stands for Engineering) and *Humanities* are the branch of knowledge of the career studied by the parents. The f stands for the father and the m for the mother. The results of the first stage are shown in Table A3.1. It is observed that only in a few cases parental effects on the decision about the degree are significant. Then, we proceed with the second stage, an estimation that uses the predicted probabilities from the first stage. The predicted values are indicated by 'pr.' before the variable name Results are shown in Table A3.2.

Table A3.1. Probit Estimations for the Field Chosen by the Students.

Variables	Science	Health	Eng	Social
Science f	0,268	0,569	0,352	−1,08***
	(0,404)	(0,37)	(0,469)	(0,434)
Science m	−0,936*	−0,506	0,598	0,356
	(0,538)	(0,387)	(0,416)	(0,33)
Health f	−0,305	−0,325	−0,583	0,084
	(0,262)	(0,248)	(0,459)	(0,206)
Health m	−0,076	0,363*	−0,036	−0,117
	(0,226)	(0,192)	(0,321)	(0,184)
Social f	−0,172	0,006	0,069	−0,019
	(0,173)	(0,157)	(0,233)	(0,142)
Social m	0,104	−0,107	−0,106	−0,108
	(0,141)	(0,136)	(0,210)	(0,123)
Eng f	−0,282	0,211	−0,212	0,007
	(0,208)	(0,171)	(0,312)	(0,164)
Eng m	−4,711	0,281	0,278	0,368
	(300,563)	(0,475)	(0,642)	(0,434)
Humanities f	0,285	0,069	0,35	−0,34
	(0,514)	(0,498)	(0,643)	(0,468)
Humanities m	−0,196	0,004	−0,031	0,201
	(0,315)	(0,292)	(0,417)	(0,262)
Public peers	−0,015***	0,166***	−0,117*	−0,055
	(0,042)	(0,039)	(0,064)	(0,035)
Private peers	0,151	−0,011	0,127*	−0,24***
	(0,053)	(0,052)	(0,07)	(0,048)
Hierarchy	0,022	0,01	0,22	−0,102
	(0,209)	(0,198)	(0,264)	(0,168)
Parent public	0,228***	0,058	0,221	−0,176*
	(0,114)	(0,109)	(0,157)	(0,1)
Parents private	−0,081	0,01	−0,021	0,024
	(0,115)	(0,109)	(0,159)	(0,099)
Avg mark	0,027	−0,068***	0,35***	−0,064
	(0,097)	(0,115)	(0,141)	(0,08)

(*Continued*)

Table A3.1. *(Continued)*

Variables	Science	Health	Eng	Social
Avg mark2	0,000	0,029***	−0,04***	−0,006
	(0,009)	(0,01)	(0,013)	(0,008)
Gender	0,212***	−0,327***	0,614***	−0,175*
	(0,105)	(0,102)	(0,147)	(0,091)
Non public school	−0,005	0,218***	−0,17	−0,346***
	(0,113)	(0,103)	(0,161)	(0,097)
Madrid	−5,003	−0,067	−4,727	−0,287
	(99,311)	(0,176)	(154,749)	(0,158)
Constant	−1,227***	−1,926***	−2,282***	1,011***
	(0,341)	(0,401)	(0,56)	(0,278)
Wald-Chi^2	96.291***	28.301*	46.165***	74.792***
Log-pseudolikelihood	−441.824	−384.061	−187.577	−558.267
AIC	810.123	925.649	417.155	1158.534
BIC	1026.593	911.066	518.098	1259.478

Notes: Standard error in parentheses: $^{***}p < 0.01$, $^{**}p < 0.05$, $^{*}p < 0.1$.

Table A3.2. Probit Estimations Using the Predicted Probabilities from the First Stage.

Variables	Public Sector	Private Sector
Public peers	0,278***	−0,053
	(0,061)	(0,061)
Private peers	−0,051	0,127
	(0,089)	(0,088)
Hierarchy	0,536***	0,161
	(0,175)	(0,175)
Parents public	0,267***	−0,187
	(0,126)	(0,128)
Parents private	−0,055	0,081
	(0,102)	(0,103)
Avg mark	−0,358***	0,184**
	(0,116)	(0,114)
Avg mark 2	0,043***	−0,028
	(0,014)	(0,014)
M_Years of Education	−0,011	−0,017
	(0,013)	(0,014)
F_Years of Education	−0,013	0,004
	(0,012)	(0,012)
Gender	−0,056	0,101
	(0,183)	(0,18)
Non public school	−0,051	0,36**
	(0,158)	(0,157)
Work exp	−0,22***	0,028
	(0,089)	(0,09)
Madrid	−0,043	0,365
	(0,516)	(0,506)
pr.science	0,996	−1,189
	(1,158)	(1,125)
pr.eng	−0,405	0,826
	(1,304)	(1,26)

Table A3.2. *(Continued)*

Variables	Public Sector	Private Sector
pr.social	−0,262	−2,462
	(1,538)	(1,505)
pr.health	0,472	−0,268
	(1,39)	(1,382)
Constant	−0,138	0,988
	(1,4)	(1,37)
Wald-Chi2	136.75***	125.46***
Log-pseudolikelihood	−538.38	−528.124
AIC	1112.761	1092.249
BIC	1199.264	1178.752

Note: Standard error in parentheses: $^{***}p < 0.01$, $^{**}p < 0.05$, $^{*}p < 0.1$.

Now some variables lose their statistical effect, while the predicted variables from the first stage are not significant. These results seem to support that the effect of parents on children's decision about the field are irrelevant for the willingness to work for neither the public or the private sector.

To be sure that there is not a significant selection problem in our model, we develop a second robustness check. In addition to the degree of children, we include in the model the degree of parents. Also, we include an interaction between the parents and the individual career, which is indicated by a '*' between the variables. The results of this model are presented in Table A3.3. The main findings of the chapter remain the same which shows that the selection bias in the sample cannot be important.

Table A3.3. Probit Estimations Including the Degree of Parents.

Variables	Public Sector	Private Sector
Public peers	0,283***	−0,012
	(0,038)	(0,039)
Private peers	0,009	0,193***
	(0,043)	(0,043)
Hierarchy	0,579***	0,265
	(0,181)	(0,18)
Parents public	0,327***	−0,135
	(0,112)	(0,113)
Parents private	−0,079	0,075
	(0,103)	(0,105)
Avg mark	−0,293***	0,238***
	(0,103)***	(0,105)
Avg mark2	0,037	−0,029***
	(0,085)	(0,09)
M_Years of Education	−0,011	−0,015
	(0,008)	(0,009)
F_Years of Education	−0,013	0,003
	(0,014)	(0,014)

(Continued)

Table A3.3. (*Continued*)

Variables	Public Sector	Private Sector
Gender	0,037	0,171*
	(0,012)	(0,012)
Non public school	−0,031	0,493***
	(0,096)	(0,096)
Work exp	−0,178*	0,041
	(0,102)	(0,101)
Madrid	−0,261	0,631***
	(0,093)	(0,094)
Science	0,227	−0,361**
	(0,173)	(0,167)
Science m	−0,253	0,209
	(0,177)	(0,173)
Science f	0,242	0,094
	(0,378)	(0,351)
Eng	−0,763***	−0,095
	(0,435)	(0,404)
Eng m	0,01	−0,182
	(0,279)	(0,222)
Eng f	−0,083	0,169
	(0,478)	(0,514)
Social m	0,182	−0,146***
	(0,172)	(0,172)
Social	0,34**	−0,838
	(0,157)	(0,155)
Social f	−0,021	0,083
	(0,166)	(0,162)
Health m	0,083	−0,061
	(0,19)	(0,185)
Health	0,658***	−0,606***
	(0,229)	(0,231)
Health f	−0,086	−0,38
	(0,172)	(0,171)
Science*Science m	1,136	−0,753
	(0,24)	(0,249)
Science*Science f	−5,414	5,77
	(4,61,176)	(4,61,406)
Eng*Eng m	−3,272	4,257
	(2,65,971)	(2,66,369)
Eng*Eng f	−3,833	−0,697
	(3,76,754)	(3,76,754)
Social*Social m	−0,368	0,087
	(2,15,922)	(0,808)
Social*Social f	−0,204	0,053
	(0,255)	(0,264)
Constant	−0,4638	−0,458
	(0,37034)	(0,391)
Wald-Chi2	160.97***	152.17***
Log-pseudolikelihood	−509.5685	−501.5603
AIC	1087.137	1071.121
BIC	1250.532	1234.515

Notes: Standard error in parentheses: ***$p < 0.01$, **$p < 0.05$, *$p < 0.1$.

APPENDIX 4. NON-ZEROS MODEL

To have non-respondents on the question of the preferred sector allows us some flexibility with the empirical model. This is what gives us the possibility of regressing two different probit models and observing changes in the marginal effects on Table 4.

However, there may have been a self-selection bias among the non-respondents, which could affect the results of the study. To test this, we have created a new variable called *Confirmed Sector*, which only includes individuals who have

Table A4.1. Probit Estimation of the Non-Zeros Model.

Variables	Confirmed Sector
Public Peers	0.161***
	(0.044)
Private Peers	−0.150***
	(0.055)
Hierarchy	0.160
	(0.194)
Parents Public	0.303**
	(0.124)
Parents Private	−0.111
	(0.113)
Avg Mark	−0.389***
	(0.106)
Avg Mark	0.048***
	(0.011)
M_years of education	0.004
	(0.016)
F_years of education	−0.012
	(0.014)
Gender	−0.135
	(0.104)
Non public School	−0.314***
	(0.107)
Work exp	−0.153
	(0.101)
Madrid	−0.591***
	(0.168)
Science	−0.133
	(0.142)
Eng	−0.964***
	(0.273)
Social	0.218*
	(0.120)
Constant	0.630
	(0.413)
Observations	721
Log Likelihood	−424.195
AIC	882.390
BIC	957.433

Notes: Standard error in parentheses: $^{***}p < 0.01$, $^{**}p < 0.05$, $^{*}p < 0.1$.

answered the question. This new variable assigns the value 1 to individuals who have declared their willingness to work for the public sector and assigns the value 0 to those who have declared their willingness to work for the private sector. The number of observations on this model is 721, which is the number of respondents. As can be seen in Table A4.1, the results are in line with those presented in the main document. There is a positive effect on the horizontal (peers) channel for both sectors and a positive and significant effect on the vertical (parents) channel for the public sector.

CHAPTER 6

ADULT HEALTH AND INEQUALITY OF OPPORTUNITY IN SPAIN

David Pérez-Mesa and Ángel S. Marrero

Department of Economics, Accounting and Finance, and CEDESOG, University of La Laguna, Spain; EQUALITAS

ABSTRACT

In this paper, the theory of inequality of opportunity is applied to examine health inequality among adults in Spain. Using a survey module conducted by the Centro de Investigaciones Sociológicas (CIS) in 2017, the role played by and the contributions of circumstances, efforts and lifestyles, and demographic variables in explaining adult health inequality are assessed. Additionally, the mediating role of individual education in the relationship between circumstances and health is analyzed. The findings underscore the significant relevance of unfair factors (circumstances) and demographics in generating adult health inequality, as opposed to the minimal contribution of fair factors (efforts and lifestyles). Furthermore, education is shown to significantly influence health, mitigating the impact of certain circumstances and serving as a transmission channel for others. In light of these results, efforts and lifestyles alone are insufficient to counterbalance unfair circumstances beyond an individual's control. Therefore, improving circumstances and early-life factors, or reducing their impact on health through the implementation of compensatory policies, is essential for reducing health inequality and promoting equal opportunities for inclusive development.

Keywords: Adult health; health inequality; inequality of opportunity; Spain; circumstances; lifestyles; education

Opportunity, Mobility and Inequality
Research on Economic Inequality, Volume 31, 153–173

ISSN: 1049-2585/doi:10.1108/S1049-258520250000031007

1. INTRODUCTION

In recent years, we have witnessed a growing theoretical and empirical literature on inequality of opportunity across different fields of economic research, including income, health and education.[1] It has been motivated by its normative relevance since this literature builds upon a fundamental distinction between unfair and fair sources of inequality (Fleurbaey & Schokkaert, 2011; Roemer, 1998). According to this framework, an individual's outcome depends on variables beyond and within his/her control, denoted as circumstances and efforts, respectively. Thus, total inequality can be seen as a combination of inequality caused by different circumstances that are considered unfair, referred to as inequality of opportunity, and inequality caused by factors more related to the willingness to exert effort, which is considered fair as it belongs to the sphere of individual responsibility.[2] Moreover, empirical evidence shows that inequality of opportunity negatively affects economic growth and could end up discouraging subsequent development (Marrero & Rodríguez, 2013, 2023; World Bank, 2006). Therefore, the analysis of the inequality of opportunity is relevant not only from a social justice and equity perspective, but also from an efficiency point of view.

Particularly, an expanding body of literature has addressed the measurement of inequality of opportunity in health (Davillas & Jones, 2020; Fleurbaey & Schokkaert, 2009; García-Gómez et al., 2015; Jusot et al., 2013; Rosa Dias, 2009; Trannoy et al., 2010). This literature has mainly focused its analysis on adult populations in developed European countries, either individually or for a sample of countries. Only few of these studies have analyzed inequality of opportunity in health in Spain (Bigorne et al., 2021; Bricard et al., 2013; Jusot et al., 2010; Kim, 2016; Pasqualini et al., 2017; Pinilla et al., 2017; Tubeuf & Jusot, 2011), all of them using data from multiple waves of the Survey of Health, Ageing and Retirement in Europe (SHARE), with the exception of Pinilla et al. (2017), who use the Spanish Survey of Household Finances (EFF).

The studies using SHARE employ multiple waves to extract different circumstances and current characteristics of the respondents, but they cover only a segment of the Spanish adult population, given that it is a longitudinal database representative of the European population aged 50 and above. Meanwhile, Pinilla et al. (2017) pooled data from four waves of the EFF, which covers the entire adult population in Spain, although they limited their analysis to the reference person in the household (aged 28–85 years) and his/her partner, and they only use one variable relating to the social background of these individuals during their childhood.

These studies use self-assessed health (SAH) as the dependent variable, while the most commonly used circumstances are parental occupation, the number of books at home as a proxy for parental education, parental longevity and parental health-related behaviours, such as smoking and drinking. In addition, effort is generally captured by the individual's education and occupation, and lifestyles by alcohol consumption, smoking, obesity and exercise status. Finally, they included the age and sex of the respondents as demographic variables.

The main goal of this chapter is to estimate inequality of opportunity in health for the Spanish adult population, disentangling the contribution of unfair (circumstances) and fair (efforts and lifestyles) components in explaining health inequality. To this end, we use a survey module conducted by the Centro de Investigaciones Sociológicas (CIS) in 2017, focusing on a representative sample of the Spanish adult population. Methodologically, we follow the two-stage estimation strategy proposed by Trannoy et al. (2010). Firstly, we estimate 'relative' efforts/lifestyles, which entails assessing individual efforts and lifestyles that are isolated from circumstances, thus exclusively attributed to personal responsibility (Jusot et al., 2013). Secondly, we conduct a regression analysis connecting adult health with circumstances and relative efforts/lifestyles, while controlling for demographic variables. Additionally, we employ the Shapley decomposition method to calculate the contribution of each variable group in explaining health inequality.

The contribution of this study rests on two main aspects. First, to the best of our knowledge, it is the first paper that examines health inequality using the CIS database. Second, we analyze a sample of the Spanish population aged 25 years and older and consider a larger set of circumstances, efforts and lifestyles compared to the aforementioned studies. Specifically, we consider parental education, parental socioeconomic status (SES), region of birth, place of residence, birth order and sex as circumstances. In terms of efforts and lifestyles, we consider education, employment status, smoking, exercise, and vegetable consumption. Additionally, compared to studies using SHARE data, we source all variables from the same wave, thereby mitigating the potential for temporal inconsistencies and response bias.

As a parallel objective of this study, our approach also allows us to analyse the transmission channels through which individual circumstances may influence health. These channels encompass factors that, to some extent, fall under individual responsibility, yet contribute to the influence of unequal opportunities on individual health. Specifically, we focus on the educational attainment of the individual, a significant channel discussed in the literature (Rosa Dias, 2009; Trannoy et al., 2010; Tubeuf et al., 2012). We examine whether the circumstances exert a direct effect on health, or whether their effect can be channelled through the individual's education.

In terms of circumstances, we find that father's education and SES, birth order, sex and age significantly affect adult health, whereas in terms of efforts and lifestyles, employment status, exercise and vegetable consumption are the significant factors. Moreover, the set of circumstances and individual age each contribute to explaining around 43% of health inequality, while the fairness component (efforts and lifestyles) only contributes 14%. Additionally, we show that the health status of the individuals is significantly influenced by their education, which also mitigates the effect on health of some circumstances, such as birth order and sex, but also acts as a channel for the effect of circumstances, such as the place of residence and the educational and socioeconomic level of the mother.

The rest of the chapter is structured as follows. Section 2 describes the database and the key variables used. Section 3 presents the methodology and decomposition approach. Section 4 shows the main results. Finally, Section 5 presents the discussion.

2. DATA

We gather information from the module 'Social Inequality and Social Mobility' (CIS 3178), based on Marrero et al. (2017) and conducted by the CIS during 2017. This database, which comprises a sample of 2,482 individuals, is representative of the Spanish adult population aged 18 years and older. The questionnaire provides information on four types of variables: respondent demographics, including sex and age; individual's outcomes, such as health status, educational attainment, employment status and income; a set of individual circumstances measured by the family background; and the individual's efforts and lifestyles, such as smoking or exercise.

From the full sample of 2,482 individuals, following the literature on inequality of opportunity (Carrieri et al., 2020; Ferreira & Gignoux, 2011), we restrict our sample to the adult population aged 25 years and older to avoid potential life-cycle bias[3] and maximize the sample size, obtaining a subsample of 2,273 individuals. From this subsample, we remove those individuals with at least 1 missing value on any of the variables used in our models.[4] By performing this procedure, we obtain our final sample of 1,819 individuals.[5] Table 1 presents the descriptive statistics of the main variables used.

2.1. Health

The variable of interest is health in adulthood as measured by SAH. Despite its subjectivity and other problems reported in the literature (Bago d'Uva et al., 2008; Black et al., 2017; Davillas et al., 2023), SAH is one of the most common measures of health collected in surveys and it is widely used in health economics (Contoyannis & Jones, 2004; Currie et al., 2015; Van Doorslaer et al., 2000). It has been validated as a good predictor of future mortality, health care utilization and a relatively reliable indicator of health at the individual level (DeSalvo et al., 2005; Doiron et al., 2015; Idler & Benyamini, 1997).

In the CIS questionnaire, individuals were asked: 'In general, would you say that your current health is... very good, good, fair, poor or very poor?' Based on this question, we have considered health as a binary variable grouping very good and good health against fair, poor and very poor health.[6] In our database, more than 60% of the individuals reported good or very good health (see Table 1), which is consistent with other studies in the related literature (Jusot et al., 2013; Pinilla et al., 2017; Trannoy et al., 2010).

2.2. Circumstances

Eight circumstances are considered: father's and mother's education, father's and mother's SES, birth order, sex, type of place of residence and region of birth.

Table 1. Descriptive Statistics.

	N	%		*N*	%
DEPENDENT VARIABLE			**Place of residence**		
Self-assessed health			Rural	763	41.95
Very good	366	20.12	Urban	1,056	58.05
Good	866	47.61	*Total*	1,819	100
Fair	460	25.29	**Region of birth**[a]		
Bad	121	6.65	Spain	1,625	89.33
Very bad	6	0.33	Abroad	194	10.67
Total	1,819	100	*Total*	1,819	100
CIRCUMSTANCES			**DEMOGRAPHICS**		
Father's education			**Age**		
No education	660	36.28	25–30	184	10.12
Primary	658	36.17	31–50	773	42.5
Secondary	336	18.47	51–70	620	34.08
Higher	165	9.07	More than 70	242	13.3
Total	1,819	100	*Total*	1,819	100
Mother's education			**EFFORTS AND LIFESTYLES**		
No education	690	37.93	**Education**		
Primary	755	41.51	No education	157	8.63
Secondary	252	13.85	Primary	535	29.41
Higher	122	6.71	Secondary	692	38.04
Total	1,819	100	Higher	435	23.91
Father's SES			*Total*	1,819	100
Unemployed/inactive	39	2.14	**Employment status**		
Lower class	141	7.75	Non-employed	919	50.52
Middle class	1,448	79.6	Employed	900	49.48
Upper class	191	10.5	*Total*	1,819	100
Total	1,819	100	**Smoking**		
Mother's SES			Smoker	510	28.04
Unemployed/inactive	1,206	66.3	Non-smoker	1,309	71.96
Lower class	134	7.37	*Total*	1,819	100
Middle class	386	21.22	**Physical activity**		
Upper class	93	5.11	Once/less than once per week	969	53.27
Total	1,819	100	Daily/several times per week	850	46.73
Birth order			*Total*	1,819	100
First	665	36.56	**Vegetables consumption**		
Second and third	819	45.02	Once/less than once per week	172	9.46
Fourth or more	335	18.42	Daily/several times per week	1,647	90.54
Total	1,819	100	*Total*	1,819	100
Sex					
Male	900	49.48			
Female	919	50.52			
Total	1,819	100			

Note: Constructed by the authors using data from CIS (2017).
[a]Details of the regions of Spain are not shown for space limitations.

Parental education is measured as the highest education level attained by the father/mother when the individual was 16 years old, categorised into no education, primary education, secondary education and higher education. Less than 10% of fathers/mothers have achieved higher education, although fathers have attained higher levels of secondary and tertiary education than mothers.

Regarding parental SES, we follow Cabrera et al. (2021) to group the parents of the individuals into three social classes (lower, middle and upper class), taking into account the 10 large occupational groups of the ISCO-08 classification.[7] In addition, since the above classification only covers employed individuals, we also include a category for unemployed/inactive parents. As shown in Table 1, while almost all fathers were employed, 66% of the mothers were unemployed/inactive (mostly inactive); moreover, 80% of the fathers and 21% of the mothers worked in occupations belonging to the middle social class, respectively.

Birth order is divided into the following categories: first, second and third, and fourth or more. Approximately 37% and 45% of the individuals are the first-born and second/third at birth, respectively. Following Davillas and Jones (2020), Balasooriya et al. (2021) and Brunori et al. (2022), among others, we also include sex as a circumstance, although we are aware that other authors argue against this consideration and classify it as a demographic variable (Deutsch et al., 2018; Jusot et al., 2013; Trannoy et al., 2010).[8] As illustrated in Table 1, each sex corresponds to half of the sample.

The type of place of residence and the region of birth during the adolescence are introduced to control for regional differences within Spain. The type of place of residence is classified into rural and urban, while the region of birth includes the 17 Autonomous Communities of Spain, a joint category for Ceuta and Melilla and another for abroad. 42% and 58% of respondents lived in a rural and urban location, respectively, while about 89% were born in Spain.

2.3. Efforts and Lifestyles

Five individual effort and lifestyle variables are included. Efforts are measured by the highest level of education of the individual, classified in the same groups as parental education (no education, primary, secondary and higher education), and by his/her employment status, divided into employed and unemployed/inactive (similar to Brunori et al., 2022). In comparison with their parents, descendants have higher levels of education, with 24% of them having tertiary education, 38% secondary education and only 9% with no education. In addition, half of the sample is employed.

Lifestyle variables refer to the health-related behaviours of the respondents with respect to smoking, physical activity and vegetable consumption.[9] While smoking classifies individuals as currently smokers or non-smokers, the other two variables refer to how often individuals are physically active and consume vegetables, grouping the responses into daily/several times per week and once/less than once per week. The majority of the sample reported a healthy lifestyle regarding smoking (almost 72% of the respondents do not smoke) and vegetable consumption (91% eat vegetables daily/several times per week), although less than half of the individuals are physically active.

Finally, we consider the age of the individual as a demographic variable, which we divide into four groups of age: under 30 years (25–30 years), 31–50 years, 51–70 years and over 70 years. The average age of the sample is 51 years, with a minimum and maximum age of 25 and 93 years, respectively.

3. METHODOLOGY

3.1. Measuring Inequality of Opportunity in Health

Let us assume that the health status H_i of the individual i is a function of a vector of circumstances C_{ki}, a vector of effort and lifestyles variables E_{ki}, a demographic variable D_i given by the individual's age and a residual term u_i:

$$H_i = \alpha + \sum_{k=1}^{K} \beta_k C_{ki} + \sum_{k=1}^{K} \omega_k E_{ki} + \gamma D_i + u_i \quad (1)$$

Circumstances are variables beyond the individual's control, while efforts are characteristics that belong to the sphere of his/her responsibility. However, efforts can also be affected by individual circumstances (Ferreira & Gignoux, 2011; Jusot et al., 2013; Roemer & Trannoy, 2016). Thus, the impact of circumstances on health occurs both through a direct effect on individual health, and an indirect effect through the influence of circumstances on the individual's efforts and lifestyles.

In order to neutralize the impact of circumstances on effort and lifestyles, we adopt the two-stage procedure proposed by Trannoy et al. (2010) and proceed as follows. First, we regress each effort and lifestyle in a separate equation against the vector of circumstances, controlling for demographics (models (2a) to (2e)). For each of these auxiliary regressions, we compute the relative residuals (i.e., purged from circumstances) and introduce them into the subsequent equations describing individual effort.[10] Finally, we regress individual health in adulthood against the vector of circumstances, the estimated relative residuals of the effort equations and demographics (model (2f)). The models are written as follows:

$$Education_i = \alpha^a + \sum_{k=1}^{K} \beta_k^a C_{ki} + \gamma^a D_i + u_i^a, \quad (2a)$$

$$Employment_i = \alpha^b + \sum_{k=1}^{K} \beta_k^b C_{ki} + \gamma^b D_i + \omega_1^b \hat{u}_i^a + u_i^b, \quad (2b)$$

$$Smoking_i = \alpha^c + \sum_{k=1}^{K} \beta_k^c C_{ki} + \gamma^c D_i + \omega_1^c \hat{u}_i^a + \omega_2^c \hat{u}_i^b + u_i^c, \quad (2c)$$

$$Physical\ act_i = \alpha^d + \sum_{k=1}^{K} \beta_k^d C_{ki} + \gamma^d D_i + \omega_1^d \hat{u}_i^a + \omega_2^d \hat{u}_i^b + \omega_3^d \hat{u}_i^c + u_i^d, \quad (2d)$$

$$Vegetables_i = \alpha^e + \sum_{k=1}^{K} \beta_k^e C_{ki} + \gamma^e D_i + \omega_1^e \hat{u}_i^a + \omega_2^e \hat{u}_i^b + \omega_3^e \hat{u}_i^c + \omega_4^e \hat{u}_i^d + u_i^e, \quad (2e)$$

$$Health_i = \alpha^f + \sum_{k=1}^{K} \beta_k^f C_{ki} + \gamma^f D_i + \omega_1^f \hat{u}_i^a + \omega_2^f \hat{u}_i^b + \omega_3^f \hat{u}_i^c + \omega_4^f \hat{u}_i^d + \omega_5^f \hat{u}_i^e + u_i^f, \quad (2f)$$

Models (2a)–(2f) are modelled using binary logit models, where the dependent variables take value 1 if the individual reports having higher education, being employed, non-smoking, exercising daily/several times per week, eating vegetables, and having good or very good health (and take value 0 otherwise), respectively. In the model (2f), the coefficients associated with the circumstances represent their overall effects (i.e., the sum of their direct and indirect effects) on health, and the estimated relative residuals reflect individual effort, unobserved circumstances and other random factors, since they are orthogonal to the circumstances.[11]

Additionally, as a parallel exercise, we analyze the mediating role of education in the relationship between circumstances and health. For this purpose, we first regress only the circumstances on adult health while controlling for the respondent's age (model (2g)). Subsequently, we introduce the individual's education level, denoted as $Educ_i$, into model (2h). This approach allows us to assess whether the influence of circumstances on health comes from their direct effect or from an indirect effect mediated through the individual's education level.

$$Health_i = \alpha^g + \sum_{k=1}^{K} \beta_k^g C_{ki} + \gamma^g D_i + u_i^g, \tag{2g}$$

$$Health_i = \alpha^h + \sum_{k=1}^{K} \beta_k^h C_{ki} + \gamma^h D_i + \delta^h Educ_i + u_i^h, \tag{2h}$$

Furthermore, if the individual's education level is significant in model (2h), we could also assess whether the circumstances are directly or indirectly (through education) affecting health by comparing their significance in models (2a) and (2h), as well as other studies that use this strategy (Fajardo-Gonzalez, 2016; Deutsch et al., 2018, among others). Thus, if a circumstance's estimated coefficient is only statistically significant in the auxiliary regression (model (2a)), this indicates that its effect on health is indirect. Conversely, if the estimated coefficient is only statistically significant in model (2h), it suggests that its effect on health is direct. Additionally, if a circumstance's estimated coefficient is significant in both models, this implies that the circumstance affects health through both direct and indirect pathways.

3.2. Decomposition of Health Inequality

We use the Shapley decomposition to estimate the contribution of each factor in explaining health inequality (Chantreuil & Trannoy, 2013; Sastre & Trannoy, 2002; Shorrocks, 2013). Taking into account all possible combinations of circumstances, efforts and lifestyles, and demographics, this approach derives the partial contribution of each factor (or group of factors) to the generation of health inequality. For each explanatory variable, it calculates all marginal effects on inequality when all other factors are sequentially removed, and the contribution of each variable is the average of these marginal effects. The estimated contributions can therefore be interpreted as the expected marginal impact of each factor on health inequality.

More specifically, we apply the Shapley decomposition to the pseudo-R^2 estimated from the health logit regression (model (2f)), which measures the explained variance of the health status (Deutsch et al., 2018; Israeli, 2007; Tubeuf et al., 2012). This method has the advantage that it produces an exact additive decomposition of the explained inequality into its factors, treating all of them symmetrically.

4. RESULTS

This section presents the results of our empirical analysis. First, we show the results of the two-step procedure proposed by Trannoy et al. (2010) and examine the determinants of individual health status. Then, we analyze the role of education as a channel of transmission of health inequality. Finally, we present the Shapley decomposition and compare the contributions of circumstances, efforts and lifestyles, and demographics to the pseudo-R^2 of the health logit regression.

4.1. Regression Results

Table 2 shows the estimation results of models (2a)–(2h), which are interpreted in terms of odds ratios. In general, they have the expected sign, and the most relevant and significant results are discussed below.

Looking at the second column of Table 2 (model (2a)), the probability of having tertiary education increases significantly with parental education (with a higher odds ratio for mother's education), and if the father's SES is high. It is also higher for younger cohorts and those who lived in an urban locality. However, this likelihood decreases with birth order and with a lower mother's SES. The latter result may derive from the fact that a working mother has less time to devote to her child than an unemployed or housewife, which could have an impact on the child's education.

Model (2b) shows that the probability of being employed is lower among women and, as expected, much higher for those under 50 compared to individuals over 70 years old. It is higher and significant for individuals born in the more developed regions of Spain (Catalonia, Madrid and the Basque Country) (see Table A1 in Appendix for birth region estimates), with an educated father or a middle-class mother. Moreover, the effort exerted to obtain a higher education also increases the likelihood of being employed.

Regarding model (2c), we observe that having a middle-class mother and having lived in an urban environment increases the probability of smoking. Being a woman and efforts for higher education reduce the probability of being smoker, although it increases for younger individuals. Moreover, with respect to the reference category, born in some regions of Spain also affects the probability of smoking, but parental education has no impact on it.

Looking at the fifth column (model (2d)), we find that the likelihood of doing regular physical activity is higher for individuals with an educated father, a mother with a high SES and those who lived in an urban area. Women are less likely to exercise daily, although surprisingly age does not affect it significantly. Besides, the relative residuals from the education and smoking regressions have a significant and positive impact on the probability of doing regular physical activity.

Table 2. Estimation Results of the Logit Models.

Model	(2a)	(2b)	(2c)	(2d)	(2e)	(2f)	(2g)	(2h)
Dependent variable	Education	Employ. sta.	Smoking	Physical act.	Veget. con.	Health	Health	Health
				CIRCUMSTANCES				
Father's education (Reference category: No education)								
Primary	1.550**	1.438**	1.301	1.310*	1.153	1.656***	1.634***	1.545***
	(0.316)	(0.249)	(0.230)	(0.198)	(0.321)	(0.268)	(0.262)	(0.250)
Secondary	2.015***	1.960***	1.179	1.389*	0.753	1.374	1.353	1.231
	(0.465)	(0.412)	(0.244)	(0.262)	(0.248)	(0.273)	(0.268)	(0.249)
Higher	4.918***	1.615	1.159	1.492	0.684	2.861***	2.761***	2.514***
	(1.513)	(0.495)	(0.357)	(0.425)	(0.303)	(0.927)	(0.869)	(0.802)
Mother's education (Reference category: No education)								
Primary	1.711***	1.141	0.785	0.796	1.212	1.165	1.166	1.120
	(0.327)	(0.189)	(0.135)	(0.117)	(0.325)	(0.182)	(0.180)	(0.174)
Secondary	2.560***	1.113	0.744	0.803	1.575	0.836	0.853	0.810
	(0.613)	(0.258)	(0.168)	(0.167)	(0.597)	(0.185)	(0.190)	(0.180)
Higher	5.907***	1.124	0.954	0.721	0.943	1.014	1.051	0.976
	(2.086)	(0.413)	(0.341)	(0.235)	(0.493)	(0.376)	(0.374)	(0.353)
Father's SES (Reference category: Unemployed/inactive)								
Lower	1.418	1.184	1.306	0.821	2.223	1.728	1.709	1.822
	(0.780)	(0.551)	(0.588)	(0.313)	(1.308)	(0.697)	(0.694)	(0.735)
Middle	1.452	1.363	0.863	0.843	2.031	1.843*	1.813*	1.859*
	(0.705)	(0.559)	(0.332)	(0.287)	(0.994)	(0.656)	(0.652)	(0.661)
Upper	2.473*	1.605	0.636	1.210	1.825	1.812	1.802	1.758
	(1.305)	(0.737)	(0.281)	(0.475)	(1.019)	(0.748)	(0.752)	(0.727)
Mother's SES (Reference category: Unemployed/inactive)								
Lower	0.415***	1.118	1.257	1.028	0.657	0.754	0.763	0.776
	(0.134)	(0.248)	(0.286)	(0.199)	(0.191)	(0.168)	(0.168)	(0.173)
Middle	1.059	1.307*	0.744**	1.094	1.274	0.802	0.811	0.815
	(0.159)	(0.193)	(0.103)	(0.141)	(0.280)	(0.116)	(0.115)	(0.116)
Upper	0.611	0.785	1.040	1.903**	2.357	0.912	0.914	0.931
	(0.221)	(0.263)	(0.342)	(0.574)	(1.230)	(0.313)	(0.309)	(0.317)
Birth order (Reference category: First)								
Second and third	0.768*	1.067	0.835	1.017	1.120	1.018	1.024	1.038
	(0.104)	(0.133)	(0.103)	(0.112)	(0.204)	(0.127)	(0.126)	(0.128)
Fourth or more	0.549***	0.954	0.867	1.092	1.498	0.715**	0.727**	0.760*
	(0.113)	(0.161)	(0.146)	(0.159)	(0.393)	(0.112)	(0.112)	(0.119)
Sex (Reference category: Man)								
Woman	1.000	0.490***	1.432***	0.766***	2.106***	0.739***	0.745***	0.757**
	(0.126)	(0.0557)	(0.158)	(0.0747)	(0.366)	(0.0808)	(0.0808)	(0.0825)
Type of place of residence (Reference category: Rural)								
Urban	1.587***	0.963	0.772**	1.290**	0.988	1.022	1.022	0.993
	(0.224)	(0.118)	(0.0944)	(0.137)	(0.179)	(0.121)	(0.120)	(0.117)
Region of birth (Reference category: Abroad)[a]								
				DEMOGRAPHICS				
Age (Reference category: More than 70)								
25–30	1.816**	154.6***	0.198***	0.937	0.292***	9.682***	9.051***	7.860***
	(0.551)	(113.6)	(0.0576)	(0.207)	(0.120)	(2.736)	(2.516)	(2.236)
31–50	1.796**	290.6***	0.216***	0.906	0.452**	4.289***	4.127***	3.680***
	(0.450)	(209.2)	(0.0532)	(0.147)	(0.153)	(0.753)	(0.717)	(0.663)
51–70	1.363	71.05***	0.327***	1.213	0.634	2.080***	2.051***	1.894***
	(0.344)	(51.12)	(0.0803)	(0.190)	(0.209)	(0.336)	(0.330)	(0.313)

Table 2. (*Continued*)

Model	(2a)	(2b)	(2c)	(2d)	(2e)	(2f)	(2g)	(2h)
Dependent variable	Education	Employ. sta.	Smoking	Physical act.	Veget. con.	Health	Health	Health
EFFORTS-LIFESTYLES (relative residuals)								
Education		1.647***	2.033***	2.226***	2.647***	1.149		
		(0.241)	(0.312)	(0.291)	(0.654)	(0.172)		
Employment status			1.037	0.961	0.827	1.712***		
			(0.133)	(0.112)	(0.164)	(0.219)		
Smoking				1.533***	1.726***	1.223		
				(0.177)	(0.308)	(0.156)		
Physical activity					2.115***	1.537***		
					(0.378)	(0.176)		
Vegetables consumption						1.396*		
						(0.266)		
EDUCATION (Reference category: No education)								
Primary								1.261
								(0.245)
Secondary								1.582**
								(0.337)
Higher								1.701**
								(0.402)
Pseudo R^2	0.192	0.252	0.077	0.048	0.089	0.116	0.099	0.101
N	1,819	1,819	1,819	1,819	1,819	1,819	1,819	1,819

Note: Constructed by the authors using data from CIS (2017).
Robust standard errors in parentheses. * $p<0.1$, ** $p<0.05$, *** $p<0.01$.
[a]Region of birth coefficients are not included because of space limitations (see Table A1 in Appendix for complete estimation results).

In relation to model (2e), parental background does not affect the likelihood of eating vegetables regularly. This likelihood is higher for women and if the individual has positive lifestyle habits, such as having higher education, non-smoking and doing regular physical activity. In addition, the younger the individual, the lower the probability of eating vegetables, and being born in some regions also has a significant influence on this habit.

Looking at the health regression model (2f), the reported odds ratios show the overall impact of circumstances and efforts on health status in adulthood. The probability of having a good or very good SAH increases as the father's level of education and SES increases, decreases significantly with age and is higher for men than for women. Mother's background does not directly influence health in adulthood, as well as the region of birth and place of residence during the adolescence. Furthermore, while being the fourth or more at birth negatively affects the likelihood of having good health, the residuals of employment status, physical activity and vegetable consumption are positively and significantly associated with good health.

In general, the results of model (2f) are consistent with the evidence of the literature on the determinants of health and health inequality. Indeed, parental education and SES significantly affects individual health in Spain, in line with the well-known relationship between family background and health (Almond et al., 2018; Case et al., 2005; Marmot, 2005). It has also been found in the literature that the likelihood of reporting good health decreases with age and among women (Jusot et al., 2013; Li Donni et al., 2014; Pinilla et al., 2017), as well as the (negative) relationship between birth order and later health in adulthood (Black et al., 2016; Hatton & Martin, 2010). Lastly, the non-significance effect of the country of birth and place of residence is in line with the mixed evidence in this regard (Fajardo-Gonzalez, 2016; Lazar, 2013; Li Donni et al., 2014), while the positive impact on adult health of the relative residuals of employment, physical activity and vegetable consumption has been found in the literature of inequality of opportunity (Bricard et al., 2013; Deutsch et al., 2018; Tubeuf et al., 2012).

In addition to the previous analysis, we also assess the mediating role of education in the relationship between circumstances and health by examining the estimates of models (2g) and (2h). Once the education of the individual is introduced into the model (2h), we can see that it has a significant impact on individual's health: having secondary and tertiary education are significant at 5%, meaning that the probability of having better health increases with the education of the individual. Regarding the circumstances, in general, both models (2g) and (2h) are very similar in terms of magnitude and significance of the coefficients (and coincide with those of model (2f)). However, birth order and sex reduce their significance and the odd-ratios of the age decrease considerably, which would indicate that education moderates the effects of these explanatory variables on health.

Furthermore, since education has a significant impact on health, we can also compare models (2a) and (2h) to analyze whether circumstances have a direct effect on health or an indirect one through their influence on education. When making this comparison, we observe that mother's education, mother's SES, and the type of place of residence are significant in model (2a) but not significant in model (2h), indicating that these circumstances have an indirect effect on health. All other circumstances (except the region of birth) are significant in both models, suggesting that they affect health both directly and indirectly through their impact on education.

In summary, our results indicate that the circumstances can affect individual's health in adulthood both through a direct impact and indirectly through their effect on effort-related variables. Moreover, the findings suggest that education has a direct influence on health and also acts as a mediator in the relationship between circumstances and health, thereby mitigating the impact of certain explanatory variables on health status. These results are in line with those shown in the literature (Rosa Dias, 2009; Trannoy et al., 2010).

4.2. The Shapley Decomposition

To estimate the contribution of circumstances, efforts and lifestyles, and demographics in explaining health inequality, we apply the Shapley decomposition to the pseudo-R^2 estimated from the health logit regression. Table 3 presents the

Table 3. Contribution of Circumstances, Efforts and Lifestyles, and Demographic Variables to Health Inequality.

	Shapley Value (a)	Contribution to the Pseudo R^2 (%) (c)
CIRCUMSTANCES	0.0491	42.49%
Father's education	0.0173	14.95%
Mother's education	0.0114	9.88%
Father's SES	0.0033	2.82%
Mother's SES	0.0019	1.64%
Birth order	0.0048	4.12%
Sex	0.0037	3.19%
Place of residence	0.001	0.85%
Region of birth	0.0058	5.04%
DEMOGRAPHICS	0.0508	43.95%
Age	0.0508	43.95%
EFFORTS AND LIFESTYLES (relative residuals)	0.0156	13.55%
Education	0.0004	0.36%
Employment status	0.0071	6.14%
Smoking	0.001	0.84%
Physical activity	0.0059	5.08%
Vegetables consumption	0.0013	1.13%
Pseudo R^2	**0.1155 (b)**	**100%**

Notes: Constructed by the authors using data from CIS (2017). The contribution of each explanatory variable is obtained dividing the Shapley value by the pseudo R^2: $(c)=(a)/(b)*100$.

contributions of each group of factors and each variable. Both circumstances and demographics explain a significant proportion of the pseudo R^2, around 43%, respectively, while the effort exerted by the individual accounts for only 14%.

Looking at the explanatory variables individually, age explains the largest proportion of the pseudo R^2 of the health logit regression (44%), followed by father's education (15%) and mother's education (10%), the latter two being the most important circumstances. Also noteworthy is the contribution of the region of birth and birth order (almost 5% and 4%, respectively), and that sex does not seem to be relevant in explaining health inequality. The efforts/lifestyles with the greatest and most significant impact are employment status and physical activity.

Comparing with the literature on inequality of opportunity that uses SAH as health outcome, and considering the differences between studies (survey sources, target samples and explanatory variables used), the relative contributions of the circumstances, efforts and demographics are similar to those presented by Jusot et al. (2013) for France. Moreover, circumstances play an important role in the explained health inequality as in Trannoy et al. (2010), and the proportion explained by circumstances (42%) is considerably higher than the one estimated by Tubeuf et al. (2012) for United Kingdom (19%), Deutsch et al. (2018) for Luxembourg (27%) and Bigorne et al. (2021) for a sample of European countries (36%). In these latter studies, the effort represents twice the effort reported in Table 3, although our magnitude of demographics is in line with Deutsch et al. (2018).

In summary, our decomposition demonstrates the great relevance of unfair factors (circumstances) and age in the generation of adult health inequality in Spain, in contrast to the minimal effect of fair factors (efforts and lifestyles). However, it is also necessary to consider the role of age since it explains half of the estimated health inequality.[12]

5. CONCLUSION

In this paper, we have analyzed the contribution of circumstances, efforts and lifestyles, and demographics in explaining health inequality among adults in Spain. In general, our results are consistent with the evidence found in the literature on the determinants of health inequality and inequality of opportunity. Parental education and SES have a positive and significant association with individual health, while the likelihood of reporting good health decreases with age, birth order and among women. In addition, the efforts and lifestyle choices made by individuals to be employed, exercise and eat healthy are positively and significantly linked to health outcomes. Furthermore, we have shown that circumstances can affect health directly but also indirectly through their effect on effort variables, highlighting in this case the mediating role of the individual's education. Finally, we also find that unfair components (circumstances) and age of individuals account for a significant proportion of the health inequality explained by our model. Among the circumstances, parental education is the most important factor, followed by the region of birth and birth order. In contrast, fair components such as efforts and lifestyles have a modest contribution.

Our study has the advantage of the large number of relevant circumstances and effort variables considered simultaneously, which have been collected from the same survey. However, it also has some limitations. First, our measure of adult health is based on a subjective indicator of health status, and this variable may suffer from reporting bias. Second, the results are generated with a sample of living individuals, thus excluding deceased individuals would narrow the health gaps among the respondents and exert downward pressure on the true effect of circumstances on health. Third, since this database does not contain all relevant variables that explain individual health status, the specification of our empirical model could suffer from potential unobserved circumstances and effort variables. Finally, we cannot perform longitudinal analyses given the characteristics of the database.

Potential lines of research include dealing with missing values in order to perform the analysis with the full sample of individuals while reducing the potential biases that this could generate. In addition, it would also be appropriate to analyze whether our results differ by sex or for different age cohorts, as well as to test the robustness of the results to other measures of health, such as height or body mass index.

Overall, our results indicate that the effort and lifestyle of individuals to achieve good health is not enough to offset the influence of the unfair circumstances. Therefore, improving circumstances and early-life factors, or reducing their impact on health through the implementation of compensatory policies, is necessary for reducing health inequality and equalize opportunities for progress in later life. In this context, the evidence shown in this study identifies the education of individuals as a key factor to explain health and health disparities. This outcome highlights the importance of equalizing educational opportunities as a means to reduce health inequality, and also underscores the potential for coordinated policies between the education and healthcare sectors. However, given that our results are descriptive and based on regression analyses, they should not be interpreted as policy recommendations but as potential lines of future exploration.

NOTES

1. See Ramos and Van de Gaer (2016), Jusot and Tubeuf (2019), and Asadullah et al. (2021) for a review of the literature on inequality of opportunity in income, health and education, respectively.
2. This distinction between different types of inequality is reasonable when dealing with adult population, but the literature of inequality of opportunity has also focused on the analysis of the child population. In the latter, all inequality must be considered inequality of opportunity since all factors related to children are beyond their control (Hufe et al., 2017; Pérez-Mesa et al., 2022; Roemer & Trannoy, 2016). Thus, the literature on inequality of opportunity is closely related to the literature on early-life factors and their long-term impact on future outcomes (Almond et al., 2018; Case & Paxson, 2010; Currie, 2011).
3. This age restriction allows us to focus on individuals who have completed their educational qualifications and with a higher proportion of employed persons, as we include the individual's education and employment status as effort variables in our analysis.
4. From the subsample of individuals older than 25 years (2273), we remove 454 individuals because of missing values, i.e., 20% of the sample. Conducting a simple exploratory analysis on the randomness of these missing values, it is observed that individuals omitting responses to certain questions, such as those pertaining to parental education and SES, tend to report poorer health and education. These patterns, along with not having the complete set of determinants of health inequality, may underestimate health gaps within our sample, thus our estimates should be considered as a lower bound of the explained inequality. Addressing these missing values (see, e.g. Brunori et al., 2022 and the literature referenced therein), although desirable, exceeds the scope of this paper.
5. It is worth noting that we have only one individual per household, therefore there is not a potential correlation within family units.
6. We categorise our dependent variable in this way because we want to compare those individuals who are at least in good health with the others, as commonly done in the literature (see, e.g., Jusot et al., 2013, among others; Tubeuf et al., 2012) and to avoid a highly unbalanced distribution of the observations across categories. However, an alternative categorisation of our health variable, such as grouping very poor and poor against the other categories (results available upon request), generates different results in terms of health inequality, as expected given the existing evidence in the literature (Wagstaff & Van Doorslaer, 1994; Van Doorslaer et al., 1997; Ziebarth, 2010).
7. Lower class is composed by the group 9 in the ISCO-08 classification, middle class by 3 to 8 groups, and upper class comprises groups 1 and 2. Regarding individuals in the armed forces, given their small number, the observations are assigned to a specific class according to the studies they indicate and their membership (officers or troops).
8. See García-Gómez et al. (2015) for a discussion on the treatment of age and sex from a normative perspective and its implications for estimating inequality of opportunity.
9. Since the database provides a rich number of lifestyles related to the frequency of consumption of particular foods, we considered grouping them into a single variable using the principal components approach (PCA) (Filmer & Pritchett, 2001; Kolenikov & Angeles, 2009). However, given that the first principal component (and even the sum of the three significant components) explained only a small part of the aggregate variability of these

habits, we decided to include only vegetable consumption based on its more widespread use in the literature (Brunori et al., 2022; Carrieri & Jones, 2018; Rosa Dias, 2009).

10. As in Trannoy et al. (2010), these residuals are computed as generalized residuals (Gourieroux et al., 1987).

11. Since the set of circumstances considered in our regressions are beyond the individual's control, they are considered exogenous. Thus, we do not concern here with endogeneity issues but focus on the correlation between health status and circumstances, which cannot be interpreted as causality.

12. García-Gómez et al. (2015) emphasize that demographics (in general, sex, but also age) and lifestyle differences are co-determined and influenced by social and behavioral factors, and are not only linked to biological factors; therefore, they should be explicitly considered in any analysis of inequality of opportunity. Moreover, some authors argue that, while it is rational to focus on avoidable differences for policy analysis, "unfair" does not necessarily coincide with "avoidable" (see Fleurbaey and Schokkaert (2009) for a detailed discussion).

ACKNOWLEDGEMENTS

We would like to thank the editors, an anonymous referee, Gustavo A. Marrero, Pedro Salas-Rojo, Sandy Tubeuf, and Raquel Sebastián for their valuable comments and suggestions. The authors acknowledge financial support from the Ministerio de Ciencia e Innovación of Spain through the projects PID2019-107161GB-C33 and PID2022-137352NB-C44. Pérez-Mesa also thanks the financial support from the Gobierno de Canarias through its FPI program (TESIS2019010156 grant), co-funded by the European Social Fund. All views and any remaining errors or omissions are our sole responsibility.

REFERENCES

Almond, D., Currie, J., & Duque, V. (2018). Childhood circumstances and adult outcomes: Act II. *Journal of Economic Literature*, *56*(4), 1360–1446.

Asadullah, M. N., Trannoy, A., Tubeuf, S., & Yalonetzky, G. (2021). Measuring educational inequality of opportunity: Pupil's effort matters. *World Development*, *138*, 105262.

Bago d'Uva, T., O'Donnell, O., & Van Doorslaer, E. (2008). Differential health reporting by education level and its impact on the measurement of health inequalities among older Europeans. *International Journal of Epidemiology*, *37*(6), 1375–1383.

Balasooriya, N. N., Bandara, J. S., & Rohde, N. (2021). The intergenerational effects of socioeconomic inequality on unhealthy bodyweight. *Health Economics*, *30*(4), 729–747.

Bigorne, A., Boggian, L., & Tubeuf, S. (2021). *Inequality of opportunity in health: The gender dimension*. ECINEQ-Society for the Study of Economic Inequality.

Black, S. E., Devereux, P. J., & Salvanes, K. G. (2016). Healthy (?), wealthy, and wise: Birth order and adult health. *Economics & Human Biology*, *23*, 27–45.

Black, N., Johnston, D. W., Shields, M. A., & Suziedelyte, A. (2017). Who provides inconsistent reports of their health status? The importance of age, cognitive ability and socioeconomic status. *Social Science & Medicine*, *191*, 9–18.

Bricard, D., Jusot, F., Trannoy, A., & Tubeuf, S. (2013). Inequality of opportunities in health and the principle of natural reward: Evidence from European countries. In P. Rosa Dias & O. O'Donnell (Eds.), *Health and inequality. Research on Economic Inequality* (Vol. 21, pp. 335–370). Emerald Group Publishing Limited.

Brunori, P., Davillas, A., Jones, A. M., & Scarchilli, G. (2022). Model-based recursive partitioning to estimate unfair health inequalities in the United Kingdom Household Longitudinal Study. *Journal of Economic Behavior & Organization*, *204*, 543–565.

Cabrera, L., Marrero, G. A., Rodríguez, J. G., & Salas-Rojo, P. (2021). Inequality of opportunity in Spain: New insights from new data. *Hacienda Publica Española/Review of Public Economics*, *237*, 153–185.
Carrieri, V., & Jones, A. M. (2018). Inequality of opportunity in health: A decomposition-based approach. *Health Economics*, *27*(12), 1981–1995.
Carrieri, V., Davillas, A., & Jones, A. M. (2020). A latent class approach to inequity in health using biomarker data. *Health Economics*, *29*(7), 808–826.
Case, A., Fertig, A., & Paxson, C. (2005). The lasting impact of childhood health and circumstance. *Journal of Health Economics*, *24*(2), 365–389.
Case, A., & Paxson, C. (2010). Causes and consequences of early-life health. *Demography*, *47*(S), S65–S85.
Chantreuil, F., & Trannoy, A. (2013). Inequality decomposition values: The trade-off between marginality and efficiency. *Journal of Economic Inequality*, *11*, 83–98.
Contoyannis, P., & Jones, A. M. (2004). Socio-economic status, health and lifestyle. *Journal of Health Economics*, *23*(5), 965–995.
Currie, J. (2011). Inequality at birth: Some causes and consequences. *American Economic Review*, *101*(3), 1–22.
Currie, J., Duque, V., & Garfinkel, I. (2015). The Great Recession and mothers' health. *Economic Journal*, *125*(588), F311–F346.
Davillas, A., de Oliveira, V. H., & Jones, A. M. (2023). Is inconsistent reporting of self-assessed health persistent and systematic? Evidence from the UKHLS. *Economics & Human Biology*, *49*, 101219.
Davillas, A., & Jones, A. M. (2020). Ex ante inequality of opportunity in health, decomposition and distributional analysis of biomarkers. *Journal of Health Economics*, *69*, 102251.
DeSalvo, K. B., Fan, V. S., McDonell, M. B., & Fihn, S. D. (2005). Predicting mortality and healthcare utilization with a single question. *Health Services Research*, *40*(4), 1234–1246.
Deutsch, J., Pi Alperin, M. N., & Silber, J. (2018). Using the Shapley decomposition to disentangle the impact of circumstances and efforts on health inequality. *Social Indicators Research*, *138*, 523–543.
Doiron, D., Fiebig, D. G., Johar, M., & Suziedelyte, A. (2015). Does self-assessed health measure health? *Applied Economics*, *47*(2), 180–194.
Fajardo-Gonzalez, J. (2016). Inequality of opportunity in adult health in Colombia. *Journal of Economic Inequality*, *14*, 395–416.
Ferreira, F. H., & Gignoux, J. (2011). The measurement of inequality of opportunity: Theory and an application to Latin America. *Review of Income and Wealth*, *57*(4), 622–657.
Filmer, D., & Pritchett, L. H. (2001). Estimating wealth effects without expenditure data—or tears: An application to educational enrollments in states of India. *Demography*, *38*(1), 115–132.
Fleurbaey, M., & Schokkaert, E. (2009). Unfair inequalities in health and health care. *Journal of Health Economics*, *28*(1), 73–90.
Fleurbaey, M., & Schokkaert, E. (2011). Equity in health and health care. In M. Pauly, T. McGuire, & P. Barros (Eds.), *Handbook of health economics* (Vol. 2, pp. 1003–1092). Elsevier.
García-Gómez, P., Schokkaert, E., Van Ourti, T., & Bago d'Uva, T. (2015). Inequity in the face of death. *Health Economics*, *24*(10), 1348–1367.
Gourieroux, C., Monfort, A., Renault, E., & Trognon, A. (1987). Generalised residuals. *Journal of Econometrics 34*(1–2), 5–32.
Hatton, T. J., & Martin, R. M. (2010). The effects on stature of poverty, family size, and birth order: British children in the 1930s. *Oxford Economic Papers*, *62*(1), 157–184.
Hufe, P., Peichl, A., Roemer, J., & Ungerer, M. (2017). Inequality of income acquisition: The role of childhood circumstances. *Social Choice and Welfare*, *49*, 499–544.
Idler, E. L., & Benyamini, Y. (1997). Self-rated health and mortality: A review of twenty-seven community studies. *Journal of Health and Social Behavior*, *38*(1), 21–37.
Israeli, O. (2007). A Shapley-based decomposition of the R-square of a linear regression. *Journal of Economic Inequality*, *5*, 199–212.
Jusot, F., Tubeuf, S., & Trannoy, A. (2010). Inequality of opportunities in health in Europe: Why so much difference across countries? *HEDG working papers*, *10*, 26.

Jusot, F., Tubeuf, S., & Trannoy, A. (2013). Circumstances and efforts: How important is their correlation for the measurement of inequality of opportunity in health? *Health Economics*, *22*(12), 1470–1495.

Jusot, F., & Tubeuf, S. (2019). Equality of opportunity in health and healthcare. In *Oxford Research Encyclopedia of economics and finance*. Oxford University Press.

Kim, B. (2016). *Inequality of opportunity for healthy aging in Europe*. KU Leuven Department of Economics, Discussion Paper Series, DPS16, 20.

Kolenikov, S., & Angeles, G. (2009). Socioeconomic status measurement with discrete proxy variables: Is principal component analysis a reliable answer? *Review of Income and Wealth*, *55*(1), 128–165.

Lazar, A. (2013). Ex-ante and ex-post measurement of inequality of opportunity in health: Evidence from Israel. In P. Rosa Dias & O. O'Donnell (Eds.), *Health and inequality. Research on Economic Inequality* (Vol. 21, pp. 371–395). Emerald Group Publishing Limited.

Li Donni, P., Peragine, V., & Pignataro, G. (2014). Ex-ante and ex-post measurement of equality of opportunity in health: A normative decomposition. *Health Economics*, *23*(2), 182–198.

Marmot, M. (2005). Social determinants of health inequalities. *The Lancet*, *365*(9464), 1099–1104.

Marrero, G. A., Betancort, M., Cabrera, L., Darias-Curvo, S., Pérez, C. N., Rodríguez, J. G., & Sánchez, D. (2017). *Desigualdad de oportunidades y movilidad intergeneracional en Canarias*. Fundación Cajacanarias.

Marrero, G. A., & Rodríguez, J. G. (2013). Inequality of opportunity and growth. *Journal of Development Economics*, *104*, 107–122.

Marrero, G. A., & Rodríguez, J. G. (2023). Unfair inequality and growth. *Scandinavian Journal of Economics (forthcoming)*.

Pasqualini, M., Lanari, D., Minelli, L., Pieroni, L., & Salmasi, L. (2017). Health and income inequalities in Europe: What is the role of circumstances? *Economics & Human Biology*, *26*, 164–173.

Pérez-Mesa, D., Marrero, G. A., & Darias-Curvo, S. (2022). Child health inequality in Sub-Saharan Africa. *Economics & Human Biology*, *47*, 101176.

Pinilla, J., Lopez-Valcarcel, B. G., & Urbanos-Garrido, R. M. (2017). Estimating direct effects of parental occupation on Spaniards' health by birth cohort. *BMC Public Health*, *17*, 1–9.

Ramos, X., & Van de Gaer, D. (2016). Approaches to inequality of opportunity: Principles, measures and evidence. *Journal of Economic Surveys*, *30*(5), 855–883.

Roemer, J. E. (1998). *Equality of opportunity*. Harvard University Press.

Roemer, J. E., & Trannoy, A. (2016). Equality of opportunity: Theory and measurement. *Journal of Economic Literature*, *54*(4), 1288–1332.

Rosa Dias, P. (2009). Inequality of opportunity in health: Evidence from a UK cohort study. *Health Economics*, *18*(9), 1057–1074.

Sastre, M., & Trannoy, A. (2002). Shapley inequality decomposition by factor components: Some methodological issues. *Journal of Economics*, *77*, 51–89.

Shorrocks, A. F. (2013). Decomposition procedures for distributional analysis: A unified framework based on the Shapley-value. *Journal of Economic Inequality*, *11*(1), 99–126.

Trannoy, A., Tubeuf, S., Jusot, F., & Devaux, M. (2010). Inequality of opportunities in health in France: A first pass. *Health Economics*, *19*(8), 921–938.

Tubeuf, S., & Jusot, F. (2011). Social health inequalities among older Europeans: the contribution of social and family background. *European Journal of Health Economics*, *12*, 61–77.

Tubeuf, S., Jusot, F., & Bricard, D. (2012). Mediating role of education and lifestyles in the relationship between early-life conditions and health: Evidence from the 1958 British cohort. *Health Economics*, *21*, 129–150.

Van Doorslaer, E., Wagstaff, A., Bleichrodt, H., Calonge, S., Gerdtham, U.G., Gerfin, M., & Winkelhake, O. (1997). Income-related inequalities in health: Some international comparisons. *Journal of Health Economics*, *16*(1), 93–112.

Van Doorslaer, E., Wagstaff, A., Van der Burg, H., Christiansen, T., De Graeve, D., Duchesne, I., & Winkelhake, O. (2000). Equity in the delivery of health care in Europe and the US. *Journal of Health Economics*, *19*(5), 553–583.

Wagstaff, A., & Van Doorslaer, E. (1994). Measuring inequalities in health in the presence of multiple-category morbidity indicators. *Health Economics*, *3*(4), 281–291.

World Bank. (2006). *World Development Report 2006: Equity and Development*. The World Bank.

Ziebarth, N. (2010). Measurement of health, health inequality, and reporting heterogeneity. *Social Science & Medicine*, *71*(1), 116–124.

APPENDIX. ESTIMATION RESULTS

Table A1. Complete Estimation Results of the Logit Models.

Model	(2a)	(2b)	(2c)	(2d)	(2e)	(2f)	(2g)	(2h)
Dependent variable	Education	Employment status	Smoking	Physical Activity	Vegetables consump.	Health	Health	Health
				CIRCUMSTANCES				
Father's education (Reference category: No education)								
Primary	1.550**	1.438**	1.301	1.310*	1.153	1.656***	1.634***	1.545***
	(0.316)	(0.249)	(0.230)	(0.198)	(0.321)	(0.268)	(0.262)	(0.250)
Secondary	2.015***	1.960***	1.179	1.389*	0.753	1.374	1.353	1.231
	(0.465)	(0.412)	(0.244)	(0.262)	(0.248)	(0.273)	(0.268)	(0.249)
Higher	4.918***	1.615	1.159	1.492	0.684	2.861***	2.761***	2.514***
	(1.513)	(0.495)	(0.357)	(0.425)	(0.303)	(0.927)	(0.869)	(0.802)
Mother's education (Reference category: No education)								
Primary	1.711***	1.141	0.785	0.796	1.212	1.165	1.166	1.120
	(0.327)	(0.189)	(0.135)	(0.117)	(0.325)	(0.182)	(0.180)	(0.174)
Secondary	2.560***	1.113	0.744	0.803	1.575	0.836	0.853	0.810
	(0.613)	(0.258)	(0.168)	(0.167)	(0.597)	(0.185)	(0.190)	(0.180)
Higher	5.907***	1.124	0.954	0.721	0.943	1.014	1.051	0.976
	(2.086)	(0.413)	(0.341)	(0.235)	(0.493)	(0.376)	(0.374)	(0.353)
Father's SES (Reference category: Unemployed/inactive)								
Lower	1.418	1.184	1.306	0.821	2.223	1.728	1.709	1.822
	(0.780)	(0.551)	(0.588)	(0.313)	(1.308)	(0.697)	(0.694)	(0.735)
Middle	1.452	1.363	0.863	0.843	2.031	1.843*	1.813*	1.859*
	(0.705)	(0.559)	(0.332)	(0.287)	(0.994)	(0.656)	(0.652)	(0.661)
Upper	2.473*	1.605	0.636	1.210	1.825	1.812	1.802	1.758
	(1.305)	(0.737)	(0.281)	(0.475)	(1.019)	(0.748)	(0.752)	(0.727)
Mother's SES (Reference category: Unemployed/inactive)								
Lower	0.415***	1.118	1.257	1.028	0.657	0.754	0.763	0.776
	(0.134)	(0.248)	(0.286)	(0.199)	(0.191)	(0.168)	(0.168)	(0.173)
Middle	1.059	1.307*	0.744**	1.094	1.274	0.802	0.811	0.815
	(0.159)	(0.193)	(0.103)	(0.141)	(0.280)	(0.116)	(0.115)	(0.116)
Upper	0.611	0.785	1.040	1.903**	2.357	0.912	0.914	0.931
	(0.221)	(0.263)	(0.342)	(0.574)	(1.230)	(0.313)	(0.309)	(0.317)
Birth order (Reference category: First)								
Second and third	0.768*	1.067	0.835	1.017	1.120	1.018	1.024	1.038
	(0.104)	(0.133)	(0.103)	(0.112)	(0.204)	(0.127)	(0.126)	(0.128)
Fourth or more	0.549***	0.954	0.867	1.092	1.498	0.715**	0.727**	0.760*
	(0.113)	(0.161)	(0.146)	(0.159)	(0.393)	(0.112)	(0.112)	(0.119)
Sex (Reference category: Man)								
Woman	1.000	0.490***	1.432***	0.766***	2.106***	0.739***	0.745***	0.757**
	(0.126)	(0.0557)	(0.158)	(0.0747)	(0.366)	(0.0808)	(0.0808)	(0.0825)
Type of place of residence (Reference category: Rural)								
Urban	1.587***	0.963	0.772**	1.290**	0.988	1.022	1.022	0.993
	(0.224)	(0.118)	(0.0944)	(0.137)	(0.179)	(0.121)	(0.120)	(0.117)
Region of birth (Reference category: Abroad)								
Andalucía	1.049	0.982	0.420***	1.041	0.543	0.999	0.984	1.017
	(0.259)	(0.212)	(0.0956)	(0.206)	(0.208)	(0.219)	(0.214)	(0.222)
Asturias	0.778	0.872	0.834	1.024	0.333**	1.196	1.140	1.165
	(0.307)	(0.293)	(0.354)	(0.359)	(0.180)	(0.451)	(0.424)	(0.426)

(*Continued*)

Table A1. (*Continued*)

Model	(2a)	(2b)	(2c)	(2d)	(2e)	(2f)	(2g)	(2h)
Dependent variable	Education	Employment status	Smoking	Physical Activity	Vegetables consump.	Health	Health	Health
Baleares	0.834	1.978	0.379**	0.877	0.541	0.965	0.949	0.945
	(0.436)	(1.009)	(0.155)	(0.342)	(0.354)	(0.404)	(0.412)	(0.403)
Canarias	0.571	0.994	0.365***	0.781	0.830	0.614	0.616	0.649
	(0.259)	(0.339)	(0.122)	(0.243)	(0.514)	(0.215)	(0.214)	(0.228)
Cantabria	1.154	1.091	0.269***	2.017*	0.267**	0.581	0.594	0.585
	(0.573)	(0.576)	(0.108)	(0.786)	(0.162)	(0.252)	(0.265)	(0.258)
Castilla y León	1.619	1.264	0.574**	1.174	0.486	1.415	1.397	1.413
	(0.500)	(0.342)	(0.162)	(0.279)	(0.218)	(0.368)	(0.363)	(0.368)
Castilla-La Mancha	0.749	1.051	0.678	1.179	0.421*	0.809	0.809	0.855
	(0.271)	(0.318)	(0.222)	(0.319)	(0.200)	(0.251)	(0.244)	(0.261)
Cataluña	1.039	2.080***	0.412***	0.797	0.570	1.132	1.113	1.114
	(0.268)	(0.517)	(0.0997)	(0.170)	(0.238)	(0.281)	(0.273)	(0.273)
Valencia	1.337	0.996	0.383***	0.982	0.544	0.996	0.980	0.996
	(0.383)	(0.250)	(0.101)	(0.222)	(0.236)	(0.262)	(0.252)	(0.256)
Extremadura	0.899	0.952	0.418**	1.042	0.334**	1.279	1.249	1.343
	(0.432)	(0.340)	(0.151)	(0.324)	(0.168)	(0.453)	(0.439)	(0.482)
Galicia	1.041	1.346	0.638	1.673**	0.406**	0.921	0.916	0.926
	(0.342)	(0.379)	(0.194)	(0.426)	(0.183)	(0.256)	(0.252)	(0.256)
Madrid	1.505	1.604*	0.498***	1.655**	0.714	0.960	0.958	0.959
	(0.385)	(0.412)	(0.128)	(0.377)	(0.306)	(0.242)	(0.243)	(0.243)
Murcia	1.013	1.065	0.452**	0.920	0.682	0.848	0.834	0.869
	(0.419)	(0.390)	(0.160)	(0.302)	(0.428)	(0.296)	(0.284)	(0.297)
País Vasco	1.538	2.486***	0.599	1.155	0.461	1.219	1.216	1.185
	(0.487)	(0.809)	(0.196)	(0.327)	(0.227)	(0.409)	(0.405)	(0.393)
Ceuta and Melilla	0.654	2.247	2.427	1.496	0.260	0.779	0.758	0.733
	(0.579)	(1.573)	(2.482)	(0.921)	(0.253)	(0.513)	(0.520)	(0.504)
DEMOGRAPHICS								
Age (Reference category: More than 70)								
25–30	1.816**	154.6***	0.198***	0.937	0.292***	9.682***	9.051***	7.860***
	(0.551)	(113.6)	(0.0576)	(0.207)	(0.120)	(2.736)	(2.516)	(2.236)
31–50	1.796**	290.6***	0.216***	0.906	0.452**	4.289***	4.127***	3.680***
	(0.450)	(209.2)	(0.0532)	(0.147)	(0.153)	(0.753)	(0.717)	(0.663)
51–70	1.363	71.05***	0.327***	1.213	0.634	2.080***	2.051***	1.894***
	(0.344)	(51.12)	(0.0803)	(0.190)	(0.209)	(0.336)	(0.330)	(0.313)
EFFORTS-LIFESTYLES (relative residuals)								
Education		1.647***	2.033***	2.226***	2.647***	1.149		
		(0.241)	(0.312)	(0.291)	(0.654)	(0.172)		
Employment status			1.037	0.961	0.827	1.712***		
			(0.133)	(0.112)	(0.164)	(0.219)		
Smoking				1.533***	1.726***	1.223		
				(0.177)	(0.308)	(0.156)		
Physical activity					2.115***	1.537***		
					(0.378)	(0.176)		
Vegetables consumption						1.396*		
						(0.266)		

Table A1. *(Continued)*

Model	(2a)	(2b)	(2c)	(2d)	(2e)	(2f)	(2g)	(2h)
Dependent variable	Education	Employment status	Smoking	Physical Activity	Vegetables consump.	Health	Health	Health
EDUCATION (Reference category: No education)								
Primary								1.261
								(0.245)
Secondary								1.582**
								(0.337)
Higher								1.701**
								(0.402)
Pseudo R^2	0.192	0.252	0.077	0.048	0.089	0.116	0.099	0.101
N	1,819	1,819	1,819	1,819	1,819	1,819	1,819	1,819

Notes: Constructed by the authors using data from CIS (2017).
Robust standard errors in parentheses. * $p<0.1$, ** $p<0.05$, *** $p<0.01$.

CHAPTER 7

INCOME INEQUALITY IN RUSSIA: *IS THE KUZNETS CURVE A VALID HYPOTHESIS?*

Inna Skriabina

CEO at group Orobianco, Alicante, Spain

ABSTRACT

In this study the effect of the level of economic development on inequality is estimated. The goal is to determine whether the classical Kuznets curve hypothesis (1955) is applicable to Russia. The idea of Kuznets was that income inequality first rises with economic growth on the low stages of development and then falls as the economy matures. The empirical evidence of the curve applicable for the Russian regions has been found. The reverse casualty problem by using internal and external instruments has been also taken into the consideration. For the internal instruments, the System GMM method, which implies two functions – one in first difference and the other one in levels, has been used. For the external instruments, the net oil export per capita and trade per capita as instruments have been applied. If the quadratic term is not implied, the estimations show a significant robust positive effect of economic development on inequality. Thus, it is assumed that it happens due to the fact that Russia is still on the first upbeat of the curve, and it has not yet reached sufficient levels of development to tear down inequality.

Keywords: Kuznets Curve; income inequality; economic growth; system GMM; Russian economy; regional analysis; economic development; instrumental variables

Opportunity, Mobility and Inequality
Research on Economic Inequality, Volume 31, 175–212

ISSN: 1049-2585/doi:10.1108/S1049-258520250000031008

1. INTRODUCTION

The relationship between income inequality and economic development is one of the most debated topics in inequality studies. How does economic development affect inequality? Does it make it go down, as the nation goes richer, or on the contrary, does it push it up benefiting the rich? The most known hypothesis that connects these two concepts is the *Kuznets curve hypothesis*, developed by Simon Kuznets back to 1955. It suggests the inverted-U relation between the two, i.e. on the earlier stages of development, the inequality goes up, as the national income grows, then it reaches a turning point and starts to go down, while the economy continues to grow.

Despite the huge research investigating the empirical existence of the curve, the conclusions of the literature are still ambiguous. Most studies use cross-sectional country-level data and a set of control variables to see, whether it is the development itself that makes the inequality to go down at the certain point in time, or whether there are other factors outside to make such an effect. However, even the most accurate results are still left open for interpretation due to reverse causality, i.e. development may affect inequality but income inequality affects development.

In this study, we try to study this topic analyzing not only the 'classic' static model, but also the dynamic and instrumental variables models. In the next section, we start with the literature review which sums up not only classical studies, but also the advances of the newest inequality-development studies. In Section 3, the database is presented. Then, we explain all the models we estimate, and the related econometric issues are explained in Section 4. In Section 5, we present our main results with extensive robustness checks. Finally, we present a brief discussion and some conclusions in Section 6.

2. LITERATURE REVIEW AND CONTRIBUTION

The main theoretical approach to assessing how growth affects income inequality is the Kuznets curve (1955), which suggests that inequality first increases and then decreases forming an inverted U as the economy develops. For a mathematical version of this curve, see Robinson (1976). This approach assumes that, initially, the national economy is composed of only two sectors: agriculture and industry, and that development is associated with the movement of workers from the first to the second.

Initially, both per capita income and inequality are low, as most of the population is employed in the agricultural sector where wages and productivity are low. As industrialization and subsequent urbanization are seen as the main sources of economic development, more and more citizens begin to move to urban areas to work in industry, where wages are higher compared to those in the agricultural sector. Later, as the size and importance of the agricultural sector declines and most of the population works in industry, inequality begins to decline, resulting in an inverted U-curve (see Fig. 1).

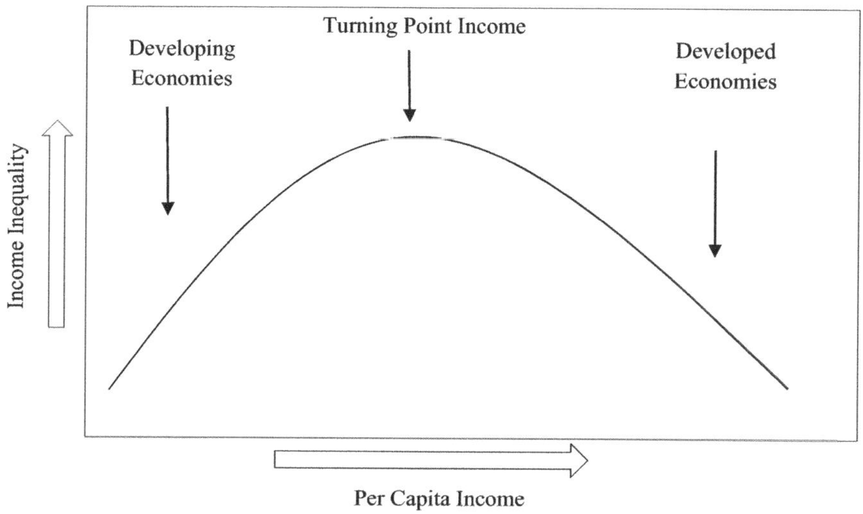

Fig. 1. The Kuznets Curve (Adapted from Kuznets, 1955).

A large number of scholars assumed this approach in their studies (among many others, Fields, 2002). More recent theoretical models, however, assume the existence of the Kuznets curve, but propose other reasons for this change. For example, Greenwood and Jovanovic (1990) argue that this change occurs due to the shift from financially unsophisticated to modern, inclusive and complex systems. Or Milanovic (1994) argues that, in addition to purely economic factors, such as the level of per capita income, the decline in inequality in developed countries is mainly due to social choice factors, such as the volume of social transfers and the level of employment in the public sector.

Likewise, Galor and Tsiddon (1997) argue that the composition of human capital is a key factor in determining the pattern between inequality and economic development. The polarization of investment in human capital in the early stages of development is crucial to enhance growth, which will later decrease inequality through a more equitable distribution of human capital. Beyond these and many other theoretical developments, a great deal of empirical research has been conducted over the past decades. Although some of them seem to confirm Kuznets' hypothesis (e.g. Anand & Kanbur, 1993; Li et al., 1998), the results remain ambiguous, as many other economists have not found evidence of the existence of this curve (see, for example, Gallup, 2012).

What makes it even more complicated is that, over the last 20 years, some researchers have detected a second increase in economic inequality in the more developed countries (see, for example, List & Gallet, 1999). One of the possible explanations would lie in the existence of another structural change: the shift from a manufacturing to a service economy. In the same vein, Milanovic (2016) himself suggests that, in the long run, the Kuznets curve is actually an attainment of Kuznets waves or cycles, characterized by alternating increases and decreases in inequality (see Fig. 2).

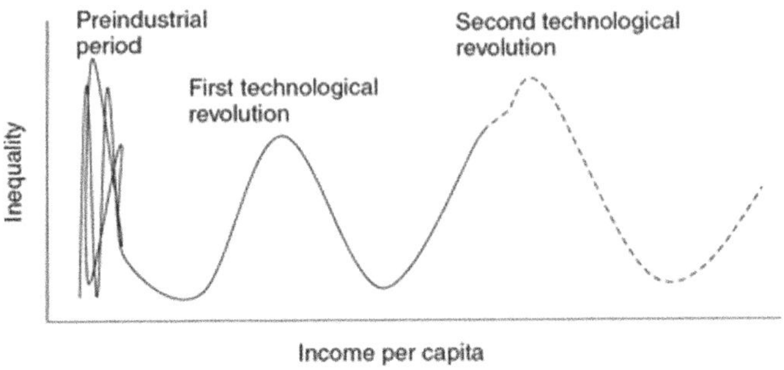

Fig. 2. The Kuznets Waves (Milanovic, 2016).

Due to the lack of data, the first empirical studies on the Kuznets Curve were conducted with cross-sectional data at the country level (Anand & Kanbur, 1993; Randolph & Lott, 1993). Numerous recent investigations have instead employed panel data for a set of countries (Barro, 2000; Desbordes & Verardi, 2012; Forbes, 2000; Gallup, 2012; Jovanovic, 2017) or time series data for the same country (Gunaydin, 2015; de la Escosura, 2008).

In our case, a panel of regional data for the same country across time (79 Russian regions and 21 years) is used. We consider that this choice gives us an important set of advantages. First, as the problem of data comparability across countries is very prominent in lots of research papers (Milanovic, 1994), if we use the data on inequality and development only for one country, we end up with a set of data much more comparable. That happens because, among other things, we do no need to adjust the price levels or make conversion to another currency. Besides, data-collecting process, sampling method and calculations are the same for all the regions. Second, the data on such a large and heterogeneous country as Russia with diverse levels of development allows us to have enough dispersion to make our analysis possible. Third, using a panel data helps us to see the actual pattern of inequality changes, as the economy develops. As Gallup (2012) points it: 'None of this research tested Kuznets hypothesis directly: that income inequality would increase and then decrease as income grew within countries'. But among all this reasons the most important one for us is that we can finally answer the question whether pure market economic powers per se can change the inequality pattern through time. This is possible because the set of factors that are specific for every country such as labour and tax regulation, institutional quality, market legislation and others, in many cases unobserved or difficult to be calculated, can significantly affect overall inequality over time, while they are controlled for if we consider the same country.

On the other hand, as we mentioned in the introduction, most empirical studies to date do not consider the endogeneity problem. Dollar and Kraay (2002), Lundberg and Squire (2003), and Brueckner et al. (2014) are some of the few papers that employ several instruments to try to diminish the problem. In this research, we employ both internal and external instruments in our models.

3. THE DATABASE

For this study, we use the Rosstat Database. Rosstat corresponds to the Russian Federal State Statistics Service, the governmental statistics agency in Russia, which was created on the base of Goskomstat after the collapse of the Soviet Union.[1] Goskomstat was created in 1987 to replace the Central Statistical Administration, while maintaining the same basic functions in the collection, analysis, publication and distribution of state statistics, including economic, social, and population statistics.

In 2007, the Unified Interdepartmental Information and Statistical System (EMISS) was created in the framework of the implementation of the federal target program 'Development of Russian State Statistics in 2007-2011'. The EMISS is operated by the Ministry of Communications and Mass Communications of the Russian Federation but is coordinated by Rosstat. The purpose of this system is to provide access to official statistical information, including metadata generated in accordance with the federal statistical work plan, using the data of state authorities, local governments, legal entities and individuals. Access to official statistical information is free of charge and non-discriminatory.

The main source of data for our research comes from the Rosstat Publication 'Regions of Russia. Socio-Economic Indicators' for the years 2002–2016.[2] The data for the publication is obtained by state statistical agencies from enterprises, organizations and the general public in the course of statistical observations, censuses, and sample surveys. Additionally, it contains the data of ministries and departments of the Russian Federation. The data for the period earlier than 2001 is from EMISS.[3]

Before estimating our models, we prepare our data set and make transformations of some variables to better suit our needs. The Rosstat Data Base gives us data for most of variables for all the eighty-three current Russian regions for the period from 1995 to 2015. However, we are to mention that during this period the regional structure of Russia has been modified several times with the grouping of some regions (in the beginning of observation, there were 89 of them). For the research goal, we consider these regions as one from the very beginning of observation by summing the data. Besides, there is very little data only on few variables on Chechen Republic due to military conflicts that have took place during the period, so we decide to drop this region, so that leaves us only with 82 regions.

Moreover, due to a peculiar organization structure of Autonomous Okrugs of Russian Federation, which are very small territorial divisions with a small population (less than 50,000 people) within a large federal subject and in fact are semi-autonomous. In the official statistics, the larger regions to which they belong do not even have the data without taking into the consideration this small subdivision. Se we also drop this three Okrugs (Nenets Autonomous Okrug, Khanty-Mansi Autonomous Okrug – Yugra, Yamalo-Nenets Autonomous Okrug), but without actually losing the information because this information counts within larger regions (Arkhangelsk Oblast, Tyumen Oblast). It leaves us with 79 regions.

As for the timespan of the research, it is to be said that as not all the variables are available for the whole period of twenty year, many of them are available only form 2000 or even 2005, so not all the regression are run for the complete period. We will specify it later with every regression. Also, we will work with averages for some of them, which will be specified later as well.

Besides, one the most important variable for our estimations is regional GDP per capita, but we cannot use it in the original state without any transformation, because of the inflation as well as price level differences that can severely disturb our estimations. Fortunately, Rosstat calculates the special index, Index of Physical Volume of Production, which depicts that actual growth of GDP without the effect of interregional price changes and inflation. This Index is calculated only from 1998, so we are to start from 1997 as the base year. We recalculate all the GDP per capita levels in 2000 basic prices, as we see it more convenient to use this year as a benchmark. For other variables, which should be used without inflation, we use inflation index, which is calculated separately for each region as well.

4. MODELS AND ECONOMETRIC ISSUES

We use several approaches and models to estimate the Kuznets curve. That gives us not only additional robustness checks, but also alleviates the endogeneity problems, which will be discussed in detail below. First, we estimate a simple static panel data model, then we proceed to estimating a dynamic panel data model and we finish up by estimating an instrumental variable panel data model.

4.1. Static Panel Data Model

The intuitive model to analyze the Kuznets curve in its pure state for panel data would be:

$$Gini_{it} = \alpha_0 + \alpha_1 GDPpc_{it} + \alpha_2 GDPpc_{it}^2 + \varepsilon_{it}, \quad (1)$$

where $Gini_{it}$ is Regional Gini Index before taxes for i region in t year, $GDPpc_{it}$ is Regional Gross Domestic Product per capita in 2000 prices (in logs) for i region in t year, $GDPpc_{it}^2$ is its quadratic term and ε_{it} is an error term.

The quadratic function is used in the model as we assume that, mathematically speaking, the inverted-U form is a concave parabola, as Kuznets (1955) suggested. So, to have a concave form, the coefficient of $GDPpc_{it}$ should be positive, and the coefficient of $GDPpc_{it}^2$ should be negative. The maximum of the function represents a turning point where inequality starts to go down as the income per capita continues rising.

Besides looking for the quadratic relationship between development and inequality, we are to include various explicative variables and controls that, according to the literature, can have a significant influence on inequality in our estimations. So, we use the following augmented model:

$$\begin{aligned} Gini_{it} = {} & \alpha_0 + \alpha_1 GDPpc_{it} + \alpha_2 GDPpc_{it}^2 + \alpha_3 Fert_{it} + \alpha_4 Life_{it} + \alpha_5 Unempl_{it} \\ & + \alpha_6 Labour_{it} + \alpha_7 Prof\ pc_{it} + \alpha_8 College\ pc_{it} + \alpha_9 Migr\ pc_{it} + \varepsilon_{it} \end{aligned} \quad (2)$$

where $Gini_{it}$ is Regional Gini Index before tax, $GDPpc_{it}$ is Regional Gross Domestic Product per capita in 2000 prices (in logs) and $GDPpc_{it}^2$ is its quadratic term, and ε_{it} is an error term. Multicollinearity tests are included in Appendix 1. In addition, we add a set of controls which corresponds to the most important demographic indexes. $Fert_{it}$ represents the fertility rate of region i in year t (children per woman in reproductive age); $Life_{it}$ is life expectancy for region i in year t (in years); $Unempl_{it}$ represents the unemployment rate (in percentage); $Labour_{it}$ is the share of people of working age for region i in year t; $Prof_{it}$ is the number of professional school students for each 10 thousand habitants in region i and year t; $College_{it}$ is the number of college students for each ten thousand habitants in region i and year t; and $Migr_{it}$ is net migration for each 10 thousand habitants. General descriptive statistics (Table A1) and panel data descriptive statistics (Table A2) as well as simple graphic analysis (Fig. A1-A4) are in the Appendix.

We add education variables, because it is assumed that education has a large impact on inequality as it affects the composition of human capital (see Galor & Tsiddon, 1997). Polarization of investment in human capital at the early stages of development is crucial to enhance growth, but later it will pull the inequality down. So, we expect that education has a negative impact on inequality. We consider two variables for different stages of education.

We include the Net Migration variable to account for the effect of emigration and immigration on inequality. According to the findings of Mckenzie and Rapoport (2007), emigration increases inequality at first (at lower levels of migration stock) and then reduces it (at higher levels). This is because, initially, only individuals in the middle part of the wealth distribution can afford to migrate, which crowds out the middle levels of the income distribution, and later, when these individuals send remittances to their countries of origin, inequality is reduced. In contrast, the effect of immigration on inequality is considered positive in most research (Card, 2009), as it widens the gap between high-skilled and low-skilled workers.

Life expectancy and fertility variables are demographic factors which also represent the development of the economy, because the more developed the economy is, the higher is the life expectancy and the lower is the fertility. Life expectancy is a good proxy for population health as well.

Unemployment and the share of people of working age are important control variables as well, because they represent labour market conditions. In some economies, such as Spain high unemployment rate is one of the main channels of inequality. The share of people of working age can affect inequality because the lower this share is, the more social pressure the working population has to maintain children and elderly people. Hence, by adding all these variables, we control not only for economic development, but also for demographics and social development.

4.2. Dynamic Panel Data Model

Although there is large empirical research on how income affects inequality in general and, on the Kuznets curve hypothesis in particular, only a few papers take into account the endogeneity problem. This issue can bias significantly the coefficients as it violates the exogeneity assumption of the Gauss-Markov theorem. In broad terms, endogeneity exists in models in which an independent variable is correlated with the error term. Endogeneity is provoked by the existence of endogenous variables, that is, variables that are determined by the model itself on the contrary of exogenous variables which are predetermined.

In our case, the possible reason can be the reverse causality, when it is inequality that provokes growth changes. Indeed, a large amount of literature exists that investigates on this problem. In addition, there is a possibility of existence of omitted variables or even variables that in fact accounts for both growth and inequality. These concerns imply the necessity of an exogenous instrument, a variable that impacts inequality only through GDP, or in the case of lack of a valid external instrument, the need for internal instruments.

In the case of panel data, we suggest the use of a dynamic model instead of the simple static model. We do it primarily because GDP per capita depends a lot on their past realizations. But moreover, it also permits us to minimize the endogeneity problem since the future cannot cause the past.

Although the question may seem philosophical, Granger (1969) tried to solve it with the econometric method, which now is known as the Granger Causality Test. The premise of Granger is that the future is not able to cause the present or the past. If one event occurs after the other, we assume that the former cannot cause the latter. However, if something occurs beforehand, it does not automatically imply that it causes something that occurs latter. For example, if the weather prediction happens before the snowfall, we cannot say it causes the snowfall. In our case, changes in GDP per capita precede changes in inequality, or is it vices a versa or maybe the changes are simultaneous and are caused by some other event? We suppose that in fact this process goes both ways in spiral.

The standard Granger causality test was developed for time series, but not for panel data. However, a test for Granger non-causality in heterogeneous models was developed later by Dumitrescu and Hurlin (2012), which was adopted for Stata by Lopez and Weber (2017).

Some recent research attempts to control for endogeneity through instrumental variables (Brueckner et al., 2014). The most recent idea of dealing with the problem has been proposed by Brueckner and Ledermann (2018). They create a new variable that controls for change in inequality caused by GDP per capita, so they can use the residual variation in inequality to estimate its effect on growth. Although there is very little research that tries to control for the endogeneity problem in models where inequality affects growth, none of them have dealt with the existence of reverse causation on the Kuznets curve.

Taking into consideration all the above written, we suggest a dynamic model instead of the classic Kuznets model. To consider the Granger causality assumption, we add lags to regional GDP per capita. Moreover, instead of using levels of Gini as dependant variable, we use changes in Gini:

$$\Delta Gini_{it} = \alpha_0 + \alpha_1 Gini_{t-s} + \alpha_2 GDPpc_{it-s} + \alpha_3 GDPpc_{it-s}^{\ 2} + \varepsilon_{it-s}, \tag{3}$$

where $\Delta Gini = Gini_{it} - Gini_{it-s}$, which is the difference between Gini Index in the current t period and previous t-s period, $GDPpc_{it-s}$ is Regional Gross Domestic

Product per capita in 2000 prices (in logs) in the previous *t-s* period, GDP^2_{it-s} is its quadratic term, and ε_{it-s} is an error term.

The best way to estimate this kind of dynamic model is to apply the Difference GMM developed by Arellano and Bover (1991) and the System GMM developed by Arellano and Bover (1995) and Blundell and Bond (1998). Both are generalized method of moments estimators designed for 'small T, large N' panels, i.e. panel data consisting of observation for many individuals, but just for a few time periods, where the dependant variable is dynamic, that is, it depends on its own past realizations. they can be used for dynamic models, where independent variables are not strictly exogenous, or correlated with past or current error terms, as well as in models with heteroscedasticity and autocorrelation within individuals.

These methods do not concern cross-sectional dependency and structural breaks. The Difference GMM estimator developed by Arellano and Bond (1991) transforms all regressors by differencing them and then uses the Generalized Method of Moments designed by Hansen (1982). The System GMM estimator (Arellano and Bover, 1995; Blundell and Bond, 1998) augments the Difference GMM estimator by making an additional assumption, which is that first differences of instrument variables are uncorrelated with fixed effects. It dramatically improves efficiency by allowing the introduction of more instrumental variables. It is named System GMM, because in fact it builds a system of two equations – the original one and the transformed one. Data Summary Statistics and test and preliminary estimations are in Appendix 1.

We should mention that normally these methods are used for linear fixed effects models, and we assume that our model is quadratic. Thus, we introduce the quadratic term as a separate variable assuming that it would cause the multicollinearity problem.

We run the augmented regression for the dynamic model:

$$\begin{aligned} Gini_{it} = {} & \alpha_0 + \alpha_1 Gini_{t-s} + \alpha_2 GDPpc_{it-s} + \alpha_3 GDPpc_{it-s}{}^2 + \ \alpha_4 Fert_{it-s} \\ & + \alpha_5 Life_{it-s} + \alpha_6 Unempl_{it-s} + \alpha_7 Labour_{it-s} + \alpha_8 Prof\ pc_{it-s} \\ & + \alpha_9 College\ pc_{it-s} + \alpha_{10} Migr\ pc_{it-s} + \varepsilon_{it} \end{aligned} \tag{4}$$

To estimate this model, we consider 5-year periods, because our data does not permit us to have longer lags (Difference and System GMM cannot be used if we have only two time periods), although in most of the literature 10-year periods are used (Bruecker et al., 2014). We assume that after five years, the endogeneity starts to lose its influence. General descriptive statistics (Table A11) and panel data descriptive statistics (Table A12) as well as simple graphic analysis (Fig. A5) are in the Appendix.

4.3. Instrumental Variables (IV) Panel Data Model

The use of Difference GMM and System GMM can alleviate the endogeneity problem, but still the best method to use in this case is the instrumental variable method (IV). Broadly speaking, an instrumental variable is a variable that is uncorrelated with the error term but correlated with the explanatory variable in the equation. The concept of instrumental variables was first derived by Philip G. Wright, in the context of simultaneous equations in his 1928 book *The Tariff on Animal and Vegetable Oils*. This method is massively used for solving not only the endogeneity problem, but also measurement errors in the variables or the omitted variable problem.

One computational method which can be used to calculate IV estimates is two-stage least squares (2SLS). In the first stage, each explanatory variable that is an endogenous covariate in the equation of interest is regressed on all the exogenous variables in the model and the excluded instruments. In the second stage, the regression of interest is estimated as usual, except that in this stage each endogenous covariate is replaced with the predicted values from the first stage.

The most important part of this method is the selection of valid and strong instruments. That means that the instrument should be both exogenous itself and strongly correlated to the endogenous variable. Normally, the precision of IV estimates is lower than that of the OLS estimates. In the presence of weak instruments (instruments only weakly correlated with included endogenous regressors), the loss of precision will be severe, and IV estimates may be no improvement over OLS. Many researchers conclude from their work that if the first-stage F statistic exceeds 10, their instruments are sufficiently strong.

We use the net oil and gas exports per capita in US dollars and the volume of internal trade per capita in roubles in 2000 basic prices to instrument the GDP per capita. We assume that since the Russian Economy in general largely depends on this kind of exports, it comes as no surprise that the most developed Russian regions are those having the highest oil and gas exports. We use trade, as it is the second source of creation of regional GDP for most regions. We consider that these variables influence inequality only through its effect on regional GDP per capita.

So, the corresponding first-stage equation for the two-stage least squares (2SLS) estimation is:

$$GDPpc_{it} = \alpha_{it} + OilExport\ pc_{it} + Trade\ pc_{it} + \varepsilon_{it} \tag{5}$$

where $GDPpc_{it}$ is Regional Gross Domestic Product per capita in 2000 prices (in logs) for i region in t year and $OilExport\ pc_{it}$ is Net Oil Export per capita in current US dollars per capita (in logs) for i region in t year, $Trade\ pc_{it}$ is Internal trade per capita in roubles in 2000 basic prices and ε_{it} is an error term. We use this variable in US dollar and not in roubles, because to our mind it is better that it reflects not only the number of exports per capita, but also fluctuations in oil prices and rouble to dollar exchange rate variations. All these elements hugely affect GDP per capita. The assumption in 2SLS estimation is that they only affect income inequality through their effect on GDP per capita. We are going to use IV estimation both in static and dynamic panel data models.

5. MAIN RESULTS

5.1. Static Model Results

If we look at the results of simple static model regressions (Table 1), we can see that the log of GDP per capita has a positive and significant effect on inequality, i.e. in general terms, the greater the level of development is, the higher the inequality is. A one percent increase in GDP per capita increases the Gini coefficient by approximately 5 points. Although, if we consider the simple quadratic model by introducing the quadratic term, we can see that although the coefficients have the signs we expected (positive for the linear term and negative for the quadratic term), the coefficient is not statistically significant. When we add more controls, we can see that only the education variables have a significant effect on inequality. However, it is worth to mention that the number of professional school students affects positively the inequality, while the number of college students (lower level of education) affects it negatively. Preliminary estimation and tests are in Appendix 1 (Tables A4–A10).

We conduct some robustness checks. First, we use regional GDP per capita without logs (Table 2). We can see that in a simple regression the effect of GDP per capita on inequality is insignificant and not very different from zero. But if we introduce the quadratic term, the Kuznets curve is confirmed, although

Table 1. Effects of Regional GDP pc on Gini Index.

	Gini (1) Base	Gini (2) Quadratic	Gini (3) Augmented
Ln (GDP00)	4.76***	6.59***	1.94
	(0.39)	(1.93)	(1.82)
Ln $(GDP00)^2$		−0.25	0.41*
		(0.23)	(0.23)
Fertility			0.13
			(0.41)
Life Expectancy			0.00
			(0.11)
Unemployment			0.03
			(0.02)
Labour			0.12
			(0.08)
Prof. School			0.06*
			(0.03)
College			−0.07***
			(0.01)
Migration			0.00
			(0.00)
Constant	0.00	0.00	0.00
	(0.00)	(0.00)	(0.00)
Observations	1,495	1,495	1,482
Number of groups	79	79	79

Notes: The method of estimation is Fixed Effects. Driscoll-Kraay errors are shown in parenthesis. Time Dummies are not shown.

*** $p<0.01$, * $p<0.1$.

Table 2. Effect of Regional GDP pc on Gini Index (No Logs).

VARIABLES	Gini (1) Base	Gini (2) Quadratic	Gini (3) Augmented
GDPpc	0.0018	0.1271***	0.1437***
	(0.0048)	(0.0102)	(0.0094)
$GDPpc^2$		−0.0004***	−0.0004***
		(0.0000)	(0.0000)
Fertility			0.4858
			(0.4407)
Life Expectancy			−0.0207
			(0.0925)
Unemployment			0.0115
			(0.0159)
Labour			0.2088**
			(0.0908)
Prof. School			0.0838**
			(0.0320)
College			−0.0689***
			(0.0061)
Migration			0.0009
			(0.0007)
Constant	33.8067***	0.0000	0.0000
	(0.1546)	(0.0000)	(0.0000)
Observations	1,495	1,495	1,482
Number of groups	79	79	79

Notes: The method of estimation is Fixed Effects. Driscoll-Kraay errors are shown in parenthesis. Time Dummies are not shown.
*** $p<0.01$, ** $p<0.05$, * $p<0.1$.

the coefficient with a quadratic term is very close to zero. When we introduce more controls, the effect holds and again education variables are significant and do not change their sign. In this regression, the variable which represents the population of working age gains its significance and affect positively the inequality.

If we change the measure of inequality and use a decile index (this index measures the proportion of income of 10% population of highest income to 10% of mean income of population with lowest income) instead of the Gini Index, the results are similar to the initial ones (see Table 3).

Now, we exclude possible outliers, such as Moscow which has a very strange inequality pattern (high inequality in the beginning of period that drops dramatically later) or huge oil producing regions. If we drop Moscow from the regression (Table 4), we observe that the only coefficient that does not lose significance is the one corresponding to regional GDP per capita in the basic regression. If we drop large oil exporting regions (with an average oil and gas exports more than 1 thousand dollars per capita per year, which also includes Moscow), we obtain similar results (Table 5).

Because we do not deal with the endogeneity problem, all these results represent only simple correlations between the variables.

Table 3. Effect of Regional GDP pc on Decile Coefficient.

VARIABLES	Decile (1) Base	Decile (2) Quadratic	Decile (3) Augmented
Ln (GDP00)	4.5799***	6.0975***	0.0495
	(0.6072)	(2.0820)	(1.1834)
Ln (GDP00)^2		−0.2089	0.6342***
		(0.2199)	(0.1389)
Fertility			0.2674
			(0.4013)
Life Expectancy			−0.0046
			(0.0580)
Unemployment			0.0242
			(0.0143)
Labour			0.1562*
			(0.0862)
Prof. School			0.1170***
			(0.0406)
College			−0.0900***
			(0.0139)
Migration			0.0013
			(0.0009)
Constant	0.0000	0.0000	0.0000
	(0.0000)	(0.0000)	(0.0000)
Observations	1,495	1,495	1,482
Number of groups	79	79	79

Notes: The method of estimation is Fixed Effects. Driscoll-Kraay errors are shown in parenthesis. Time Dummies are not shown.
*** $p<0.01$, * $p<0.1$.

Table 4. Effect of Regional GDP pc on Gini (Without Moscow).

VARIABLES	Gini (1) Base	Gini (2) Quadratic	Gini (3) Augmented
Ln (GDP00)	4.0985***	2.6500	1.9795
	(0.1994)	(1.9532)	(1.8782)
Ln (GDP00)^2		0.1987	0.2965
		(0.2613)	(0.2501)
Fertility			−0.1116
			(0.3478)
Life Expectancy			0.0381
			(0.1292)
Unemployment			0.0262
			(0.0203)
Labour			0.0515
			(0.0579)
Prof. School			−0.0183
			(0.0264)
College			0.0062
			(0.0128)
Migration			0.0006
			(0.0005)
Constant	22.7516***	24.3576***	0.0000
	(0.7881)	(3.6056)	(0.0000)
Observations	1,476	1,476	1,463
Number of groups	78	78	78

Notes: The method of estimation is Fixed Effects. Driscoll-Kraay errors are shown in parenthesis. Time Dummies are not shown.
*** $p<0.01$.

Table 5. Effect of Regional GDP pc on Gini (Without Huge Oil-Exporting Regions).

VARIABLES	Gini (1) Base	Gini (2) Quadratic	Gini (3) Augmented
Ln (GDP00)	2.8546***	0.5274	0.3642
	(0.4826)	(2.5715)	(2.1377)
Ln $(GDP00)^2$		0.3659	0.3343
		(0.3567)	(0.2971)
Fertility			0.2640
			(0.3738)
Life Expectancy			−0.0474
			(0.1095)
Unemployment			0.0239
			(0.0197)
Labour			0.0731
			(0.0503)
Prof. School			−0.0237
			(0.0286)
College			0.0047
			(0.0129)
Migration			0.0002
			(0.0004)
Constant	27.6429***	31.1042***	0.0000
	(1.8550)	(4.6406)	(0.0000)
Observations	1,289	1,289	1,283
Number of groups	68	68	68

Notes: The excluded regions are: Arkhangelsk Oblast, Chukotka Autonomous Okrug, Leningrad Oblast, Moscow, Novosibirsk Oblast, Tyumen Oblast, Republic of Tatarstan, Republic of Bashkortastan, Saint Petersburg, Sahklin Oblast and Samara Oblast. The method of estimation is Fixed Effects. Driscoll-Kraay errors are shown in parenthesis. Time Dummies are not shown.
*** $p<0.01$.

5.2. Dynamic Model Results

The results from the estimation of the dynamic model (Table 6) show both the positive effect of GDP per capita on the change in inequality and the presence of the Kuznets Curve in all models. Also, they show that the inequality in the previous period affects negatively its change in the next period. That is, the higher the inequality, the lesser it goes up in the future. Cross-Sectional Dependence Test (Table A13) is in the appendix.

Again, the college education affects negatively the inequality, while professional school education affects it positively. But in comparison with the static model, where unemployment in the same period does not significantly affects inequality, now unemployment in the previous period affects it positively. Fertility has a negative effect on inequality. It also may confirm our hypothesis that the higher is the development, the higher is inequality and the lower is the fertility. In every quadric equation, the test of validity of instruments does not work. That may be because of the multicollinearity problem between the two explicative variables.

We conduct a variety of robustness checks for our dynamic model. First, we run the model using levels of the Gini Index as the dependant variable, not the

Table 6. Effects of Regional GDP pc on Gini (Dynamic Model, System GMM).

VARIABLES	Δ Gini (1) Base	Δ Gini (2) Square	Δ Gini (3) Augmented
Gini (lag)	−0.625***	−0.361***	−0.322***
	(0.0262)	(0.0388)	(0.0396)
Ln (GDP)pc (lag)	0.857***	3.259***	8.360***
	(0.244)	(1.109)	(2.296)
Ln (GDP)pc^2 (lag)		−0.327**	−0.976***
		(0.153)	(0.276)
College (lag)			−0.0134**
			(0.00550)
Prof. School (lag)			0.0810***
			(0.0222)
Migration (lag)			−0.000587
			(0.000909)
Life Expectancy (lag)			0.0863
			(0.0548)
Fertility (lag)			−1.710**
			(0.724)
Unemployment (lag)			0.130***
			(0.0426)
Labour (lag)			0.0480
			(0.0721)
Constant	0	6.715**	−10.75*
	(0)	(2.769)	(6.327)
Observations	237	237	235
Number of Regions	79	79	79
Number of Instruments	15	16	41
AR (1) *p*-value	0.578	0.084	0.071
Hansen *p*-value	0.167	0.004	0.159

Notes: Time dummies are included in all models. Estimations are by one-step System GMM, reducing the number of lags to two. AR(1) test is for first-order correlation in the first-differenced residuals. It is above 0.5, so even the *t*-1 instruments are valid. The *p*-value for the Hansen over-identifying restriction test is above 0.5 for base and augmented equations, so we assume that the instruments are strong. It is above 0.5 for the quadratic equation, but it can occur due to multicollinearity problem because of the usage of the quadratic term. Standard errors in parentheses.
*** $p<0.01$, ** $p<0.05$, * $p<0.1$.

change of Gini Index (Table 7). Then we use Difference GMM estimator instead of System GMM estimator (Table 8). We proceed with estimating the model without using the logarithms for regional GDP per capita (Table 9), and finally we drop Moscow as a possible outlier (Table 10) and huge oil-exporting regions from the model (Table 11).

It is important to mention, that in all the robustness checks the Kuznets Curve persists. The same thing happens with the education variables except for the regression without Moscow, where the coefficient of college education is not significant. This may happen because Moscow has the highest number of university students per ten thousand habitants and the most dramatic decline in inequality during those years.

Table 7. Effects of Regional GDP pc on Gini (Dynamic Model, System GMM).

VARIABLES	Gini (1) Base	Gini (2) Square	Gini (3) Augmented
Gini (lag)	0.377***	0.506***	0.662***
	(0.0259)	(0.0275)	(0.0375)
Ln (GDP)pc (lag)	0.862***	13.10***	6.491***
	(0.213)	(1.629)	(2.014)
Ln (GDP)pc^2 (lag)		−1.578***	−0.728***
		(0.221)	(0.245)
College (lag)			−0.0125**
			(0.00517)
Prof. School (lag)			0.0808***
			(0.0189)
Migration (lag)			−0.000670
			(0.000881)
Life Expectancy (lag)			0.0750
			(0.0477)
Fertility (lag)			−0.863
			(0.631)
Unemployment (lag)			0.0833**
			(0.0327)
Labour (lag)			0.0178
			(0.0612)
Constant	21.10***	−7.047**	0
	(0.985)	(3.451)	(0)
Observations	237	237	235
Number of Regions	79	79	79
Number of Instruments	17	13	51
AR (1) *p*-value	0.584	0.238	0.106
Hansen *p*-value	0.376	0.001	0.598

Notes: Time dummies are included in all models. Estimations are by one-step System GMM, reducing the number of lags to two. AR (1) test is for first-order correlation in the first-differenced residuals. It is above 0.5, so even the *t*-1 instruments are valid. The *p*-value for the Hansen over-identifying restriction test is above 0.5 for base and augmented equations, so we assume that the instruments are strong. It is above 0.5 for the quadratic equation, but it can occur due to multicollinearity problem because of the usage of the quadratic term. Standard errors in parentheses.
*** $p<0.01$, ** $p<0.05$, * $p<0.1$.

Table 8. Effects of Regional GDP pc on Delta Gini (Dynamic Model, Difference GMM).

VARIABLES	ΔGini (1) Base	ΔGini (2) Square	ΔGini (3) Augmented
Gini (lag)	−0.679***	−0.329***	−0.461***
	(0.0529)	(0.0748)	(0.0869)
Ln (GDP)pc (lag)	1.379*	14.58***	13.51***
	(0.759)	(4.020)	(3.927)
Ln (GDP)pc^2 (lag)		−1.746***	−1.223**
		(0.304)	(0.506)

Table 8. *(Continued)*

VARIABLES	ΔGini (1) Base	ΔGini (2) Square	ΔGini (3) Augmented
College (lag)			−0.0416***
			(0.0151)
Prof. School (lag)			0.250*
			(0.141)
Migration (lag)			−0.00514**
			(0.00207)
Life Expectancy (lag)			−0.198
			(0.217)
Fertility (lag)			−0.385
			(2.344)
Unemployment (lag)			0.108
			(0.102)
Labour (lag)			0.00389
			(0.157)
Observations	158	158	156
Number of Regions	79	79	79
Number of Instruments	10	9	20
AR (1) *p*-value	0.257	0.059	0.193
Hansen *p*-value	0.376	0.005	0.107

Notes: Time dummies are included in all models. Estimations are by one-step Difference GMM, reducing the number of lags to three. AR (1) test is for first-order correlation in the first-differenced residuals. It is above 0.5, so even the *t*-1 instruments are valid. The *p*-value for the Hansen over-identifying restriction test is above 0.5 for base and augmented equations, so we assume that the instruments are strong. It is above 0.5 for the quadratic equation, but it can occur due to multicollinearity problem because of the usage of the quadratic term. Standard errors in parentheses.
*** $p<0.01$, ** $p<0.05$, * $p<0.1$.

Table 9. Effects of Regional GDP pc on Delta Gini (Dynamic Model, System GMM). Without logs.

VARIABLES	Δ Gini (1) Base	Δ Gini (2) Square	Δ Gini (3) Augmented
Gini (lag)	−0.620***	−0.512***	−0.363***
	(0.0300)	(0.0684)	(0.0391)
GDPpc (lag)	0.0243***	0.0501***	0.0159
	(0.00293)	(0.00972)	(0.0100)
GDPpc^2 (lag)		−0.000149***	−5.39e-05
		(3.25e-05)	(3.50e-05)
College (lag)			−0.0164***
			(0.00487)
Prof. School (lag)			0.0987***
			(0.0175)
Migration (lag)			−0.000309
			(0.000872)
Life Expectancy (lag)			0.0545
			(0.0486)

(Continued)

Table 9. (*Continued*)

VARIABLES	Δ Gini (1) Base	Δ Gini (2) Square	Δ Gini (3) Augmented
Fertility (lag)			−0.713
			(0.674)
Unemployment (lag)			−0.00110
			(0.0262)
Labour (lag)			0.131***
			(0.0496)
Constant	22.98***	18.08***	3.920
	(1.070)	(2.370)	(4.945)
Observations	237	237	235
Number of Regions	79	79	79
Number of Instruments	15	16	51
AR (1) *p*-value	0.192	0.729	0.235
Hansen *p*-value	0.006	0.000	0.257

Notes: Time dummies are included in all models. Estimations are by one-step System GMM, reducing the number of lags to three. AR (1) test is for first-order correlation in the first-differenced residuals. It is above 0.5, so even the *t*-1 instruments are valid. The *p*-value for the Hansen over-identifying restriction test is above 0.5 for base and augmented equations, so we assume that the instruments are strong. It is above 0.5 for the quadratic equation, but it can occur due to multicollinearity problem because of the usage of the quadratic term. Standard errors in parentheses.
*** $p < 0.01$.

Table 10. Effects of Regional GDP pc on Delta Gini (Dynamic Model, System GMM). Without Moscow.

VARIABLES	(1) Base	(2) Square	(3) Augmented
Gini (lag)	−0.808***	−0.513***	−0.469***
	(0.0313)	(0.0557)	(0.0473)
Ln (GDP)pc (lag)	1.233***	2.282**	7.740***
	(0.181)	(0.990)	(1.989)
Ln (GDP)pc^2 (lag)		−0.152	−0.855***
		(0.138)	(0.240)
College (lag)			0.00420
			(0.0127)
Prof. School (lag)			0.0619**
			(0.0258)
Migration (lag)			−0.00128
			(0.000815)
Life Expectancy (lag)			0.121**
			(0.0481)
Fertility (lag)			−0.591
			(0.673)
Unemployment (lag)			0.0986***
			(0.0375)
Labour (lag)			0.0461
			(0.0629)
Constant	0	0	−9.856*
	(0)	(0)	(5.776)
Observations	234	234	232
Number of Regions	78	78	78
Number of Instruments	17	16	41

Table 10. *(Continued)*

VARIABLES	(1) Base	(2) Square	(3) Augmented
AR (1) *p*-value	0.804	0.098	0.138
Hansen *p*-value	0.337	0.013	0.411

Notes: Time dummies are included in all models. Estimations are by one-step System GMM, reducing the number of lags to three. AR (1) test is for first-order correlation in the first-differenced residuals. It is above 0.5, so even the *t*-1 instruments are valid. The *p*-value for the Hansen over-identifying restriction test is above 0.5 for base and augmented equations, so we assume that the instruments are strong. It is above 0.5 for the quadratic equation, but it can occur due to multicollinearity problem because of the usage of the quadratic term. Standard errors in parentheses.
*** $p<0.01$, ** $p<0.05$, * $p<0.1$.

Table 11. Effects of Regional GDP pc on Delta Gini (Dynamic Model, System GMM). Without Huge Oil-Exporting Regions.

VARIABLES	Δ Gini (1) Base	Δ Gini (2) Square	Δ Gini (3) Augmented
Gini (lag)	−0.808***	−0.454***	−0.466***
	(0.0347)	(0.0575)	(0.0524)
Ln (GDP)pc (lag)	0.673***	3.270**	11.90***
	(0.237)	(1.351)	(2.479)
Ln (GDP)pc² (lag)		−0.345*	−1.519***
		(0.205)	(0.329)
College (lag)			−0.0133
			(0.0238)
Prof. School (lag)			0.0708**
			(0.0356)
Migration (lag)			−0.00193**
			(0.000824)
Life Expectancy (lag)			0.110**
			(0.0486)
Fertility (lag)			−0.838
			(0.700)
Unemployment (lag)			0.123***
			(0.0382)
Labour (lag)			−0.00223
			(0.0616)
Constant	0	0	0
	(0)	(0)	(0)
Observations	204	204	204
Number of Regions	68	68	68
Number of Instruments	15	16	41
AR (1) *p*-value	0.258	0.396	0.258
Hansen *p*-value	0.017	0.422	0.094

Notes: Time dummies are included in all models. Estimations are by one-step System GMM, reducing the number of lags to three. AR (1) test is for first-order correlation in the first-differenced residuals. It is above 0.5, so even the *t*-1 instruments are valid. The *p*-value for the Hansen over-identifying restriction test is above 0.5 for base and augmented equations, so we assume that the instruments are strong. It is above 0.5 for the quadratic equation, but it can occur due to multicollinearity problem because of the usage of the quadratic term. Standard errors in parentheses.

The regions which are excluded are Arkhangelsk Oblast, Chukotka Autonomous Okrug, Leningrad Oblast, Moscow, Novosibirsk Oblast, Tyumen Oblast, Republic of Tatarstan, Republic of Bashkortastan, Saint Petersburg, Sahklin Oblast and Samara Oblast.

*** $p<0.01$, ** $p<0.05$, * $p<0.1$.

6. IV RESULTS

IV regression results show us the existence of the Kuznets curve both in static (Table 12) and dynamic models (Table 13). It should be mentioned that in static and dynamic models the significance of control variables is very different. In the dynamic model the only coefficient that is significant is that of college education that maintains its negative effect on inequality. In the static model, on the contrary, it is the only coefficient that is not significant, although is also negative. All the rest coefficients affect positively inequality, except fertility whose effect is negative. The instruments prove to be valid in all regressions.

First, we check whether our instrumental variable, which is net oil export per capita, affects inequality beyond its effect through GDP per capita (Table 14). We see that its effect is not significant, so this instrument is exogenous. Then we proceed to analyze the static model but using 5-year periods (Table 15) and then using 5-year periods with lags (Table 16). We can see that the results stay, only in the augmented model log of Regional GDP per capita loses its significance.

Table 12. Effect of Regional GDP pc on Gini (IV Model, Static Model).

VARIABLES	Gini (1) Base	Gini (2) Square	Gini (3) Augmented
Ln (GDP pc)	22.46***	36.66***	33.24***
	(1.945)	(3.458)	(4.737)
Ln (GDP pc)^2		−2.454***	−1.777***
		(0.407)	(0.506)
Fertility			−0.0544***
			(0.0101)
Life Expectancy			0.0575**
			(0.0280)
Unemployment			0.0103***
			(0.00227)
Labour			0.305***
			(0.105)
Prof. School			4.424***
			(1.139)
College			−0.00229
			(0.132)
Migration			0.319***
			(0.0539)
Constant	−42.55***	−61.55***	−86.27***
	(6.778)	(7.900)	(12.45)
Observations	676	676	670
Number of Regions	68	68	67
Wu-Hausman *p*-value (endogeneity test)	0.000	0.000	0.000
Wald Statistic for Validity of Instruments	91.3252 (0.000)	57.9146 (0.000)	42.1419 (0.000)

Notes: The method of estimation is 2SLS FE. Time dummies are included in every regression. The instrumental variable for ln (GDP)pc are net oil and gas export per capita y internal trade per capita. Standard errors in parentheses.

*** $p<0.01$, ** $p<0.05$, * $p<0.1$.

Table 13. Effect of Regional GDP pc on Gini (IV Model, Dynamic Model).

VARIABLES	ΔGini (1) Base	ΔGini (2) Square	ΔGini (3) Augmented
Ln (GDP) pc (lag)	6.069**	19.26***	12.12**
	(3.096)	(4.878)	(5.434)
Ln (GDP) pc^2 (lag)		−2.365***	−1.162*
		(0.577)	(0.704)
Gini (lag)	−0.501***	−0.413***	−0.626***
	(0.107)	(0.0802)	(0.0993)
College (lag)			−0.0464***
			(0.0151)
Prof. School (lag)			0.144
			(0.103)
Life Expectancy (lag)			−0.211
			(0.157)
Migration (lag)			−0.000647
			(0.00445)
Unemployment (lag)			0.00539
			(0.0810)
Fertility (lag)			0.684
			(1.824)
Labour (lag)			−0.0963
			(0.204)
Constant	−1.167	−21.07**	14.24
	(8.708)	(9.997)	(17.43)
Observations	150	150	148
Number of Regions	63	63	62
Wu-Hausman *p*-value (endogeneity test)	0.00210.9312	0.01147.4888	0.06516.2214
Wald Statistic for Validity of Instruments	(0.10)	(0.20)	(0.25)

Notes: The method of estimation is 2SLS FE. Time dummies are included in every regression. The instrumental variable for ln (GDP)pc are net oil and gas export per capita y internal trade per capita. Standard errors in parentheses.
*** $p<0.01$, ** $p<0.05$, * $p<0.1$.

Table 14. Effect of Oil Export pc on Gini beyond GDP pc.

VARIABLES	Gini (2) 1 year	Gini (3) 5 years
Ln (GDP pc)	26.59***	24.51***
	(6.924)	(2.272)
Ln (Oil Export pc)	0.212	−0.0517
	(0.196)	(0.0543)
Constant	−58.47**	−50.90***
	(25.00)	(8.093)
Observations	150	574
Number of Regions	63	62
Wald test	74.121	23.450
	(0.000)	(0.000)

Notes: The method of estimation is 2SLS FE. Time dummies are included in all regressions. Standard errors in parentheses.
*** $p<0.01$, ** $p<0.05$, * $p<0.1$.

Table 15. Effect of Regional GDP pc on Gini (IV Model, Static Model, 5 Years).

VARIABLES	Gini (1) Base	Gini (2) Square	Gini (3) Augmented
Ln (GDPpc)	27.02***	43.74***	36.34***
	(6.486)	(8.778)	(12.62)
Ln $(GDPpc)^2$		−3.708***	−2.034
		(1.206)	(1.394)
College			−0.0773**
			(0.0317)
Prof. School			0.0680
			(0.0829)
Migration			0.0148
			(0.00920)
Life Expectancy			0.119
			(0.307)
Fertility			2.209
			(3.425)
Unemployment			0.550***
			(0.190)
Labour			−0.0368
			(0.380)
Constant	−60.65***	−71.48***	−79.70**
	(23.39)	(19.71)	(34.15)
Observations	150	150	149
Number of num_reg	63	63	63
Wu-Hausman *p*-value (endogeneity test)	0.000	0.000	0.000
Wald Statistic for Validity of Instruments	10.1418	4.4062	4.8022
	(0.01)	(0.11)	(0.05)

Notes: The method of estimation is 2SLS FE. Time dummies are included in every regression. The instrumental variable for ln (GDP)pc are net oil and gas export per capita y internal trade per capita. Standard errors in parentheses.
*** $p<0.01$, ** $p<0.05$, * $p<0.1$.

Table 16. Effect of regional GDP pc on Gini (IV Model, Model with Lags).

VARIABLES	Gini (1) Base	Gini (2) Square	Gini (3) Augmented
Ln (GDPpc) (lag)	29.35***	29.35***	20.34***
	(6.991)	(6.991)	(7.316)
Ln $(GDPpc)^2$ (lag)	−3.558***	−3.558***	−1.912**
	(0.820)	(0.820)	(0.896)
College (lag)			−0.0422**
			(0.0167)
Prof. School (lag)			0.249
			(0.204)
Migration (lag)			0.0121

(*Continued*)

Table 16. *(Continued)*

VARIABLES	Gini (1) Base	Gini (2) Square	Gini (3) Augmented
			(0.00837)
Life Expectancy (lag)			0.0642
			(0.208)
Fertility (lag)			−3.669
			(2.418)
Unemployment (lag)			0.312***
			(0.114)
Labour (lag)			0.126
			(0.319)
Constant	−19.13	−19.13	−19.95
	(16.86)	(16.86)	(24.42)
Observations	106	106	105
Number of Regions	62	62	62
Wu-Hausman *p*-value (endogeneity test)	0.001	0.000	0.002
Wald Statistic for Validity of Instruments	6.9240	4.1236	3.7980
	(0.15)	(0.15)	(0.15)

Notes: The method of estimation is 2SLS FE. Time dummies are included in every regression. The instrumental variable for ln (GDP)pc is net oil and gas export per capita y internal trade per capita. Standard errors in parentheses.
*** $p<0.01$, ** $p<0.05$, * $p<0.1$.

7. CONCLUSIONS

In this chapter, we have analyzed the inequality-development relationship based on the famous Kuznets curve hypothesis. After running three different models and plenty of robustness checks, we can sum up our main findings.

First, we have found strong evidence that in the Russian Federation, economic growth increases inequality. That is quite different from the results in other papers, where the estimation was conducted on state level (Brueckner et al., 2014). Our result may be caused by the fact that Russia is not a high-developed country, so it is still situated in the upbeat of the first Kuznets wave, according to Milanovic (2016). In most of the Russian regions, the average income is still on the level of the developing world.

Second, the inverted U-shaped relationship between development and economic inequality exists at the regional level in the Russian Federation. A few regions that are 'the engine' of Russian economic growth (the regions with the highest net oil exports per capita) are the ones that pull down the pattern of inequality in it.

Third, while the positive effect of GDP per capita on inequality appears to hold intact against all types of robustness checks, its quadratic term appears only in instrumented models. That is, only if we somehow control for the endogeneity problem, the Kuznets Curve appears. This contradicts to hypothesis of other researchers who argue that inequality eventually goes down due to other factors, such as redistributive social policies.

Fourth, one peculiar pattern that we detected in most of the regressions is the impact of higher education on inequality. Its significant negative effect on inequality appears almost in every regression. Sometimes this variable takes off the significance of the quadratic term which may reflect the fact that it is the level of education which tears inequality down through GDP per capita. However, this point requires further exhaustive research.

Finally, we highlight the case of Moscow, as it has its unique pattern of inequality in comparison with all the other regions: it starts with an extremely high level of inequality and then it drastically drops down throughout the years. It is notable that Moscow also has the highest number of college students and the most drastic increase in its number as well.

NOTES

1. In Russian, Государственный комитет по статистике, Gosudarstvennyi komitet po statistike, or, in English, the State Committee for Statistics.
2. This publication is available in the following link: http://www.gks.ru/wps/wcm/connect/rosstat_main/rosstat/ru/statistics/publications/catalog/doc_1138623506156
3. The data can be found on https://fedstat.ru/organizations/

REFERENCES

Anand, S., & Kanbur, S. R. (1993). The Kuznets process and the inequality—development relationship. *Journal of Development Economics*, *40*(1), 25–52.

Arellano, M. (1987). Computing robust standard errors for within-groups estimators. *Oxford Bulletin of Economics & Statistics*, *49*(4).

Arellano, M., & Bond, S. (1991). Some tests of specification for panel data: Monte Carlo evidence and an application to employment equations. *The Review of Economic Studies*, *58*(2), 277–297.

Arellano, M., & Bover, O. (1995). Another look at the instrumental variable estimation of error-components models. *Journal of Econometrics*, *68*(1), 29–51.

Barro, R. J. (2000). Inequality and growth in a panel of countries. *Journal of Economic Growth*, *5*(1), 5–32.

Beck, N., & Katz, J. N. (1995). What to do (and not to do) with time-series cross-section data. *American Political Science Review*, *89*(3), 634–647.

Blundell, R., & Bond, S. (1998). Initial conditions and moment restrictions in dynamic panel data models. *Journal of Econometrics*, *87*(1), 115–143.

Breusch, T. S., & Pagan, A. R. (1980). The Lagrange multiplier test and its applications to model specification in econometrics. *The Review of Economic Studies*, *47*(1), 239–253.

Brueckner, M., & Lederman, D. (2018). Inequality and economic growth: the role of initial income. *Journal of Economic Growth*, *23*, 341–366.

Brueckner, M., Dabla Norris, E., & Gradstein, M. (2015). National income and its distribution. *Journal of Economic Growth*, *20*, 149–175.

Card, D. (2009). Immigration and inequality. *American Economic Review*, *99*(2), 1–21.

De Hoyos, R. E., & Sarafidis, V. (2006). Testing for cross-sectional dependence in panel-data models. *The Stata Journal*, *6*(4), 482–496.

De La Escosura, L. P. (2008). Inequality, poverty and the Kuznets curve in Spain, 1850–2000. *European Review of Economic History*, *12*(3), 287–324.

Desbordes, R., & Verardi, V. (2012). Refitting the Kuznets curve. *Economics Letters*, *116*(2), 258–261.

Dollar, D., & Kraay, A. (2002). Growth is Good for the Poor. *Journal of Economic Growth*, *7*, 195–225.

Dumitrescu, E., & Hurlin, C. (2012). Testing for Granger non-causality in heterogeneous panels. *Economic Modelling*, *29*(4), 1450–1460.
Driscoll, J. C., & Kraay, A. C. (1998). Consistent covariance matrix estimation with spatially dependent panel data. *Review of Economics and Statistics*, *80*(4), 549–560.
Fields, G. S. (2002). *Distribution and development: A new look at the developing world*. MIT Press.
Forbes, K. J. (2000). A reassessment of the relationship between inequality and growth. *The American Economic Review*, *90*(4), 869–887.
Frees, E. W. (2004). *Longitudinal and panel data: Analysis and applications in the social sciences*. Cambridge University Press.
Frees, E. W. (1995). Assessing cross-sectional correlation in panel data. *Journal of Econometrics*, *69*(2), 393–414.
Friedman, M. (1937). The use of ranks to avoid the assumption of normality implicit in the analysis of variance. *Journal of the American Statistical Association*, *32*(200), 675–701.
Froot, K. A. (1989). Consistent covariance matrix estimation with cross-sectional dependence and heteroskedasticity in financial data. *Journal of Financial and Quantitative Analysis*, *24*(3), 333–355.
Gallup, J. L. (2012). *Is there a Kuznets curve*. Portland State University.
Galor, O., & Tsiddon, D. (1997). The distribution of human capital and economic growth. *Journal of Economic Growth*, *2*(1), 93–124.
Granger, C. W. (1969). Investigating causal relations by econometric models and cross-spectral methods. *Econometrica: Journal of the Econometric Society*, 424–438.
Greenwood, J., & Jovanovic, B. (1990). Financial development, growth, and the redistribution of income. *Journal of Political Economy*, *98*(5), 1076–1107.
Günaydın, D., & Çetin, M. (2015). The impact of economic growth and trade openness on income inequality: An empirical analysis for Turkish economy. *IIB International Refereed Academic Social Sciences Journal*.
Hansen, L. P. (1982). Large sample properties of generalized method of moments estimators. *Econometrica: Journal of the Econometric Society*, 1029–1054.
Hoechle, D. (2007). Robust standard errors for panel regressions with cross-sectional dependence. *The stata journal*, *7*(3), 281–312.
Jovanovic, B. (2017). When is there a Kuznets curve? Some evidence from the ex-socialist countries.
Kuznets, S. (1955). Economic growth and income inequality. *The American Economic Review*, *45*, 1–28.
Li, H., Squire, L., & Zou, H. (1998). Explaining international and intertemporal variations in income inequality. *The Economic Journal*, *108*(446), 26–43.
List, G. A., & Gallet, C. A. (1999). The Kuznets curve: What happens after the inverted-U? *Review of Development Economics*, *3*(2), 200–206.
Lopez, L., & Weber, S. (2017). *Testing for Granger causality in panel data*. University of Neuchatel, Institute of Economic Research.
Lopez, L., & Weber, S. (2017). Testing for Granger causality in panel data. *The Stata Journal*, *17*(4), 972–984.
Lundberg, M., & Squire, L. (2003). The simultaneous evolution of growth and inequality. *The Economic Journal*, *113*(487), 326–344.
Maddala, G. S., & Lahiri, K. (2009). *Introduction to econometrics*. Wiley.
Mckenzie, D., & Rapoport, H. (2007). Network effects and the dynamics of migration and inequality: Theory and evidence from Mexico. *Journal of Development Economics*, *84*(1), 1–24.
Milanovic, B. (2016). Inequality within countries. Introducing Kuznets waves to explain long-term trends in inequality. *Global inequality. A new approach for the age of globalization* (pp. 46–117). The Belknap Press of Harvard University Press.
Milanovic, B. (1994). Determinants of cross-country income inequality. *An 'Augmented'; Kuznets Hypothesis*. Policy Research Working Paper, The World Bank.
Pesaran, M. H. (2015). *Time series and panel data econometrics*. Oxford University Press.
Pesaran, M. H. (2004). General diagnostic tests for cross section dependence in panels. Cambridge Working Papers. *Economics*, *1240*(1), 1.
Randolph, S. M., & Lott, W. F. (1993). Can the Kuznets effect be relied on to induce equalizing growth? *World Development*, *21*(5), 829–840.
Reed, W. R., & Ye, H. (2011). Which panel data estimator should I use? *Applied Economics*, *43*(8), 985–1000.

Robinson, S. (1976). A note on the U hypothesis relating income inequality and economic development. *The American Economic Review*, *66*(3), 437–440.

Rogers, W. (1993). sg17: Regression standard errors in clustered samples. *Stata Technical Bulletin*, *13*, 19.

Sarafidis, V., & Robertson, D. (2006). *On the impact of cross section dependence in short dynamic panel estimation*. University of Cambridge, http://www.econ.cam.ac.uk/faculty/robertson/csd.pdf

Sukiassyan, G. (2007). Inequality and growth: What does the transition economy data say? *Journal of Comparative Economics*, *35*, 35–56.

White, H. (1980). Using least squares to approximate unknown regression functions. *International Economic Review*, 149–170.

APPENDIX: THE KUZNETS CURVE STATIC MODEL ESTIMATIONS

Table A1. General Descriptive Statistics.

Variable	Obs	Mean	Std. Dev.	Min	Max
GINI	1,700	37.18535	4.370966	23.1	62.3
LN_GDP00	1,549	3.729522	.7442882	1.507062	6.837386
MIGR	1,743	−10.20763	118.9764	−1170.1	2522.5
REDISTR	1,549	46.44267	46.15811	−41.48574	470.2448
PROF_SCH	1,737	6.976717	5.927025	.07	34.5
COLLEGE	1,711	12.46815	23.27152	0	275.4
LIFE_EXP	1,733	66.62674	3.436411	53.8	80.05
UNEMPL	1,724	9.77819	6.54295	.8	66.9

Table A2. Panel Data Descriptive Statistics.

Variable		Mean	Std. Dev.	Min	Max	Observations
GINI	overall	37.18535	4.370966	23.1	62.3	$N = 1700$
	between		3.312903	32.63333	54.83333	$n = 83$
	within		2.902927	23.74726	50.48059	T-bar = 20.4819
LN_GDP00	overall	3.729522	.7442882	1.507062	6.837386	$N = 1549$
	between		.7198538	1.886785	6.448588	$n = 82$
	within		.2661147	2.844212	4.348252	T-bar = 18.8902
MIGR	overall	−10.20763	118.9764	−1170.1	2522.5	$N = 1743$
	between		69.45153	−302.0186	144.2419	$n = 83$
	within		96.88785	−1028.743	2394.653	T = 21
REDISTR	overall	46.44267	46.15811	−41.48574	470.2448	$N = 1549$
	between		39.26359	−36.47636	256.4423	$n = 82$
	within		25.03702	−181.2563	260.2451	T-bar = 18.8902
PROF_SCH	overall	6.976717	5.927025	.07	34.5	$N = 1737$
	between		5.474708	.1648095	25.8879	$n = 83$
	within		2.334135	−11.41119	15.58881	T-bar = 20.9277
COLLEGE	overall	12.46815	23.27152	0	275.4	$N = 1711$
	between		21.38652	0	181.849	$n = 83$
	within		9.142	−94.5668	106.0192	T-bar = 20.6145
LIFE_EXP	overall	66.62674	3.436411	53.8	80.05	$N = 1733$
	between		2.60551	57.83762	74.01905	$n = 83$
	within		2.28084	57.67483	74.03483	T-bar = 20.8795
UNEMPL	overall	9.77819	6.54295	.8	66.9	$N = 1724$
	between		5.926338	2.595238	46.52857	$n = 83$
	within		3.511716	−9.75181	40.04819	T-bar = 20.7711

As we observe in Fig. A3, there was a large dispersion of the Gini Index in 1995, but it has been shrinking over time to reach convergence, which is known as the 'shrinkage' effect.

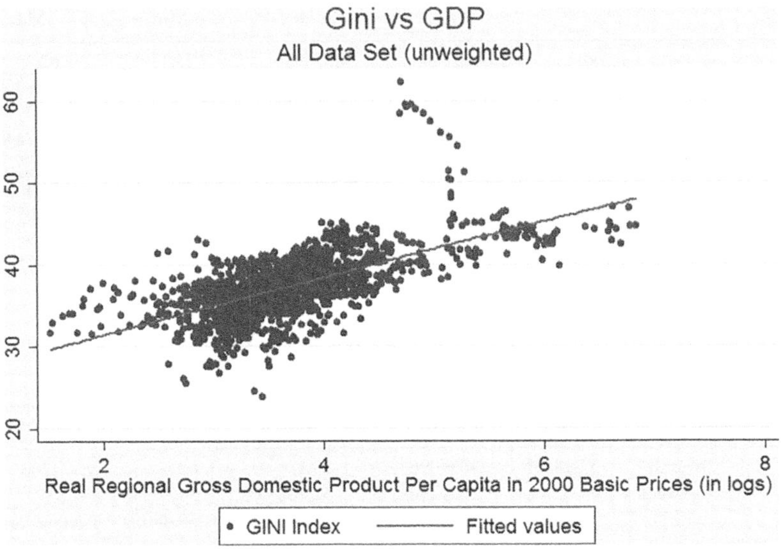

Fig. A1. Gini Versus GDP OLS Fitted Values (Unweighted).

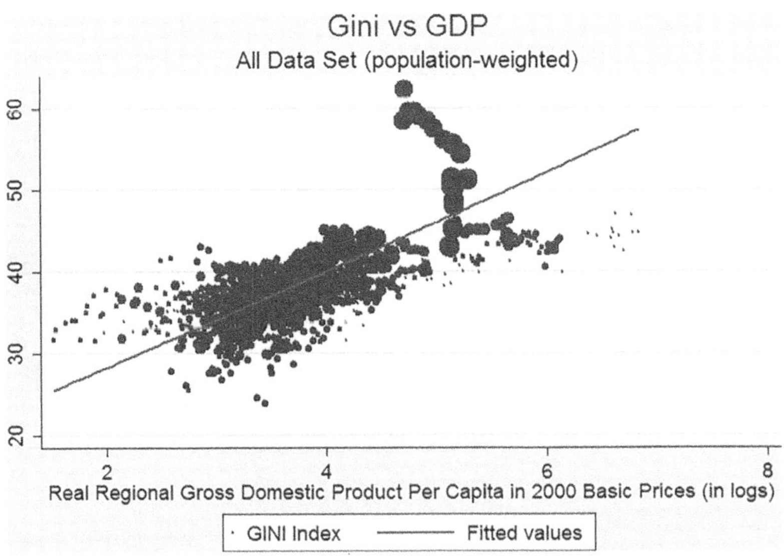

Fig. A2. OLS Fitted Values (Population-Weighted).

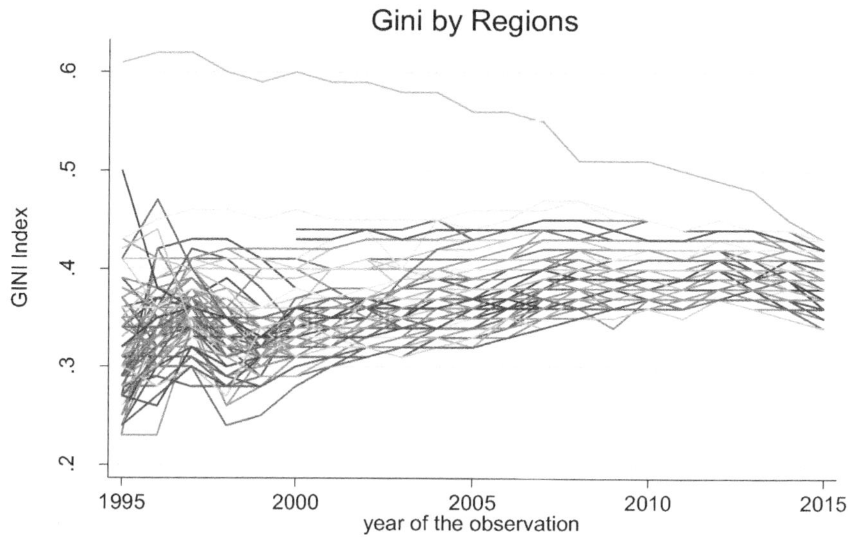

Fig. A3. Gini by Regions.

Fig. A4 shows large heterogeneity across Russian regions.

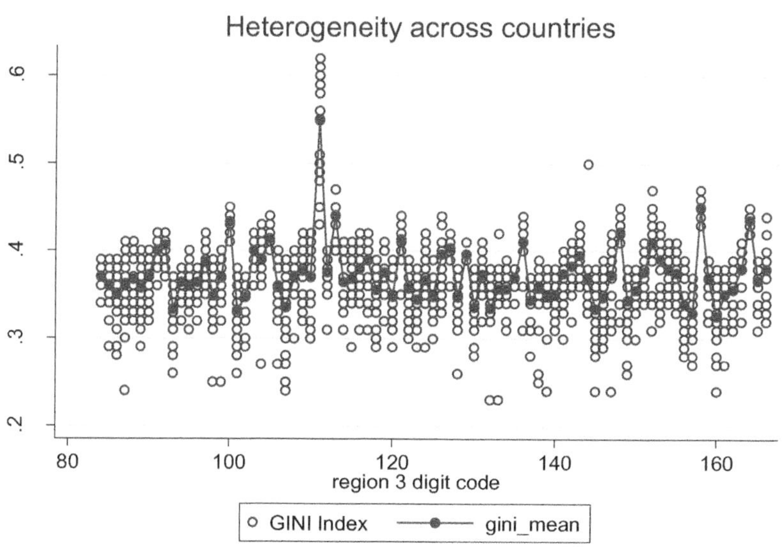

Fig. A4. Heterogeneity Across Regions.

As we add a set of additional variables to construct the augmented model, first, we check whether the explanatory variables we suggest do not have a multicollinearity problem.

To start, we check out correlation coefficients between explanatory variables, although according to Maddala and Lahiri (2009), 'high intercorrelations among the explanatory variables are *neither necessary nor sufficient* to cause the multicollinearity problem'. They add, that 'the best indicators of the problem are the *t*-ratios of the individual coefficients'.

Table A3. Correlation Table.

	LN_GDP00	MIGR	REDISTR	PROF_SCH	COLLEGE	LIFE_EXP	UNEMPL
LN_GDP00	1.0000						
MIGR	−0.0573	1.0000					
REDISTR	−0.5384	−0.0228	1.0000				
PROF_SCH	0.1290	0.2259	−0.1501	1.0000			
COLLEGE	0.2689	0.2338	−0.0197	0.5708	1.0000		
LIFE_EXP	0.0915	0.2313	0.3624	0.0767	0.3243	1.0000	
UNEMPL	−0.5343	−0.0802	0.4585	−0.2396	−0.2597	−0.0051	1.0000

Then, we look for Variance Inflation Factors (VIF) factors. As a rule of thumb, if the mean VIF is less than 10, we conclude that there is no multicollinearity in the model.

Table A4. Collinearity Diagnostics.

Collinearity Diagnostics				
Variable	VIF	SQRT VIF	Tolerance	R-Squared
LN_GDP00	2.02	1.42	0.4941	0.5059
MIGR	1.18	1.09	0.8474	0.1526
REDISTR	2.09	1.45	0.4778	0.5222
PROF_SCH	1.60	1.26	0.6265	0.3735
COLLEGE	1.82	1.35	0.5481	0.4519
LIFE_EXP	1.54	1.24	0.6484	0.3516
UNEMPL	1.56	1.25	0.6410	0.3590
Mean VIF	1.69			

	Eigenval	Cond Index
1	5.2109	1.0000
2	1.2205	2.0663
3	0.7500	2.6359
4	0.4390	3.4454
5	0.1990	5.1171
6	0.1692	5.5490
7	0.0106	22.1919
8	0.0009	76.5380
Condition Number	76.5380	

Eigenvalues & Cond Index computed from scaled raw sscp (w/ intercept)

Det(correlation matrix) 0.1558

ECONOMETRIC ISSUES

Panel data takes advantage of the cross-section variability, the identification and estimation of the parameters of a response function exploiting this variation of the included variables. If the variables do not show excessive time variability but cross-sectional one, the approximation with panel data would provide extra capacity for that estimation.

$$Y_{it} = \alpha + \beta_1 X_{1it} + e_{it}$$

where i means the ith cross unit and t time t (year). This formulation allows the combination of multiple individuals and temporal parameters. Among the many models of Panel Data, the most used are the Fixed Effects (FE) model and the Random Effects (RE) model. The difference between fixed and random effects does not lie in the morphology of the model, which is always the same. The difference is that instead of considering α as fixed, it is assumed that this variable is random with a mean value and a random deviation from this mean value. Substituting $\alpha_i = \alpha + u_i$ in $Y_{it} = \alpha_i + \beta_1 X_{1it} + e_{it}$ we obtain:

$$Y_{it} = \alpha + \beta_1 X_{1it} + u_i + e_{it}$$

where u_i represents unobservable cross-sectional heterogeneity.

However, we suggest that the best method for estimating this kind of relationship is the FE model, because we assume that the constant term is fixed for all the regions.

RESULTS

Preliminary Estimations

Although our research goal is to estimate models (1) and (2), in the first place, we run various tests on the data to be sure that the method that we use is the best fit to our data set. To do this we start with the simple linear model. As for the methods, we start out estimating our linear basic model with Pooled OLS, Fixed Effects and Random Effects.

Table A5. Pooled OLS, Fixed Effects and Random Effects Comparison.

Variable	OLS	FE	RE
LN_GDP00	3.4336552***	6.8169688***	6.1876713***
_cons	24.760895***	12.141957***	14.430912***
N	1543	1543	1543
*r*2	.4129131	.54653498	

legend: * p<0.05; ** p<0.01; *** p<0.001

As we can see from the table, our initial analysis shows that Regional GDP per capita has a positive and significant effect on the Gini coefficient. However, we need to conduct some test to choose the best econometric methods from the three that we have used.

First, we compare Pooled OLS with Random Effects. To decide on which model has better statistical properties, whether the RE model or the pooled data, we use the Breusch and Pagan Lagrangian Multiplier Test for Random Effects. The null hypothesis of this test is that H_0: $\sigma_u^2 = 0$. If the test is rejected, there is a difference between the Pooled OLS model and the RE model, and it is preferable to use the RE method.

Table A6. Breusch and Pagan Test.

Breusch and Pagan Lagrangian multiplier test for random effects

GINI[id,t] = Xb + u[id] + e[id,t]

Estimated results:	Var	sd = sqrt(Var)
GINI	15.83314	3.979088
e	2.840359	1.685336
u	5.636046	2.374036

Test: Var(u) = 0

chibar2(01) = 5049.65

Prob > chibar2 = 0.0000

Observing Table A6, we reject the Ho. Since its Probability is less than 0.05, the random effect estimators are better than the ordinary least squares estimators (Pooled).

Now the next step is to decide which model is better, FE or RE. To do this, we use the Hausman Test. The Hausman test evaluates the consistency of the RE estimator. The null hypothesis can be interpreted as that these estimates are consistent, that is, the requirement of orthogonality of model errors and repressors is satisfactory.

Table A7. The Hausman Test.

	Coefficients (b) FE	(B) RE	(b-B) Difference	sqrt(diag(V_b-V_B)) S.E.
LN_GDP00	6.816969	6.187671	.6292975	.0542083

b = consistent under Ho and Ha; obtained from xtreg

B = inconsistent under Ha, efficient under Ho; obtained from xtreg

Test: Ho: difference in coefficients not systematic

chi2(1) = (b-B)'[(V_b-V_B)^(-1)](b-B)

= 134.77

Prob>chi2 = 0.000

As we can see, the *p*-value is less than 5% of fixed significance, so the random effects estimator is inconsistent. Therefore, we will use the fixed effects estimator.

The Breusch and Pagan test and the Hausman test allow us to choose between traditional models, but these models are not effective in the presence of autocorrelation and heteroscedasticity, for which we will use formal tests to identify what kind of problems are present in our model (see Table A8).

Table A8. Panel Data Tests.

Test	*H0*		Result in Our Model (FE)
Testing for cross- sectional dependence/contemporaneous correlation	The null hypothesis is that residuals are not correlated	Frees' test of cross sectional independence = 12.047 Critical values from Frees' Q distribution alpha = 0.10 : 0.1612 alpha = 0.05 : 0.2116 alpha = 0.01 : 0.3125 Pesaran's test of cross sectional independence = 52.276, Pr = 0.0000 Average absolute value of the off-diagonal elements = 0.422	We have cross-sectional dependence.
Testing for serial correlation.	The null is no serial correlation.	Wooldridge test for autocorrelation in panel data H0: no first order autocorrelation F(1, 81) = 152.733 Prob > F = 0.0000	We have presence of autocorrelation type AR (1)
Unit root for panels LN_GDP00		Fisher-type unit-root test for LN_GDP00 Based on augmented Dickey-Fuller tests Ho: All panels contain unit roots — Number of panels = 82 Ha: At least one panel is stationary — Avg. number of periods = 18.89 AR parameter: Panel-specific — Asymptotics: T -> Infinity Panel means: Included Time trend: Not included Drift term: Included — ADF regressions: 3 lags Statistic / p-value Inverse chi-squared(164) P 545.1253 0.0000 Inverse normal Z -14.9514 0.0000 Inverse logit t(414) L* -15.7906 0.0000 Modified inv. chi-squared Pm 21.0441 0.0000 P statistic requires number of panels to be finite. Other statistics are suitable for finite or infinite number of panels.	No test shows the presence of unit roots.
Unit root for panels GINI		Fisher-type unit-root test for GINI Based on augmented Dickey-Fuller tests Ho: All panels contain unit roots — Number of panels = 83 Ha: At least one panel is stationary — Avg. number of periods = 20.48 AR parameter: Panel-specific — Asymptotics: T -> Infinity Panel means: Included Time trend: Not included Drift term: Included — ADF regressions: 3 lags Statistic / p-value Inverse chi-squared(164) P 533.1326 0.0000 Inverse normal Z -14.6604 0.0000 Inverse logit t(414) L* -15.4937 0.0000 Modified inv. chi-squared Pm 20.3819 0.0000 P statistic requires number of panels to be finite. Other statistics are suitable for finite or infinite number of panels.	No test shows the presence of unit roots.
Testing for heteroscedasticity	The null hypothesis is homoscedasticity (or constant variance)	Modified Wald test for groupwise heteroskedasticity in fixed effect regression model H0: sigma(i)^2 = sigma^2 for all i chi2 (82) = 4834.87 Prob>chi2 = 0.0000	We have the heteroscedasticity.

As we can see, we have several problems with our data which put at risk the asymptotic properties of the estimators. Ignoring such kind of problems in the estimation of panel models can lead to severely biased statistical results.

Fixed Effects Regression with Driscoll and Kraay Standard Errors

There are several methods that are commonly used in econometrics to address the violation of classic linear model assumptions. To address the heteroscedasticity problem, heteroscedasticity-consistent or so-called 'White' standard errors are used (White, 1980). Developing White's work, Arellano (1987), Froot (1989), and Rogers (1993) came up with generalized estimator that produces consistent standard errors if the residuals are correlated within, but uncorrelated between clusters. However, according to Reed and Ye (2011), the best method for estimating models with heteroscedasticity, contemporaneous cross-section correlation and autocorrelation of type AR (1) is Panel-Corrected Standard Error (PCSE) estimation suggested by Beck and Katz (1995), but that is only viable for OLS estimation.

On the contrary, Hoeckle (2007) argues that in the case of panel's cross-sectional dimension N is large compared to the time dimension T, the best way to estimate that kind of data is to use Driscoll and Kraay (1998) standard errors. This method can be used both for Pooled OLS and FE estimators.

DK Standard Errors for FE are implemented in two steps. First, all model variables $z_{it} \in \{y_{it} + x_{it}\}$ are within-transformed as follows:

$$\tilde{z}_{it} = z_{it} - \bar{z}_i + \bar{\bar{z}}_i \quad \text{where} \quad \bar{z}_i = T_i^{-1} \sum_{t=t_{i,1}}^{T_i} z_{it} \quad \text{and} \quad \bar{\bar{z}} = (\sum T_i)^{-1} \sum_i \sum_t z_{it}$$

As the within-estimator corresponds to the OLS estimator of $\tilde{y}_{it} = \tilde{x}_{it}^{'}\theta + \tilde{\varepsilon}_{it}$, the second step is to estimate the transformed regression model by Pooled OLS with DK SE.

In the table below we show the difference of estimation conducted by these four methods in our basic and quadratic models.

As we can see from Tables A9 and A10, application of DK SE did not change the coefficients and only changes the significance of the quadratic term in quadratic regression from 0.1% to 1%. Moreover, our hypothesis about the coefficients is confirmed and the relationship between inequality and development has the inverted-U form, at least in the basic model and in the basic quadratic model.

Table A9. Comparison of Standard Error Estimates for FE Regression (Basic Model).

Variable	FE	White	Rogers	DriscollKraay
LN_GDP00	6.8169688***	6.8169688***	6.8169688***	6.8169688***
_cons	12.141957***	12.141957***	12.141957***	12.141957***
N	1543	1543	1543	1543
*r*2	.54653498	.54653498	.54653498	

legend: * p<0.05; ** p<0.01; *** p<0.001

Table A10. Comparison of Standard Error Estimates for FE Regression for Quadratic Model.

Variable	FE	White	Rogers	DriscollKraay
LN_GDP00	11.058718***	11.058718***	11.058718***	11.058718***
SQRLN_GDP00	−.57358786***	−.57358786	−.57358786	−.57358786**
_cons	4.6183484**	4.6183484	4.6183484	4.6183484
N	1543	1543	1543	1543
*r*2	.55356422	.55356422	.55356422	

legend: * p<0.05; ** p<0.01; *** p<0.001

Basic and Augmented Models Estimations

Now we proceed to augment our model step by step by adding control variables. As we can see, by adding more variables, first, we take off the significance of the quadratic term, and then it becomes positive that means that the curve starts to have a normal U-form, that is, the inequality does not start to go down automatically, when our factors enter in the interplay.

Besides, from all the control variables we choose, only two affects inequality negatively – life expectancy and number of college students, that is, health and education. The curious thing is the number of professional training schools affects inequality positively.

One of our secondary research goals was to see the effects of migration and redistribution on overall inequality. As we can see they have positive and significant effect, although the coefficients are very small. It is interesting to notice that in case of Russia, unemployment has no significant effect on inequality.

Again, for comparison we show the results of augmented model estimation for four above mentioned methods of estimation.

KUZNETS CURVE DYNAMIC AND IV MODEL ESTIMATIONS

Table A11. Descriptive Statistics.

Variable	Obs	Mean	Std. Dev.	Min	Max
dGini	237	1.470127	1.78334	−5.579998	5.895
mean_gini_5	317	37.23464	3.812496	26.425	59.95
mean_ln_g~00	316	3.637527	.6201163	1.621768	5.649567
mean_sqrl~00	316	13.61966	4.676757	2.639016	31.91778
mean_college	318	13.16681	23.83268	0	248.44
mean_prof_~h	319	7.268915	5.893808	.14	32.2922
mean_migr	320	−10.96917	100.3074	−784.275	914.15
mean_life	319	66.77509	3.337149	55.1	78.48
mean_fert	319	1.483665	.3420623	.91	3.38
mean_unempl	318	9.930708	6.50094	1.44	52.68
mean_labour	320	60.79538	3.127324	54.87584	70.624
mean_gini_5	317	37.23464	3.812496	26.425	59.95
mean_gdp00	316	46.94074	37.80927	5.084672	284.1935
mean_gdp2	316	3646.294	8632.729	26.0868	80780.16
mean_net_exp	234	.7756138	2.812202	−.0654406	29.58972
p_trade	1,328	36962.95	24198.03	0	164360.5

Table A12. Panel Data Descriptive Statistics.

> n_life mean_fert mean_unempl mean_labour mean_gini_5 mean_gdp00 mean_gdp2 mean

Variable		Mean	Std. Dev	Min	Max	Observations
dGini	overall	1.470127	1.78334	−5.579998	5.895	$N = 237$
	between		1.080192	−4.303333	3.918334	$n = 79$
	within		1.422453	−3.243208	4.45513	T = 3
mean_g~5	overall	37.23464	3.812496	26.425	59.95	$N = 317$
	between		3.061605	33.135	54.4175	$n = 80$
	within		2.284483	29.85714	42.76714	T-bar = 3.9625
mean_l~0	overall	3.637527	.6201163	1.621768	5.649567	$N = 316$
	between		.5636384	1.895955	5.461908	$n = 79$
	within		.2643512	2.849379	4.258444	T = 4
mean_s~0	overall	13.61966	4.676757	2.639016	31.91778	$N = 316$
	between		4.271126	3.638017	29.87131	$n = 79$
	within		1.950198	6.415299	19.603	T = 4
mean_c~e	overall	13.16681	23.83268	0	248.44	$N = 318$
	between		22.45981	.04	188.3851	$n = 80$
	within		8.137897	−73.13181	73.22169	T-bar = 3.975
mean_p~h	overall	7.268915	5.893808	.14	32.2922	$N = 319$
	between		5.534956	.225125	25.80542	$n = 80$
	within		2.084237	−7.73651	13.75569	T-bar = 3.9875
mean_m~r	overall	−10.96917	100.3074	−784.275	914.15	$N = 320$
	between		68.78252	−282.9833	159.9577	$n = 80$
	within		73.31462	−512.2609	766.7018	T = 4
mean_l~e	overall	66.77509	3.337149	55.1	78.48	$N = 319$
	between		2.618986	58.0195	74.335	$n = 80$
	within		2.099	62.34009	71.13835	T-bar = 3.9875
mean_f~t	overall	1.483665	.3420623	.91	3.38	$N = 319$
	between		.2773591	1.109375	2.751333	$n = 80$
	within		.2135415	.7123313	2.332415	T-bar = 3.9875
mean_u~l	overall	9.930708	6.50094	1.44	52.68	$N = 318$
	between		6.095919	2.2975	47.50125	$n = 80$
	within		3.11265	−.1792931	22.81446	T-bar = 3.975
mean_l~r	overall	60.79538	3.127324	54.87584	70.624	$N = 320$
	between		2.432249	57.23073	69.13475	$n = 80$
	within		1.979888	55.72393	64.20988	T = 4
mean_g~5	overall	37.23464	3.812496	26.425	59.95	$N = 317$
	between		3.061605	33.135	54.4175	$n = 80$
	within		2.284483	29.85714	42.76714	T-bar = 3.9625
mean_g~0	overall	46.94074	37.80927	5.084672	284.1935	$N = 316$
	between		34.90097	6.802269	240.0171	$n = 79$
	within		14.93531	−35.34227	129.5597	T = 4
mean_g~2	overall	3646.294	8632.729	26.0868	80780.16	$N = 316$
	between		7849.138	48.18938	59630.65	$n = 79$
	within		3674.479	−24297.32	28482.6	T = 4
mean_n~p	overall	.7756138	2.812202	−.0654406	29.58972	$N = 234$
	between		2.32975	−.0389982	14.59918	$n = 78$
	within		1.58976	−12.92811	15.76615	T = 3
p_trade	overall	36962.95	24198.03	0	164360.5	$N = 1328$
	between		14382.28	8779.004	107240.6	$n = 83$
	within		19520.06	−24175.78	121892.7	T = 16

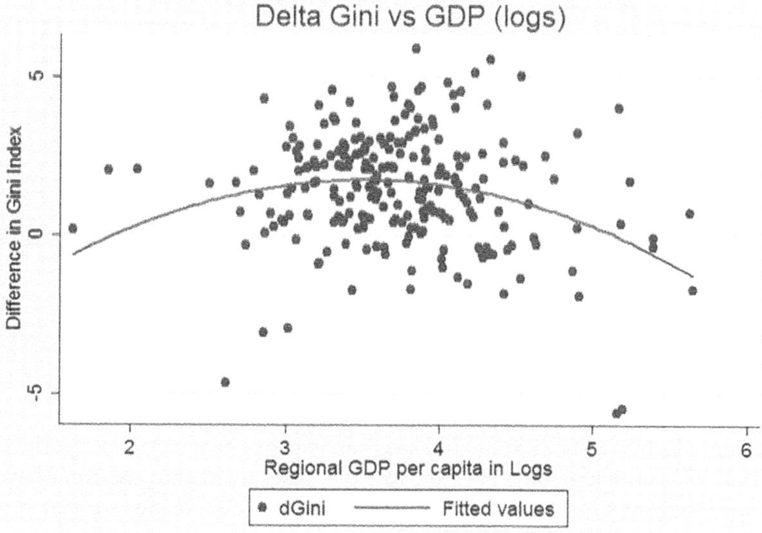

Fig. A5. Difference in Gini Versus GDP OLS Fitted Values.

As we already mentioned, the main problems of Difference GMM and System GMM is that it does not consider cross-sectional dependency. That is why we need to perform cross-sectional independency tests to make sure we can apply these methods. According to Sarafidis and Robertson (2006), while dealing specifically with short dynamic panel-data models show that if there is cross-sectional dependence in the disturbances, all estimation procedures that rely on IV and the generalized method of moments (GMM) – such as Arellano and Bond (1991), and Blundell and Bond (1998) – are inconsistent as N (the cross-sectional dimension) grows large, for fixed T (the panel's time dimension).

That is why we run some tests on cross-sectional dependence on our data. However, as these tests are based on FE and RE models, first of all we'll run these regressions together with Pooled OLS to see the difference (time dummies included).

In our case, we cannot use Lagrange multiplier, also known as the LM test statistics, proposed by Breusch and Pagan (1980), as it is developed for cases when $T > N$, and in the case of $N > T$ it is not valid. In these cases, we should test the hypothesis of cross-sectional independence in paneldata models by implementing two semi-parametric tests developed by Friedman (1937) and Frees (1995, 2004), together with the parametric testing procedure proposed by Pesaran (2004). According to De Hoyos and Sarafidis (2006), in dynamic panels, Pesaran's test remains valid under FE/RE estimation (even if the estimated parameters are biased) and therefore it may be the preferred choice, since the properties of the remaining tests in dynamic panels are not yet known.

Table A13. Cross-sectional Dependence Tests.

```
. xtcsd, pesaran abs
Pesaran's test of cross sectional independence = -1.615, Pr = 0.1064
Average absolute value of the off-diagonal elements = 0.428
. xtcsd, frees abs
   Frees' test of cross sectional independence = 2.384
Critical values from Frees' Q distribution
                                   alpha = 0.10 : 0.4892
                                   alpha = 0.05 : 0.6860
                                   alpha = 0.01 : 1.1046
Average absolute value of the off-diagonal elements = 0.457
. xtcsd, friedman abs
Friedman's test of cross sectional independence = 0.507, Pr = 1.0000
Average absolute value of the off-diagonal elements = 0.457
```

We run all three tests in Stata and see that, except Frees' test that produces the error due to insufficient time periods, rest two tests show that we don't have any cross-sectional dependency, as *p*-value is much above 0.05. So, we can proceed with Difference and System GMM estimations.

INDEX

Printed and bound by CPI Group (UK) Ltd, Croydon, CR0 4YY
15/09/2026
14962485-0003